D0501434

THE BIAS
AGAINST GUNS

THE BIAS
AGAINST GUNS

WHY ALMOST EVERYTHING
YOU'VE HEARD ABOUT
GUN CONTROL IS WRONG

JOHN R. LOTT, JR.

Since 1947
**REGNERY
PUBLISHING, INC.**
An Eagle Publishing Company • Washington, DC

Copyright © 2003 by John Lott

All rights reserved. No part of this publication may be reproduced or transmitted in any form or by any means electronic or mechanical, including photocopy, recording, or any information storage and retrieval system now known or to be invented, without permission in writing from the publisher, except by a reviewer who wishes to quote brief passages in connection with a review written for inclusion in a magazine, newspaper, broadcast, or website.

Library of Congress Cataloging-in-Publication Data

Lott, John R., Jr.
The bias against guns : why almost everything you've heard about gun control is wrong / John R. Lott, Jr.
p. cm.
Includes index.
ISBN 0-89526-114-6
1. Gun control—United States—Public opinion. 2. Firearms—Law and legislation—United States. 3. Violent crimes—United States. I. Title.
HV7436 .L68 2002
363.3'3'0973—dc21
2002154527

Published in the United States by
Regnery Publishing, Inc.
An Eagle Publishing Company
One Massachusetts Avenue, NW
Washington, DC 20001

Visit us at www.regnery.com

Distributed to the trade by
National Book Network
4720-A Boston Way
Lanham, MD 20706
Printed on acid-free paper
Manufactured in the United States of America

10 9 8 7 6 5 4 3 2 1

Books are available in quantity for promotional or premium use. Write to Director of Special Sales, Regnery Publishing, Inc., One Massachusetts Avenue, NW, Washington, DC 20001, for information on discounts and terms or call (202) 216-0600.

For my children,
Maxim, Ryan, Roger, Sherwin, and Dagny.

CONTENTS

PART I

THE PERVASIVE BIAS

WHY ALMOST EVERYTHING YOU'VE EVER HEARD ABOUT GUN CONTROL CONTAINS BIAS

In the aftermath of September 11, 2001, some surveys indicated that over ten million adults were seriously considering buying a gun for the first time.[1] Actual sales soared. During the following six months, 470,000 more people bought handguns and at least 130,000 more background checks were conducted for concealed handgun permits than during the same six-month period a year earlier.[2] Many people viewed this increase with alarm. With so many more people having access to deadly weapons, wouldn't incidents of deadly violence increase?

In 1998, I published a book filled with statistics concluding just the opposite. Its title was *More Guns, Less Crime*. Using various comparisons of changing gun ownership and concealed handgun laws, I examined how crime rates changed in states over time. I found that gun control disarmed law-abiding citizens more than criminals, which meant that criminals had less to fear from potential victims.

Guns not only make it easier for people to harm others, guns also make it easier for people to protect themselves and prevent criminal acts from happening in the first place. But one rarely hears this argument. This book seeks to explain why.

With gun control, there are many trade-offs that deserve serious consideration. On one side, rules governing gun use can hinder people's ability to deter or stop criminal attacks. But on the other, these same rules have the potential to prevent the harm that guns cause. Every gun law faces this trade-off.

For example, waiting periods provide a cooling-off period, but they can also prevent would-be victims from obtaining a gun to defend

3

themselves if needed. Likewise, banning relatively inexpensive guns (so-called Saturday night specials) would prevent some criminals from obtaining weapons. But it would also discourage would-be victims—especially those with modest incomes—from purchasing guns to defend themselves. Registration laws may help the police solve crimes involving guns by providing them access to ownership records, but they drain police resources away from other law enforcement activities—such as patroling streets and catching criminals. And besides, few criminals register their weapons.

The debate over gun control is skewed in favor of stricter laws because we almost never discuss the positive effects of guns: that they often save innocent lives. Everyone agrees that rules taking guns away from criminals ought to reduce crime. But do laws that take guns away primarily from law-abiding citizens also reduce crime?

This book is written for a much broader audience than was *More Guns, Less Crime*, because I am convinced that even many pro-gun people fail to understand the essential lessons evident in patterns of defensive gun use in the United States and abroad. Though not always intentionally, the media and government have so utterly skewed the debate over gun control that many people have a hard time believing that defensive gun use occurs—let alone that it is common or desirable.

Yet, as I will show, there is compelling evidence indicating that guns make us safer. In any society where law-abiding citizens greatly outnumber criminals, this stands to reason. Even in the most totalitarian countries, criminals find ways to get guns. Police are extremely important in deterring crime, but, unfortunately, they almost always arrive on the scene after the crime has been committed. Studies show simply telling people to behave passively turns out not to be very good advice, so it is important that gun laws allow would-be victims to defend themselves.

Because the statistics on defensive gun use were so striking, my earlier book received a great deal of attention. Yet, it basically presented the current state of research, and did not attempt to answer many questions that swirl in public debates. Some readers found the evidence compelling, but many others dismissed the argument out of hand. No matter what the numbers indicate, many people simply react negatively to the idea of concealed handguns or firearms in the home. America may have a long tradition of gun sportsmanship and gun ownership, but even avid gun owners have a hard time arguing against the media and the government's campaigns for "gun-free" schools and other idyllic notions.

A well-known bumper sticker reads: "If you outlaw guns, only outlaws will have guns." This lies at the heart of the problem of gun control: Those who would turn in their guns—if a government were to outlaw them—would be the law-abiding citizens of a society. Less dramatic restrictions than an outright ban on all guns also reduce gun ownership among law-abiding citizens relative to criminals, as this book will explain. And that can increase violent crime.

Recent civil suits brought by cities such as Chicago and Boston against gun manufacturers also show how the debate is biased. The cities' suits are based upon the notion that there are no benefits from guns—only costs. These suits charge that gun makers specifically design their weapons to make them attractive to gang members and other criminals, and thus they should be held legally liable for any costs that arise from the guns. What characteristics of these guns make them attractive to criminals? Low price, easy concealability (small size and light weight), corrosion resistance, accurate firing, and high firepower.

Yet, while all these characteristics are undoubtedly desired by criminals, citizens who use guns defensively also desire them. If one has to fire a gun, accuracy is always a benefit. High firepower translates into greater stopping power, which could be crucial if an attacker is charging at someone. Lightweight, concealable guns help criminals, but they also help protect law-abiding citizens and lower crime rates in the forty-three states that allow concealed handguns. Women, especially, benefit from easier-to-use, smaller, lightweight guns.

In 1999 Chicago's city officials made much of a statement attributed to a gun store clerk recommending that an undercover police officer buy a particular type of bullet because it was less likely to travel through the human target and hit unintended victims, such as "a little girl on the next block."[3] Mayor Richard Daley interpreted this to be "code" designed to appeal to gang members concerned about accidentally shooting one of their own group. But it seems just as likely that a law-abiding citizen defending his home or defending himself in public also doesn't want a bullet he fires at an attacker to accidentally strike someone else. (Ironically, the clerk who allegedly offered this advice was actually an undercover agent for the Bureau of Alcohol, Tobacco, and Firearms.)[4]

In 2002 one state senator in California advocated taxing bullets because "Bullets cause injuries that are expensive to treat, and generally speaking, the public is footing the bill."[5] Indeed, most of those harmed by bullets are criminals (frequently gang members) without health insurance.[6] But using this kind of logic, if bullets *also* allow people to defend themselves and prevent injuries and deaths, shouldn't they receive a tax subsidy?

The issue with guns isn't whether there are benefits or costs. Clearly both exist. Rather, the question is which of these two effects is greater. And rarely—if ever—are the benefits of guns considered by the media or in government studies.

Concerns over terrorist threats now focus people's attention on the costs and benefits of guns. Issues such as the "gun show loophole" or "assault weapons" take on new meaning as the media and gun control groups raise fears about terrorists possibly acquiring weapons at gun shows or using certain firearms that are described as being more lethal than others. Newspaper articles in prominent publications such as the *Washington Post* stress quotes such as "It's understandable that in times of stress people want to protect their families. They incorrectly think getting a gun allows them to do that, when in fact they are putting their families at risk by having a gun in the home."[7]

Others complain that it's a "very cynical exercise" to encourage more people to own guns as a result of September 11,[8] that "gun manufacturers have continued to prey upon the public's fears with their campaign to sell guns to Americans frightened by the terrorist attacks,"[9] and that "our desire to defend ourselves from terrorism by buying firearms will mean, almost certainly, that thousands more Americans will die in the years ahead from gunfire."[10]

But Americans are not the first to experience terrorism. Israelis have borne this burden since their country's inception. Israelis also have the highest gun possession rate in the world.[11] The issues involving guns and terrorism are closely related to guns and crime. Guns might make terrorism easier, but they also make it easier for people to defend themselves against terrorist attacks. Many of the issues debated in the U.S. have been discussed for decades in Israel.

For example, will armed citizens create more problems than they solve? Will increasing the number of guns possessed by citizens make it easier for terrorists to get access to guns? The terrorist attacks suffered by Israel even provide potential lessons for the multiple victim public shootings in the U.S.

Two stories probably put the trade-off of guns in the starkest terms. All too typical in the media are the gut-wrenching stories about the harm caused by guns, such as this one:

> DeKalb police said the 10-year-old boy found a loaded 12-gauge shotgun under his older brother's bed and showed it to Netwian. The boys were playing inside Matthew's home. The shotgun went off and a single round hit Netwian in the head, killing the Chapel Hill Elementary School student instantly, police said. No charges have been filed against the 10-year-old boy or his 20-year-old brother.[12]

But there are also dramatic stories in which guns save lives—even cases where access to guns by young children have made a difference. Take this one:

> When Tony D. Murry held a box cutter to Sue Gay's neck Monday night, Gay's 11-year-old adopted son ran upstairs at the home at 1348 N. Huey St. and grabbed a gun. "He hit the bottom of the stairs with the .45 and stood ready stance with the gun," said Gay with feet spread apart and her hands outstretched as if holding a handgun. The boy shot one round and hit Murry, 27, in the chest, even though the man was shielding himself with Gay. "I don't know how he did that. One shot and he got him. He's my little hero," Gay said of the grandson she adopted. The fifth-grader may not have been just a lucky shot. This is a family that knows guns. "Before his dad

died, they'd go target shooting. He knows they're not toys and
not something to mess with," Gay said.[13]

People's horrified reactions to tragic stories such as the one about
young Netwian are to be expected. Some people respond by getting
rid of their guns; others by locking them up. But are these the safest
courses of action for a family?[14] Perhaps in some cases they are. But
unfortunately, too often the debate is played out in the media with
only anecdotal stories as evidence against guns. Many press accounts
start out with a tragedy to illustrate the need for some gun law. Surely
the stories help galvanize emotions, but the real issue should be the
net effect that guns have on safety. How frequently are guns used by
children to harm other children? How frequently are guns used to
save lives? Will requiring guns to be locked up save lives or cost lives?

Many other areas of the gun debate take place without any reference to evidence. Take the debate over the "gun show loophole" that
dominated much of the 2000 elections. The word "loophole" gives
the impression that there are different rules for buying a gun at a gun
show than there are for buying one elsewhere. That is not the case, as
we shall later see.[15] But the outcry against "loopholes" has pressured
many legislatures to "do something." Despite seventeen states regulating the private transfers of weapons between individuals at gun
shows, no evidence supports the conclusion that these regulations
actually lower crime.

GUNS' DETERRENT EFFECT ON VIOLENCE

"Apparently it was a female suicide bomber," Jerusalem
police chief Mickey Levy told reporters at the scene of the
blast. "The female terrorist, based on her appearance and
what I saw from her face, her crushed skull, was a young
woman." Levy said it appeared her target was the bustling
Mahane Yehuda open-air market where crowds of Israelis
were doing last minute shopping before the start of the
Jewish Sabbath at sundown. He said she apparently
changed course at the sight of police guarding the market's
entrance. "She did not succeed at getting into the market

and set off her bomb at a bus stop when a bus came to let off passengers," Levy said. "She set off a very powerful bomb."[16]

In the attack on the Jewish community center in Los Angeles that left 5 people wounded, the killer had "scouted three prominent Jewish institutions in Los Angeles as he looked for places to kill Jews, but found security too tight. He then stumbled on the lesser-known North Valley Jewish Community Center in suburban Granada Hills, they say."[17]

[His killer] also has admitted stalking [Yitzhak] Rabin on two previous occasions.... [The killer] tried again in September at a ribbon-cutting ceremony for a new highway interchange, but found security was too tight.[18]

Each of these brief stories represents a different case where very determined and motivated criminals altered their plans because of increased security. Each of the criminals eventually committed a crime, though in each case the outcome could have been far more deadly. At least in the case of the bomber, many lives were apparently saved because she was unable to set off the bomb where the greatest number of potential victims were gathered. If security had been tighter near other attempted targets, possibly the killers would have given up on their attacks.

I have come across this deterrent phenomenon many times in my own work. While serving as chief economist at the United States Sentencing Commission during the late 1980s, I read hundreds of trial transcripts in which criminals testified against their accomplices. So many cases fit the exact same pattern. These criminals were frequently asked the exact same questions about why they had chosen a particular victim. Robbers would relate how they had considered several opportunities for stealing a lot of money, such as a drug dealer who had made a big score or a taxi cab driver who would have cash on him. But the criminals would then decide against those options because the drug dealer would naturally be well armed, or the cab driver would possibly have a gun. Frequently the criminals would then relate how they had come across a potential victim viewed as an easy target, a male of unimpressive build, or a woman, or an elderly person—all of them far less likely than the drug dealer or cab driver to be carrying a weapon.

Sometimes simply the threat of self-defense with a gun is enough to stop criminals, even in the middle of a crime.[19] Take a couple of news stories from 2001:

> A bearded man, approximately 65 years old, pulled out a folding knife and threatened the owner of a convenience store.... The owner said he kept a gun behind the store counter and the attacker fled.[20]

> A gunman wearing a ski mask knocked on a door. When a man answered, the gunman tried to force his way in by using the butt of his gun to break out a storm-door window and screen, then pointed the gun at the man. When the man tried to shut the door, the gunman put his foot in the door. The man yelled to his wife to get his gun and call the police, and the gunman fled.[21]

In fact, because many Americans keep guns in their homes, burglars in the United States spend more time than burgulars in other countries "casing" a house to ensure that nobody is home. As a result, countries with high gun ownership rates experience dramatically fewer break-ins during periods when the residents are at home.[22]

Felons frequently comment in trial transcripts that they avoid late-night burglaries because "that's the way to get shot."[23] A National Institute of Justice survey found that 74 percent of the convicts who had committed a burglary or violent crime agreed: "One reason burglars avoid houses when people are at home is that they fear being shot."[24] A survey of burglars in St. Louis produced similar responses by burglar after burglar. One burglar stated, "I don't think about gettin' caught, I think about gettin' gunned down, shot."[25] Or another said:

> Hey, wouldn't you blow somebody away if someone broke into your house and you didn't know them? You hear this noise and they come breakin' in the window tryin' to get into your house, they gon' want to kill you anyway. See, with the police, they gon' say, "Come out with your hands up and don't do nothing foolish!" Okay, you still alive, but you goin' to jail. But you alive. You sneak into somebody's house and they wait 'til you get in the house and then they shoot you.... See what I'm sayin'? You can't explain nothin' to nobody; you layin' down in there dead![26]

To an economist such as myself, the notion of deterrence—which causes criminals to avoid drug dealers, cab drivers, and homes where the residents are present—is not too surprising. We see the same basic relationships in all other areas of life: If you make something more difficult, people will be less likely to engage in it. This well-known principle applies to products: When the price of apples rises relative to oranges, people buy fewer apples and more oranges.

To the noneconomist, it may appear cold to compare apples to human victims. But just as grocery shoppers switch between different types of produce depending on costs, criminals switch between different kinds of prey depending on the cost of attacking. Economists call this, appropriately enough, "the substitution effect."

Deterrent actions can help more people than just the person who takes the action. When people defend themselves, they may indirectly benefit other citizens. Burglars don't know for sure whether the occupants of a home will be armed until they actually confront them. But if you live in an area with higher gun ownership rates, the risk that a burglar faces when entering a home is obviously also high.

Homeowners who defend themselves make burglars wary of breaking into homes in general. This protects others in the neighborhood from more break-ins. Such spillover effects are frequently referred to as "third-party effects" or "external benefits." Non–gun owners in some sense are "free riders"—another economic term—on the defensive efforts provided by their gun-owning neighbors.

An Overview of This Book

Guns receive tremendous attention from the media and government. But do these institutions do a good job of informing people about the costs and benefits of guns? Do people get an accurate picture of the trade-offs we face with guns? The job the media and government do in educating people about guns has real implications for people's safety. Just as ignoring the risks of guns can put families in danger, exaggerating the risks of gun ownership can frighten people and discourage them from owning guns to defend themselves and their families. The first few chapters lay out the case that the media and government have failed to give people a balanced picture of guns.

While this book will discuss many gun control laws, from one-gun-a-month restrictions to waiting periods to background checks to concealed handgun laws, the primary focus is on several gun control issues that have received much attention recently: How to reduce possible terror attacks with guns (multiple victim public killings), the risks of increased gun ownership in the home and whether those guns should be locked, gun show loopholes, and assault weapons bans.

All four issues have been raised in the debate over terrorism, though in different forms. Multiple victim public shootings are related to one method of terrorist attack. We have seen gun sales increase despite the media's constant warnings about the risks of guns in the home. And finally, gun show loopholes and assault weapons have supposedly provided criminals—as well as terrorists—with an important source of guns.

In addition to the implications for terrorism, it is also important to understand multiple victim shootings from a purely theoretical perspective. Many criminals who shoot into crowds of people are diagnosed as being mentally instable. But the evidence in this book shows that even these supposedly "insane" criminals generally respond to the deterrent effect of guns the way a sane person would.

Indeed, the importance of incentives can be seen throughout the rest of this book. As in my past work, this book finds that law enforcement generally plays a central role in stopping crime. Still, there are some surprises about the role of law enforcement in deterring multiple victim shootings that are quite different than for other types of crimes. The surprises of what works and what doesn't can only be thoroughly understood when considering what happens to the criminals at the crime scene. The data allow us to answer some questions on how gun laws should be structured. Are mass killings prevented by gun-free zones? Does more training for permit holders help? Other issues are examined, such as whether shootings (or the news coverage of those attacks) lead to copycat attacks.

The findings regarding accidental gun deaths also defy conventional wisdom. For example, the level of accidental gun deaths is not easily related to the level of gun ownership, though there is a simple explanation for this. Similarly, when gun ownership falls or guns are locked up, it is not just that general crime increases; also criminals become emboldened to attack people in their homes and their attacks are more successful.

This book provides the first evidence on the impact of gun show regulations on crime rates. Does closing the "gun show loophole" reduce crime? Do the rules impact law-abiding people's ability to obtain guns? Given the loud debate over gun shows, these seem like basic questions, but they have not previously been examined.

The Bias Against Guns will answer all of these questions from an economic—not philosophical—perspective. My role as an economist is not to consider whether Americans have a "right" to own guns, to keep them unlocked, to sell them at gun shows, to carry guns with them wherever they go, and so on. My only objective is to study the measurable effect that gun laws have on incidents of violence, and to let the facts speak for themselves.

CHAPTER 1

THE GOOD AND THE BAD

...The audience [of 1,700 high school students] turned respectfully silent when testimonials were delivered by two other people who have been touched by the tragedy of gun violence. Most poignant was the 10-minute talk given by Wanda Faulkner, mother of Tatiana Cannon, the Bolingbrook High School freshman who died June 7, 2001, of an accidental gunshot to the chest while attending a party at a private residence in Bolingbrook.... It was Faulkner's riveting recounting of that day's events—and her plea to the students to understand the dangers of handguns—that had many in the audience wiping their eyes. Wearing the necklace that her daughter was wearing the day she died, Faulkner walked slowly in circles while holding a microphone, speaking of the personal anguish and helplessness she felt as she drove to Edward Hospital after officials had notified her of the incident.... "I am here today to tell you the truth. What is the truth? The truth is that guns were designed to kill, and when that happens a life ceases to exist," she said.... As Faulkner left the center of the gymnasium, the entire audience stood and applauded. Moments later, students sat down again and watched in the dimly lit gymnasium as Chris Pesavento, former football star at Plainfield High School, appeared in a motorized wheelchair.... paralyzed from the neck down [by a gang shooting].... The message struck home for Jermaine Austin, 19. ... "It made me think a lot about how dangerous guns are, because he was so athletic, and I am an athlete."

A 2002 newspaper article describing a program on gun violence presented to students at an Illinois high school [1]

This 2002 story from a local Chicago newspaper illustrates how the debate over guns often comes across as purely emotional. Facts do matter, but too often the facts that people rely on are much more than simply statistical numbers. Programs on guns such as the one described above at an Illinois high school constitute just a small part of the information received in the learning process about guns. People can't pick up a newspaper in the morning or listen to the national or local evening news without hearing about a criminal act involving a gun. People are unlikely to change their positions against guns when a single new fact is introduced, because that new information is merely a drop in the bucket, overwhelmed by all the other information circulating about guns.

People are inundated with information, but the information is very lopsided. We are inundated with bad news about guns and rarely hear about the benefits. After all, when was the last time that you saw a story on a national evening news broadcast about someone using a gun to save lives? As the next chapter will show, in the few cases defensive gun use is reported, the stories tend to receive brief, few-hundred-word mentions in the back of small, more rural newspapers. This is the case even though most defensive uses occur in high crime urban areas.

And because killings and injuries are news, the defensive gun use stories that are covered tend to be—with few exceptions—almost exclusively the rare cases where the criminals have been killed or seriously wounded by the would-be victim—not the cases where everything ends peacefully. The preponderance of those stories can add to the fears law-abiding citizens have about guns.

If one visits the website of the antigun Brady Campaign (formerly Handgun Control, Inc.), on any day one is greeted with a list of bad events that have occurred across the nation. For example, during the weekend of April 12–14, 2001, the site listed four stories:

— Man accused of helping his wife commit suicide (Alaska).[2]

— Monroe woman is slain in home (New York).[3]

— Man enters guilty plea in death of taxi driver (North Carolina).[4]

— Guns found in toilet tank believed murder weapons (Oklahoma).[5]

The headlines accurately reflect what happened. In the suicide case, the man thought that his wife was "jokin" [sic] about committing suicide when she asked him for the gun. The Monroe woman was shot by her estranged husband. The taxicab driver was murdered during a robbery. The Oklahoma case involved two men who forced their way into a woman's car and made her drive to a secluded area in 1999. The two killers shot to death the woman, as well as a man who happened to be passing by when they were killing her. These and other horrible stories are all too common and remind us of ones we hear about every day.

It can be difficult to remember that there's also a good side to guns. The same weekend that the Brady Campaign ran their report, the gun rights organization KeepandBearArms.com listed several examples in which guns were used to save lives.

— A 31-year-old male was shot after "forcing his way into a 33-year-old woman's home" (California).[6]

— One of two robbers stealing from a jewelry store was wounded by an employee (Washington).[7]

— A man "called 911 to report that an intruder was in his apartment threatening him." The man was forced to shoot the intruder fatally before the police were able to arrive (Texas).[8]

Possibly the first set of anecdotal cases is more disturbing than the other, but both sets raise questions about "what might have been." In the suicide case, would the woman have gotten a gun on her own or committed suicide some other way? Very possibly. Could the Monroe woman have been killed in another way by her estranged husband? Of course. In the Oklahoma case, could the two male carjackers have been able to kill the woman even if they hadn't had guns? Unfortunately, the answer is probably yes.

Similar questions can be raised about the stories listed in the second set of stories. Might the two people whose homes were broken into have defended themselves in some other way? Maybe yes, maybe no. In the cases where guns have been used to kill, the harm is clear. By contrast, with the defensive gun cases one can only guess what physical harm, if any, the criminals would have done to the victims.

There is no reason to limit the bad stories about guns to those mentioned over a particular weekend. For example, public school shootings where multiple students have been killed took place in: West Paducah, Kentucky; Jonesboro, Arkansas; Springfield, Oregon; Littleton, Colorado; and Santee, California.[9] Similar shootings near schools include Pearl, Mississippi and Savannah, Georgia. These seven killing sprees are etched into our memory with many hundreds of news stories covering each event.

Anecdotal stories dominate the media debate over guns, in part because of their obvious emotional appeal. The biggest problem with using these stories for policy discussions is the "what if" questions that cannot be adequately answered for a particular case. Academics such as myself can collect data and propose the safest course of action for people to take on average, even breaking down the estimates by the type of crime, the weapon used, and the characteristics of the victim and criminal. We will go through some of this work later. But there is not always enough information to make more than the roughest guesses in a particular case about what would have happened in the absence of a gun.

A question I hear repeatedly from audiences when I give talks is: "If defensive gun use occurs, why haven't I ever heard of even one story?" It is particularly difficult for people to accept academic and private survey data on defensive gun use that show people using guns defensively anywhere from 1.5 to 3.4 million times a year. Relying on the few anecdotal stories that were published in newspapers is unlikely to prove that these events are so numerous, but they will at least deal with the question of whether these events occur.

During 2001 I did two detailed searches on defensive gun uses: one for a piece I wrote for the *Los Angeles Times* that covered defensive gun uses from March 11 to 17, and another for a *New York Post* piece covering cases from July 22 to 28. While the search was not meant to be comprehensive, I found a total of forty defensive gun uses over those two weeks.[10] Here is a representative group from those stories.

March 11–17, 2001:

— Clearwater, Florida: At 1:05 A.M., a man started banging on a patio door, briefly left to beat on the family's truck, but returned and tore open the patio door. At that point, after numerous shouts not to break into the home, a 16-year-old boy fired a single rifle shot, wounding the attacker.[11]

— Columbia, South Carolina: As two gas station employees left work just after midnight, two men attempted to rob them. The sheriff told a local television station: "Two men came out of the bushes, one of the men had a shovel handle that had been broken off and began to beat the male employee...about the head, neck and then the arms." The male employee broke away long enough to draw a handgun from his pocket and wound his attacker, who later died. The second suspect, turned in by relatives, faces armed robbery and possible murder charges.[12]

— Little Rock, Arkansas: By firing one shot with a rifle, a 19-year-old man defended himself against three armed men who were threatening to assault him. One of them was treated for a flesh wound.[13]

— Detroit, Michigan: A mentally disturbed man yelled that the president was going to have him killed and started firing at people in passing cars. A man at the scene, who had a permit to carry a concealed handgun, fired shots that forced the attacker to stop shooting and run away. The attacker barricaded himself in an empty apartment, fired at police, and ultimately committed suicide.[14]

— West Palm Beach, Florida: After being beaten during a robbery at his home just two days earlier, a homeowner began carrying a handgun in his pocket. When another robber attacked him, the homeowner shot and wounded his assailant.[15]

— Grand Junction, Colorado: On his way home from work, a contractor picked up three young hitchhikers. He fixed them a steak dinner at his house and was preparing to offer them jobs. Two of the men grabbed his kitchen knives and started stabbing him in the back, head and hands. The attackers stopped only when he told them that he could give them money. Instead of money, the contractor grabbed a pistol and shot one of the attackers. The contractor said, "If I'd had a trigger lock, I'd be dead."[16]

— Columbia Falls, Montana: An ex-boyfriend was accused of entering a woman's home and sexually assaulting her. She got away long enough to get her handgun and hold her attacker at gun point until police arrived.[17]

— Salt Lake City, Utah: Two robbers began firing their guns as soon as they entered a pawn shop. The owner and his son returned fire. One of the robbers was shot in the arm; both later were arrested. The shop owner's statement said it all: "If we did not have our guns, we would have had several people dead here."[18]

— Baton Rouge, Louisiana: At 5:45 A.M., a crack addict kicked in the back door of a house and went in. The attacker was fatally shot as he charged toward the homeowner.[19]

July 22–28, 2001:

— Augusta, Georgia: At 5 A.M., a man awaiting trial for previously assaulting his former girlfriend, shattered a window next to her front door with a piece of concrete and let himself in. According to the coroner, "When he raised back with a piece of concrete in his hand, she fired [the weapon] and struck him dead center in the right eye."[20]

— Spartanburg, South Carolina: Arriving home at night, a man found a burglar with firearms in his kitchen. The homeowner pulled out his permitted concealed handgun and shot the intruder twice, killing him. According to police, the burglar had an outstanding "violence charge."[21]

— Near Nashville, Tennessee: A car with two men was being driven erratically and almost ran several other cars off a

highway. The car then followed another car off the highway until they both stopped at a stoplight. Then two men
from the pursuing car walked over. One man hit the driver
and the other pointed a gun, and they demanded his wallet.
The 24-year-old victim, carrying a permitted concealed
handgun, wounded an attacker. At that point the attackers
fled.[22]

— Gainesville, Florida: A newspaper carrier was dragged from
his car and beaten. Police said that at 3:15 A.M., "Five guys
get out and start running toward [the victim]. All five guys
converged on him, breaking the windshield and beating up
his car." After being pulled from his car, the victim shot
one attacker in the chest, wounding him. A police officer
said: "If you have a concealed weapons permit, that's what
it's for ... it very easily saved [the victim's] life. ... But as far
as criminals go, when you're thinking about committing a
crime, people may be carrying weapons and this is a defi-
nite result of what could happen."[23]

— East Nashville, Tennessee: Just before midnight, a woman
fatally shot an intruder who had entered her home and
tried to sexually assault her.[24]

— Tampa, Florida: Two teenage armed robbers committed a
four-hour crime spree, carjacking cars, robbing people, and
hospitalizing one victim with serious injuries. They were
only stopped by one intended victim, a pizza store owner
who shot and wounded one attacker. The wounded robber
was arrested later at a hospital.[25]

— Charleston, South Carolina: A carjacking was successfully
stopped by a 27-year-old victim who shot one of his attackers. The victim had stopped to ask directions when several
men, at least one with a lengthy criminal record, jumped
into the car.[26]

While it is doubtful that readers of this book have heard of any of
these cases, many represent gripping life and death stories. And these
stories represent only a fraction of defensive gun uses. A survey that
I conducted of 1,015 people during November and December 2002

indicates that 2.3 million defensive gun uses occurred over the previous year.[27]

The stories raise questions about what advice should have been given to these victims. Should they have behaved passively? Is there something else they could have done besides reach for a firearm? Should the woman threatened with the piece of concrete simply have tried to duck? What should the newspaper carrier beaten by five men have done? What else could the contractor in Colorado have done other than reach for his gun?

Guns do make it easier for bad things to happen, but, as these stories show, they also make it easier for people to defend themselves in situations where few other alternatives are available. That is why it is so important that people receive an accurate, balanced accounting of how guns are used. Unfortunately, neither the media nor the government is doing a very good job.

CHAPTER 2

THE MEDIA ON GUNS

WHAT CONSTITUTES NEWS ABOUT GUNS?

And nothing has happened.

Peter Bronson, a columnist for the Cincinnati Enquirer,
*commenting on the violence that was predicted in the
media after a state appeals court found Ohio's law
banning concealed handguns unconstitutional*[1]

In early 2002 the Ohio Court of Appeals struck down a state law banning the carrying of concealed handguns. The court ruled it was an
unconstitutional infringement on rights guaranteed by the state constitution. Once the court struck down the law, Hamilton County,
where the urban center of Cincinnati is located, was temporarily left
without any restrictions against law-abiding citizens carrying concealed weapons.

If any violence had been attributed to this change in Cincinnati
and its environs, there certainly would have been extensive news coverage in Ohio. But in the weeks after the decision, images of Wild
West scenarios never materialized, and the discussion of violence dis-
appeared from the media. Peter Bronson's column noting that "nothing has happened" was the media's sole acknowledgment of this.

A 1985 *Los Angeles Times* survey of about three thousand journalists found that while only half the public supported stricter handgun controls, 78 percent of journalists wanted more regulations.[2]
While the results of this survey are noteworthy, I don't allege that

they explain the vast majority of decisions behind what gun stories the media decide to cover. The media have a natural inclination to report only dramatic events, which are "news," while ignoring *potentially* tragic events, which are "not news."

Even though the survey I conducted during the fall of 2002 indicates that simply brandishing a gun stops crimes 95 percent of the time, and other surveys have also found high rates, it is very rare to see such a story. No conspiracy is really needed to explain why an editor finds a dead body on the ground very newsworthy (particularly if it is a sympathetic person like a victim of a gunshot). Take a story in which a woman brandishes a gun and a criminal flees: No shots are fired, no crime is committed, and no one is even sure what crime would have been committed had a weapon not been drawn. Nothing bad actually happened. It is not emotionally gripping enough to make the story "newsworthy."[3]

To put it differently, airplane crashes get news coverage. Successful airplane take-offs and landings do not.

The importance of newsworthiness can be seen in other ways. For example, even though fewer than one out of 1,000 defensive gun uses result in the attacker's death, "newsworthiness" means the media will only cover the bloodier cases, where the attacker is virtually always shot and usually killed. Woundings might be about six times more frequent than killings, but one could never tell that from the stories the media chooses to cover.[4]

Newsworthiness might explain the majority of negative media stories on guns, but it doesn't explain all of them. For example, as I discussed in detail in my previous book, *More Guns, Less Crime*, why did the torrential news coverage of public school shootings in the 1990s fail to acknowledge when attacks were halted by citizens with guns?

A similar example of selective reporting occurred during January 2002 in a shooting that left three dead at the Appalachian Law School in Virginia. The event made international headlines from Australia to Nigeria and produced more calls for gun control. Yet in this age in which media and government officials clamor in favor of "gun-free school zones," one fact was missing from virtually all the news coverage: The attack was stopped by two students who had guns in their cars.

The fast responses of two male students, Mikael Gross, thirty-four, and Tracy Bridges, twenty-five, undoubtedly saved many lives.[5] Mikael was outside the law school and just returning from lunch when Peter Odighizuwa started his attack. Tracy was in a classroom waiting for class to start. When the shots rang out, utter chaos erupted. Mikael said, "People were running everywhere. They were jumping behind cars, running out in front of traffic, trying to get away."

Mikael and Tracy were prepared to do something quite different: Both immediately ran to their cars and got their guns. Mikael had to run about one hundred yards to get to his car. Along with Ted Besen (who was unarmed), they approached Peter from different sides.

As Tracy explained it, "I stopped at my vehicle and got a handgun, a revolver. Ted went toward Peter, and I aimed my gun at [Peter], and Peter tossed his gun down. Ted approached Peter, and Peter hit Ted in the jaw. Ted pushed him back and we all jumped on."

Isn't it remarkable that out of 208 news stories (from a computerized Nexis-Lexis search) in the week after the event, just four stories mentioned that the students who stopped the attack had guns?[6] Only two local newspapers (the *Richmond Times-Dispatch* and the *Charlotte Observer*) mentioned that the students actually pointed their guns at the attacker.[7]

Much more typical was the description given by the *Washington Post*: "three students pounced on the gunman and held him until help arrived."[8] New York's *Newsday* noted only that the attacker was "restrained by students."[9] Many stories mentioned the law enforcement or military background of these student heroes, but virtually all of the media who discussed how the attack was stopped said things such as: "students tackled the man while he was still armed," "students tackled the gunman," the attacker "dropped his gun after being confronted by students, who then tackled him to the ground," or "Students ended the rampage by confronting and then tackling the gunman, who dropped his weapon."[10]

In all, seventy-two stories described how the attacker was stopped, without mentioning that the student heroes had guns. But almost the same number of stories (sixty-eight) provided precise details on the gun used in the attack: the *New York Times* described the gun of the attacker as "a .380 semiautomatic handgun";[11] the *Los Angeles Times* as "a .380-caliber semiautomatic pistol."[12]

A week and a half after the attack, I appeared on Larry Elder's KABC radio program in Los Angeles, along with Tracy Bridges, one of the Appalachian Law School heroes.[13] Tracy related how "shocked" he had been by the news coverage. While Tracy had carefully described to over fifty reporters what had happened, discussing how he had to point his gun at Peter and yell at Peter to drop his gun, the media had consistently reported that the incident had ended by the students tackling the killer. When I relayed what the *Washington Post* had reported, Tracy quickly mentioned that he had spent a considerable amount of time talking about what actually happened, face-to-face, with Maria Glod of the *Post*. He sounded stunned that the *Post* would report the events the way it did.[14]

After finishing the radio show with Tracy, I telephoned the *Washington Post*, and Maria Glod confirmed that she talked to both Tracy Bridges and Mikael Gross and that both had told her the same story. She said that describing the students as "pouncing" and not using their guns was not "intentional," but that the story she had written together with Fredrick Kunkle had "focused" on the impact the attack had on the town rather than on the attack itself. The way that things had come out was simply due to "space constraints."[15]

I later talked to Mike Getler, the ombudsman for the *Post*. Getler was quoted in the *Kansas City Star* as saying that the reporters simply did not know that bystanders had gotten their guns.[16] But after being informed that Glod had been told by the students about using their guns, yet excluded that information because of space constraints, Getler said, "She should have included it."[17] However, Getler said that he had no power to do anything about it. Getler noted that readers had sent in letters and comments expressing concern about the coverage of the halted attack. But none of the letters was ever published.

The *Kansas City Star* piece contained a particularly interesting interview with Jack Stokes, media relations manager at the Associated Press, who "dismissed accusations that news groups deliberately downplayed the role gun owners may have played in stopping Odighizuwa.... But [Stokes] did acknowledge being 'shocked' upon learning that students carrying guns had helped subdue the gunman.

'I thought, my God, they're putting into jeopardy even more people by bringing out these guns,' Stokes said."

Larry Elder also had a particularly disheartening discussion with a "readers' representative" for the *Los Angeles Times*. The *Times* claimed that the attack was stopped when "Other students tackled the gunman minutes after he stalked through the tiny campus of the Appalachian School of Law where he wounded three others during the shooting spree."[18] The representative told Elder that "Even if there was a good guy with a gun, I don't know that he played a key role in this case....It might be that the coverage that said the man was tackled was accurate in naming 'tackling' as being the key thing that brought him down. Even if you're for gun rights, that doesn't necessarily mean that the person who had a gun was the key part of the process of subduing the man."[19]

It's no wonder people find it hard to believe that research shows that there are two million defensive gun uses each year. After all, people frequently say to me, if these events were really happening, wouldn't we hear about them on the news? But when was the last time you saw a story on the national evening news (or even the local news) about a citizen using his gun to stop a crime?

Selective reporting of crimes such as the Appalachian Law School attack isn't just poor journalism, it could actually endanger people's lives. By turning a defensive gun use story into one where students merely "overpowered a gunman," the media gives potential victims the wrong impression of what works when confronted by violence. Research consistently shows that having a gun (usually just brandishing it) is the safest way to respond to any type of criminal attack.[20]

Yet, whatever the impact that such coverage has on safety, it is clear that the decision to cover only the crimes committed with guns—and not the crimes stopped with guns—has a real impact on people's perceptions of the desirability of guns.

WHEN THE MEDIA CREATES ITS OWN NEWS ABOUT GUNS

Recently the *New York Times* ran an unusually long twenty-thousand-word series of articles on so-called "rampage killings," which the newspaper defined as any type of nonpolitical murder of two or more people in a public place.[21] The series reported the results of research conducted by the *Times* itself.

The series is interesting if only because the *Times* is viewed as the objective "publication of record" for so much of the media. Among the *Times*'s conclusions? Its research "confirmed the public perception that [rampage killings] appear to be increasing" and that another "crucial factor in rampage killings, access to guns, can be affected through legislation and regulation."[22] The tighter gun control laws mentioned included everything from "background checks at gun shows" to "trigger locks." The national editor at the *Times* proudly noted that "most experts have praised [the series] as an aggressive and objective look at a complex, emotion-laden problem."[23]

The *Times* reported that 100 such attacks took place during the fifty-one years from 1949 to 1999, with over half (51) during the five years between 1995 and 1999. Newspapers across the country started debating why these particular crimes were increasing.[24] With such a shockingly large increase, the *Times* concluded: "the nation needs tighter gun laws for everyone."[25]

It immediately caught my attention that the *Times* study reported exactly 100 cases, a nice round number. And, as the data shown in Chapter 6 indicate, it was immediately obvious that the *Times* had simply left out most cases prior to 1995.

While a sidebar to one of the articles briefly noted that the series "does not include every attack," the omissions were major and systematic. Those omissions created the most alarming claim of a roughly fivefold increase in attacks between the 1977–1994 and 1995–1999 periods (a ninefold increase between the 1949–1994 and 1995–1999 periods). For instance, the *Times* claimed that from 1977 to 1994 there was an annual average of only 2.6 attacks where at least one person was killed in a public multiple victim attack (not including robberies or political killings). Yet, the research provided later in Chapter 6 uncovered more than six times as many cases—an average of 17 per year.

It is only by consistently counting recent cases and ignoring most old ones that the *Times* reached the conclusion that mass killings increased dramatically during the mid-1990s. Contrary to its claim, there exists no upward national trend whatsoever, at least not since the mid-1970s. The national data show lots of ups and downs, but with no generally rising or falling pattern. For instance, 1996 had an unusually large number of attacks, though the level began to recede in 1997.

When questioned over the telephone, Ford Fessenden (the reporter at the *Times* who wrote the first article in its series) initially denied missing any cases.[26] But after I went through several cases, he admitted that they had concentrated mainly on cases for the years after 1994. For the early years, they had only retrieved the "easily obtainable" cases. He said that there was nothing magical about the number 100, but it had simply seemed like a convenient number at which to stop searching.

Responding to his inquiry of how long it had taken Bill Landes and me to collect the research data on multiple victim attacks, I told him, "a couple of thousand hours." His reaction was that there was "no way" they could have devoted that much time to the project. Fessenden also acknowledged that he was familiar with the research that I had done with Bill Landes and that the *Times* series may have "unintentionally" given the false impression that they were the first ones to compile this type of data. When asked if he had compared his data with ours to double-check things, his answer was "no."[27]

The *Times* claimed that attacks increased modestly in the late 1980s and that this increase coincided with the period during which the "production of semi-automatic pistols overtook the production of revolvers." But again, there was no such increase in the late 1980s. If anything, just the opposite was occurring. When one examined all the cases during this earlier period, even though there was a significant variation from year to year in the rate of attacks, the general trend was downward. The number of public shootings per ten million people fell from 1 in 1985 to 0.9 in 1990 to 0.5 in 1995.

The *Times* asserts, without explaining exactly why, that their data show the necessity of the Brady Law to stop these crimes.[28] But this conclusion can't be reached even when using the *Times*'s own, flawed data. The Brady Law went into effect during 1994, but their data purportedly show dramatic increase in "rampage killings" in 1995.

The *Times* asserted that "tighter gun laws" were required to reverse what it claimed was a sharp increase in deaths from rampages starting in 1995 (an average of thirty-three people died per year from 1995 to 1999). Unfortunately, the reporters simply assumed that tighter gun laws would save lives. Fox Butterfield, another reporter who wrote part of this series, told me that no formal statistical tests were done on their data. He said that some academics had told him that there was "no way that [they] would get any statistically significant results," and that the *Times* never checked to see whether that was true.[29]

But Butterfield's answer also creates some disturbing problems for the *Times* study. Why would the newspaper, or any institution doing research, assert benefits to gun laws if they seriously doubted that their data would produce any statistically significant results?

In fact, the policies proposed by the *Times* have proven useless at stopping these "rampage killings." As we will see in Chapter 6, different sentencing policies and gun laws (such as waiting periods, background checks, and one-gun-a-month restrictions) have not deterred the rate at which these killings occur in different states. Indeed, Ford Fessenden and Fox Butterfield both acknowledged that they knew of previous research on multiple victim shootings that Bill Landes and I had done, but they never mentioned this, and the *Times* still went ahead with its recommendations even though it had no results of its own.

While higher arrest and conviction rates, longer prison sentences, and the death penalty all reduce murders generally, none of these measures had a consistent impact on mass public shootings. Nor did any of the restrictive gun laws. Only one single policy was found to effectively reduce these attacks: the passage of right-to-carry laws, which permit law-abiding citizens to carry concealed handguns. But the *Times* never mentioned concealed handgun laws in their series, despite having knowledge of this research.

Giving law-abiding adults the right to carry concealed handguns has a dramatic impact on crime. Thirty-three states now make such allowances. When states passed such right-to-carry laws, the number of multiple victim public shootings plummeted by more than four-fifths with an even greater drop in deaths. To the extent that attacks still occur in states after these laws are enacted, they typically take place in those areas in which concealed handguns are forbidden, such as schools or government buildings. Unfortunately, nationwide the drop in attacks in states adopting right-to-carry laws has been offset by increases in states without these laws.

It is not surprising that the *New York Times* data show a sudden increase in the number of attacks, since it included all the multiple victim attacks from 1995 to 1999, but only a sixth of the attacks that actually took place in the years prior to that. Instead of simply claiming that restrictive gun laws would reduce crime, one ought to test to see whether any claims are statistically significant and also try to account for changes in other factors that might explain the results. Unfortunately, the *Times* never ran a correction explaining how the data were collected and the biases that it might imply. Nor did the *Times* print any of the letters to the editor that I submitted.[30]

The studies that the media produced represent only a small part of how the media affect our views on guns. Possibly an even more important influence is how the media cover the research of others. Again, an analysis of *New York Times* news articles over the last two years reveals some interesting patterns. Overwhelmingly, the *Times*'s news reporters tend to cite procontrol academics in their articles.[31] (While Fox Butterfield wrote nine of the fifteen stories, the pattern was the same for all the *Times* reporters.) Surveying news stories on gun control research over the last two years shows that reporters referenced nine procontrol academics a total of twenty times and one moderate-control academic was referenced in one article (see Table 2.1). The same procontrol academics seemed to be referenced again and again, with Philip Cook at Duke, Alfred Blumstein at Carnegie Mellon, and Garen Wintemute at the University of California at Davis being the most popular. No academic who believes that gun control can lead to more crime was referenced even once.[32]

Classifying these people as pro–gun control is fairly easy. For example, Alfred Blumstein argues that "the more guns that are out on the street, the greater the risk for deadly violence."[33] Philip Cook has made the same claim for over twenty years,[34] and Cook and his frequent co-author Jens Ludwig are regularly described by other researchers as being "pro-control."[35] As to David Kennedy, "he believes that strengthening gun laws, expanding drug treatment for chronic users and focusing on community policing programs must all be priorities to avoid an upsurge in crime."[36] At a recent National

Table 2.1: Academics Referenced in the *New York Times*
News Articles on Gun Control Research and Studies Over Two-Year
Period from February 28, 2000, to February 28, 2002

Name	Affiliation	References
Academics who strongly support gun control		
Alfred Blumstein	*Carnegie Mellon University*	3
Philip Cook	*Duke University*	4
James Alan Fox	*Northeastern University*	2
David Kennedy	*Harvard*	2
Jens Ludwig	*Georgetown University*	2
Matthew Miller	*Harvard*	1
Daniel Webster	*Johns Hopkins Center for Gun Policy and Research*	2
Garen Wintemute	*UC-Davis*	3
Franklin Zimring	*UC-Berkeley*	1
Academics who believe that guns have no net impact on crime, but still support gun control laws such as banning the private transfer of guns		
Gary Kleck	*Florida State University*	1
Academics who generally oppose gun control		
none		

Academy of Sciences panel on gun control, Kennedy, Ludwig, and
Dan Webster all disagreed with the statement that "it might be possible, not for sure but just possible, that existing gun control produces
more problems than benefits."[37] Similar statements by and about the
others listed as "procontrol" are easy to find.[38]

Some of these same academics were the experts interviewed by the
Times to evaluate its series on rampage shootings. For example,
Alfred Blumstein was quoted by the *Times* as saying that the study
was "careful."

The imbalance in the experts interviewed by the *Times* cannot
simply be explained by an inability to find academics who believe that
most gun control laws are ill advised. I am certainly not the only one.
For example, 294 academics from institutions as diverse as Harvard,
Stanford, Northwestern, University of Pennsylvania, and UCLA
released an open letter to Congress in 1999 stating that the new gun
laws being proposed at that time were "ill advised."[39] The signers were
diverse in terms of their areas of expertise, though most professors
were economists, lawyers, and criminologists. The academics wrote
that, "With the 20,000 gun laws already on the books, we advise Congress, before enacting yet more new laws, to investigate whether many

of the existing laws may have contributed to the problems we currently face." Not surprisingly, none of the academics referenced in the various *New York Times* news articles signed the letter.[40]

USING POLLS TO CREATE NEWS ABOUT GUNS AND SHAPE PEOPLE'S OPINIONS

> Your online gun control poll allows people only to vote in favor of stronger permitting, outlawing guns or gun exchange programs or to say things are fine the way they are. The *Tribune* offers extreme choices in the liberal domain, yet it doesn't offer the simple option of "there's already too much gun control."
>
> *A September 19, 1998, letter to the editor in the*
> Tampa Tribune *(Florida)*

Polls frequently serve as a source of news stories. Indeed, polls often *are* the news, paid for and conducted by news organizations. While they can provide us with important insights into people's views, they can also mislead in subtle ways. In the case of guns, consider the questions asked about the impact of gun control on crime rates. From some well-known national polls:

> Do you think that stricter gun control laws would reduce the amount of violent crime in this country a lot, a little, or not at all?
>
> *Pew Research Center, April 12–16, 2000, and*
> Newsweek, *August 12–13, 1999*

> Do you think stricter gun control laws would reduce the amount of violent crime in this country, or not?
>
> *ABC News/*Washington Post *Poll,*
> *March 30–April 2, 2000*

> Do you think stricter gun control laws would, or would not reduce violent crime?
>
> *CBS News, August 15, 1999*

In all, I reviewed seventeen national and seven state surveys that, with small variations, asked whether gun control laws reduce crime.[41] Not one of the surveys asked whether gun control would increase crime. The notion that gun control laws could primarily reduce legitimate gun ownership and therefore increase crime apparently never entered the pollsters' minds.

The omission in such polls of "would increase crime" as an option creates a bias in two different ways. First, there is an "anchoring" effect: the impact the omission has on the people polled.[42] The range of options affects how respondents answer the question. Including a different range of choices can make some options appear to be more reasonable, more "middle ground." By only providing options that gun control reduces crime from "a lot" to "not at all," the middle ground becomes "a little." Furthermore, the lack of options could even cause individuals who indeed believe that gun control increases crime to second-guess their own beliefs.

Second, polls affect the terms of debate. The possibility of gun control causing crime is removed from popular notice when it is not mentioned as an option. Even those who believe that gun control will leave law-abiding citizens defenseless against criminals will think that few people share their opinions. The survey options imply that gun control either makes society better or has no impact, but there is no hint that gun control could make things worse. Given that range of options, people's natural response will be: Why not try more gun control? What do we have to lose?

There are other subtle biases in the construction of these surveys. For example, when a survey asks whether gun control will be "very important" in their vote for president,[43] or "How important will be handling the issue of gun control?"[44] the media and those who hear the results interpret a higher percentage answering "yes" as evidence that more people *support* gun control.[45] Rarely do they consider that respondents might regard gun control as important because they *oppose* it.

Gun control doesn't rank particularly high on the list of top election issues (an ABC News/*Washington Post* survey ranked it as the fourteenth most pressing issue going into the 2000 election),[46] but the traditional polling formulation leads gun control to be ranked more highly than it should. It compares issues such as "protecting the environment" (which has supporters only on one side of the issue answering "yes") with the gun control category (where both pro- and anti–gun control sides answer "yes" when asked if it is important). Including both pro- and anti–gun control respondents in the same "importance" category illustrates this apples v. oranges problem. Categories should clearly gauge either how much people on both sides (for and against gun control) care about an issue, or on only one side.

Other recent survey evidence suggests that "gun control" means different things to different people. Shortly before the 2000 election, the *Los Angeles Times* noted that "surveys often find pluralities agreeing with the NRA and Bush that tougher enforcement of existing law is more important than passing new measures."[47] Indeed, some surveys indicate this difference could be as large as almost four-to-one (72 percent to 19 percent).[48]

But there is a puzzle: the survey data indicate that the percentage listing "gun control" as a very important priority usually greatly exceeds the percentage supporting new laws over tougher enforcement. One possible explanation is that many believe "gun control" is important because they are opposed to new laws. Some may prefer both more enforcement and more laws, but even this implies that what might be driving the "gun control" priority is enforcement of existing laws. Neither explanation fits with the interpretation normally provided: that more people listing "gun control" as a priority means greater support for new laws.

Yet, even the polls that ask whether more enforcement of existing laws is preferred to new gun control regulations create wrong impressions. Take the wording of fairly representative polls conducted by CBS News and Zogby:[49]

> **CBS News:** When it comes to gun control, which comes closer to your view?...We need stricter gun control laws in this country to limit the availability of guns. Existing gun control laws are sufficient, but they need to be better enforced.[50]

> **Zogby:** Which of the following statements best represents your position on gun control? Statement A: There needs to be more new and tougher gun control legislation to help in the

fight against gun crime. Statement B: There are enough gun
laws on the books. What is needed is better enforcement of
current laws regarding gun control.[51]

Both questions assume that everyone views gun control as beneficial.
The existing laws must be good, or no one would seriously argue that
they be more thoroughly enforced. Obviously, those who support additional gun control laws must think that they are valuable. The notion
that gun control laws might be counterproductive is never given any
credence. For that matter, what would someone answer if they
thought that gun control was ineffectual, that it neither makes things
worse nor better? The only other option given is "Don't Know," which
implies only that one is undecided about which of these two options
is correct, not that one thinks both options are wrong.[52]

Like everyone else, pollsters sometimes hold strong views. Unfortunately, those biases are easier to hide on policy questions than on
polls predicting election results. If a pollster incorrectly predicts who
will win an election or whether a ballot proposition will win, everyone will see that the pollster made a mistake, and it will hurt his rep-
utation. But survey results on whether people believe that gun control
reduces crime or whether gun control is an important priority are
much more difficult to evaluate. It is easy to word these polls ambigu-
ously to achieve a desired response. Of course, this is true for surveys
on many other public policy issues as well.

A few years ago, while I was doing research at the University of
Chicago, I had lunch with Tom Smith, who is the director of the General Social Survey at the National Opinion Research Center (NORC).
This private organization conducts many important national surveys
for the government as well as other clients. During lunch Tom mentioned how important he thought the General Social Survey was. He
felt the large drop in gun ownership implied by his survey would
"make it easier for politicians to do the right thing on guns" and pass
more restrictive regulations.[53] His surveys have traditionally shown
one of the lowest gun ownership rates among any of the surveys: for
example, almost 20 percentage points lower than recent polling by
John Zogby. After Tom made his comment about politicians, I didn't
ask him whether he had deliberately phrased his questions in such a

manner to obtain an artificially low gun ownership rate. But the question certainly crossed my mind. Possibly Tom is still right and Zogby and others are wrong.

Despite my concerns with the General Social Survey on guns, I still use its data later in the book. No other survey data on gun ownership re-asks the same question over enough years so that I can make comparisons before and after states change their laws. Hopefully any biases will likely affect all states uniformly and thus still allow comparisons showing why gun ownership rates have changed in some states more than in others.

HOW THE PRINT MEDIA COVER DEFENSIVE GUN USES

"[Ed] Rendell (former co-chairman of the Democratic National Committee in 2000 and governor of Pennsylvania) said that . . . he had never heard of a defensive gun use. He said that he didn't believe they occurred."[54]

Rendell's philosophy is a telling summary of how the media cover defensive gun use. Stories about defensive gun use might rarely be covered, but interesting patterns can be noted in the stories that do run. The fact is that most defensive gun use appears to occur in high crime urban areas, and that attackers are killed in fewer than one out of every one thousand defensive uses. Woundings are more common than killings (probably six or seven times more common), but they are still extremely rare.

As noted earlier, certain events will surely be considered more "newsworthy" than other events: A dead body will get more attention than a wounding, which in turn definitely gets more attention than a simple brandishing of a gun, with the criminal running away.

Unfortunately, this unbalanced pattern of gun coverage by the media gives people a distorted perception of what happens when guns are used defensively. People are in fact reluctant to fire a gun and kill another person, even when their own life is endangered.[55] By failing to cover the stories in which no one is killed, the media exaggerate the risk of defensive gun use. They create the false impression that the gun is often fired and that either the attacker or the victim ends up being wounded or killed.

To systematically study how the press covers defensive gun use, I
examined stories collected by KeepandBearArms.com and the NRA
Armed Citizen's archive during 2001. To my knowledge, these are the
only two comprehensive sources that collect stories over the entire
year. (Searches I have conducted in the past indicate that these two
organizations account for at most 60 percent of defensive news stories.[56]) The sources could provide a very uneven picture across publications and states simply because the volunteers who compiled the
stories may be more numerous or more active in different states.
However, the additional stories that I collected were very similar in
terms of the size of the paper and the characteristics of the stories
that made the news.

Between KeepandBearArms.com and the NRA Armed Citizen's
archive, there were 459 different news stories that identified defensive
gun uses. Out of these, 404 news stories appeared in newspapers, and
the rest ran on the Associated Press wire service or the web pages of
local television or radio stations. About 10 percent of the newspaper
stories were different versions of the same event. At least some information on the victims or their attackers was available in most articles.
The victims who used a gun defensively varied greatly, ranging from a
couple of twelve-year-old girls to a ninety-three-year-old man.

Excluding duplicate stories, 310 of the defensive gun users were
identified as men and 59 as women. In 4 cases a victim was killed,
and in 72 a victim was injured. The criminals were virtually always
men: 398 men and 2 women. Most stories entail criminals in their
teens (58), twenties (115), and thirties (66). Twenty-seven cases
involved multiple male attackers.[57]

Eighty percent of the news stories mentioned that the criminals
were shot. Forty-eight percent of the time the attacker was killed and
32 percent of the time he was wounded. Of the other cases, 7 percent
of the time the victim held the criminal at gunpoint until police
arrived and 13 percent reported that the criminal fled the scene after
the intended victim brandished a gun. Five cases involved defenses
against animals: two pit bulls, two cougars, and one bobcat.

Surprisingly, 20 percent of the stories covered instances where the
intended victims merely scared away their attackers or held them for
the police. These stories tended to be reported in much smaller media

markets, which appear more willing to publish articles on topics that major newspapers would consider too minor to be "newsworthy." While 35 percent of all the newspaper articles on defensive gun use were published in the top 50 newspapers, only 16 percent of the "fleeing criminal" and the "holding criminal" stories fell in that category.

The number of stories is very uneven across states. Two states alone accounted for over a fifth of all defensive gun use stories: Florida with 47, and Texas with 42. Other states with relatively high rates of reported stories were North Carolina with 19, Tennessee with 18, and 15 each in Ohio, Louisiana, and Georgia.

Although most defensive gun use occurs in major cities, most of the stories reported were outside those areas. Almost 40 percent of the stories were not even in the top 100 newspapers.

Of the 37 stories in the top 10 newspapers, 26 were accounted for by just two Texas newspapers, the *Houston Chronicle* and the *Dallas Morning News*. It is possible that Houston and Dallas are simply extremely unusual in the number of defensive gun uses, but it is also possible that those newspapers are doing a better job giving readers a more balanced view of the gun issue. A conversation with Dale Lezon, a police reporter with the *Dallas Morning News*, provides some evidence for this. He thought that the difference might arise because the *Morning News* is considered the newspaper of record for Dallas and it reports all the stories involving deaths—even if it is just a couple of paragraphs.[58] But, he said, this policy also explains why the paper only included cases where the attacker is killed, and not just deterred or wounded.[59]

Out of the nation's three largest newspapers (*USA Today*, the *Wall Street Journal*, and the *New York Times*), only the *Times* carried even a single news story on defensive gun use. (The instance involved a retired New York City Department of Corrections worker who shot a man who was holding up his gasoline station.[60]) Other smaller New York City–area newspapers were not much better, carrying seven different stories of defensive gun use [*New York Post* (3), *New York Daily News* (2), and *Newsday* (2)]. Among the other top ten papers, the *Los Angeles Times* and the *Chicago Tribune* each managed three such stories—all cases where the criminals were killed and one where a victim was seriously injured. The *Washington Post* also had three short news stories about two different cases involving gas station attendants who defended themselves against armed robbers.[61]

To get an idea of the imbalance in a major paper between stories about gun crime and guns stopping crimes, I again looked through the *New York Times* to find how much coverage the paper gave to crimes committed with guns during 2001. To be fair to the *Times*, I excluded court case coverage of crimes, crimes committed with BB or pellet guns, guns recovered at the crime scene when the guns were not directly involved in the crime, wrongful shootings by police, and the illegal transportation or sale of guns. Despite all these exclusions, the *New York Times* published 104 gun crime news articles (69 metropolitan New York stories and 35 from the rest of the country). The stories on gun crimes ranged in length from a 66-word blurb in a Sunday paper regarding a bar shooting to a major 1,675 word front page story on a school shooting,[62] for a total of 50,745 words.[63] In comparison, the one defensive gun use story amounted to 163 words.[64]

USA Today contained 5,660 words on crimes committed with guns and zero words on examples of defensive gun use. The *Washington Post* provided the least lopsided coverage with 46,884 words worth of stories on crimes committed with guns and 953 words on defensive stories.[65]

Another striking finding is that the few defensive news stories that get coverage are all local stories. While articles about crimes with guns attract both local and national coverage, defensive stories attract only local, if any, coverage. One-third of the *New York Times*'s gun crime stories are national stories, not just New York–area stories.[66] In the *Washington Post*, about a quarter of gun crime stories are national stories.[67] Yet, neither the *Washington Post* nor the *New York Times* carries a defensive gun story from outside their local area. In the full sample of defensive gun stories that I have collected, less than one percent took place outside the local coverage area. News about guns only seems to travel if it's bad news.

Possibly this pattern helps explain why residents of urban areas are so in favor of gun control. Most crime occurs in the biggest cities, and, as just described above, people are bombarded with stories about guns facilitating crime. Even though most defensive gun use also occurs in these big cities, it simply isn't reported. Hearing only the bad events leaves its impact on urban residents.

In contrast, rural areas have fewer violent crimes and thus fewer gun crime stories. But residents of rural areas are also much more likely to hear about guns saving lives, because their local newspapers cover those incidents. Rural newspaper coverage isn't balanced, but it comes much closer to balance than that of its bigger cousins. Given that so much of the broadcast media seems to rely on the *New York Times* to direct their own news coverage,[68] perhaps its imbalance can also help explain the imbalance of some of the television networks.

Ironically, Ford Fessenden, the *New York Times* reporter who worked on the "rampage killing" series mentioned earlier, complained to me that the killings the series examined did not get as much news coverage as they "deserved." I responded that most of the time that Bill Landes and I spent compiling the data for our research entailed reading through dozens or even hundreds of stories about the same event, simply to make sure that we had gotten all the important details. Some cases such as the ones where public school shootings were stopped by citizens with guns might have 600 articles or more, but only a couple of news stories might contain important information on how the attack ended. It may be difficult to agree on how much coverage such cases "deserve," but everyone can name a long list of attacks they have heard or read about in the media. The same cannot be said of defensive gun uses.[69]

Of course, the imbalance in the print media isn't just limited to newspapers. Take the special issue of *Newsweek* during 1999 entitled "America Under the Gun." Though over 15,000 words and numerous graphics were provided in an attempt to address gun ownership, there was not one mention of defensive gun use. Under the heading "America's Weapons of Choice," the table captions were: "Top firearms traced to crimes, 1998"; "Firearm deaths per 100,000 people"; and "Percent of homicides using firearms." Nothing on the "Top firearms used in self-defense." Graphic, gut-wrenching pictures showed people who had been wounded by guns. No pictures were offered of people who had used guns defensively to save lives or prevent injuries.[70]

How Guns Are Treated in Television News

By my count, we have more states rejecting new gun control legislation than have passed it. We have fifteen states that have passed prohibitions on cities suing gun manufacturers. That hardly seems like progress.

Charles Gibson, Good Morning America, *May 12, 2000*

This Congress has so far seemed somewhat unwilling to do anything about guns. Realistically, realistically—I mean, we all hope for the best—but realistically, do you think Sunday's march is going to make a difference?

Bryant Gumbel discussing the Million Mom March on
CBS's The Early Show, *May 12, 2000*

It's been a week since a six-year-old Michigan girl was shot dead by another six-year-old. As CBS's Diana Olick reports, the little girl's death has many wondering what, if anything, more can be done and asking why Congress hasn't done anything for months.

Dan Rather on CBS's Evening News, *March 7, 2000*

As lopsided as the print media are on guns, television news seems even worse.[71] Gripping pictures of chaos and of wounded and dead people make for much more riveting news than an interview with someone who testifies that a gun saved her life. With around-the-clock cable news programs in need of material that grabs viewers' attention, shoot-outs regularly fill airtime.

To investigate television coverage, I collected stories reported on the evening news broadcasts and morning news shows on the three major networks (ABC, CBS, and NBC) during 2001.[72] In 2001 there were several segments discussing the increase in gun sales after September 11, and a couple of these shows went so far as to give the desire for self-defense as a reason. But despite slightly over 190,000 words of coverage on gun crimes,[73] merely 580 words were devoted by one news broadcast to an armed off-duty police officer who helped stop a school shooting.[74] None of the three networks mentioned any other defensive gun use—certainly not one by a civilian.[75]

ABC's *Good Morning America* program is fairly typical of broad-casting in the way it treats gun stories. It unquestionably leads its competitors in terms of the sheer volume of stories it does on guns, with almost 77,000 words spent on stories discussing gun crimes. Guests supporting gun control included Rosie O'Donnell, Randy Graves (who lost a child at Columbine), an academic from Emory University urging people to "remove the guns from the home," and Representative Carolyn McCarthy from New York, whose husband was killed in Colin Ferguson's 1993 rampage on the Long Island Rail Road. Not one single guest provided an alternative viewpoint.[76] Twelve segments covered the Santana High School shooting in San-tee, California, where two students were killed. Eight segments examined the Williamsport, Pennsylvania, shooting, where one stu-dent was wounded. And four segments were devoted to an attack at a California Community College, where a student was caught before he could act out his plan.

Other topics on *Good Morning America* during 2001 included a September discussion of school shootings that had taken place during previous academic years, the second anniversary of the Columbine attack, a town meeting on school violence, a mother who shot her six-year-old son, celebrity shootings allededly involving Robert Blake and rapper Sean "Puffy" Combs, Texas prison escapees who were committing crimes with guns, a former IRS employee who shot at the White House, and the murder of a Dekalb County, Georgia, sheriff.

ABC's other news program, *World News Tonight*, covered many of the same topics as well as a few others. Among the additional stories were two different shootings where a man killed someone at a plant and then committed suicide (in Indiana and Illinois), some general pieces on school shootings, and an examination of "Secret Service Techniques Used in Threat Assessment." Even a story about the mentally ill managed to raise the issue of crimes committed with guns.

If I were a TV news director, I admit I would probably also cover many of these same stories. Yet, while a murder/suicide at a plant in Indiana or Illinois is interesting, does it really merit coverage on the national evening news? A mother who shoots her son is also impor-tant, and so is the murder of a Georgia sheriff. But surely at least one defensive gun story, such as those listed earlier, would also be as newsworthy. Within just the randomly selected two-week period studied discussed in Chapter 1, a killer in Michigan was stopped from firing his gun at passing cars by a concealed permit holder. In other cases not covered on television news, multiple lives were saved— more lives than were lost in some of the stories that made the national news.

The imbalance of viewpoints on television news is even more difficult to explain than the choice of stories covered. Of the morning show hosts, only Katie Couric interviewed NRA president Charlton Heston (March 13).[77] One interview with Charlton Heston by the *Today Show* doesn't balance extensive interviews with Rosie O'Donnell, Million Mom March founder Donna Dees-Thomases, multiple parents who had lost their children to gun violence, and an extensive discussion about how people should try to convince their neighbors not to own guns. Not one person, including Heston during his brief interview, suggested that gun control could increase crime. If stories on lives lost by guns are interesting, why not interview a heroic youngster who saved lives with a gun? If asking neighbors to stop owning guns makes for interesting television, it ought to be equally interesting to interview researchers whose work shows that increased gun ownership saves lives.

The television media's support for more gun control in news reports is often quite explicit and frequently takes the form of lobbying. Take a segment on CBS's *Early Show*:

> **Diana Olick** (reporter): When shots rang out in the halls of Santana High last week, they fell, some say, on deaf ears in the halls of Congress....
> **Representative Carolyn McCarthy:** I've had an awful lot of members say to me, "'Carolyn, I wish I could vote with you. I can't.'" That's how powerful the NRA is.
> **Olick:** But the facts don't support the fear. In Election 2000, five new senators won their seats running on the gun issue. And according to the Million Mom Organization, five out of seven congressional candidates won with strong positions on gun control.

Ms. Donna Dees-Thomases (Million Mom Organization): I believe that some of these elected officials, quite frankly, are just cowards. They are afraid of the gun lobby. But shame on them.

Olick: ... Representative Carolyn McCarthy says that in the next few months she'll introduce another bill trying once again to require background checks at gun shows. Such a bill did not pass in the last session. Julie.

Julie Chen (anchor): All right. Thanks, Diana. Diana Olick on Capitol Hill. And just ahead, we'll hear from the mother of one of the victims of the Santana High shooting.

Segment on "Members of Congress Slow to React to Santana Shooting," CBS's The Early Show, March 16, 2001

As the quotes at the beginning of this section also indicate, anchors and reporters always assume that more gun control is the answer.

Their bias shows up in the questioning of guests. A challenging interviewer would ask gun control advocates about the strongest objections provided by their opponents. Opponents of controls should of course face the same critical questioning. Instead, gun control advocates are frequently pushed to support more restrictions than they are currently advocating. All too typical was Bryant Gumbel's questioning of Senator John McCain when Gumbel asked what McCain would do if his current gun control efforts on gun show regulations failed. Gumbel didn't ask whether McCain would reconsider his support of control. Instead, Gumbel wanted to know "Could you see your position reaching the point where you might support registration; where you might support longer waiting periods?"[78]

Television anchors encourage gun control advocates in ways one could never imagine them treating gun control opponents. Katie Couric worried aloud about the charges of hypocrisy Rosie O'Donnell faced when her bodyguards applied for concealed handgun permits: "And you were demonized by the people who believe in the right to carry guns."[79]

However, there is a notable exception to all this one-sided coverage on the television news. I concentrated on the major networks simply because they have by far the largest audiences, but since the late 1990s the Fox News Channel has been providing an alternative approach. Even though Fox provides extensive live coverage of bad events involving guns, at least several news stories[80] during 2001 and the first half of 2002 have explicitly discussed defensive gun use by citizens.

Whatever the motivation for this imbalance by the networks, the constant bombardment of bad news about guns has an impact on people's views.

How the Media Rationalize Their Stand Against Guns

Carlos Gilmer was shot in the neck Saturday at the home of his godmother, Beulah Lindsay, who took care of him. The younger boy is Lindsay's grandson, who visited her home regularly. At the time of the shooting, Lindsay was upstairs preparing a party for Carlos, and neighbors said she had hung up a "Happy Birthday" banner. Authorities said the boys found the .38-cal. pistol in a purse in the house. Police did not say whether the gun belonged to Lindsay.[81]

Morris pleaded guilty in Washington County Circuit Court to gun and drug charges filed after his 4-year-old stepson, Jason Gacs, was accidentally killed Oct. 31 by a gun in their home. The lives of Cody and his parents have spun into a confusing web since then. Morris, who had prior felony convictions, was not supposed to have guns because of his criminal history.[82]

A 12-year-old girl who shot and killed her mother's attacker will not be charged, police said. The girl was asleep in her room when Anthony Fox chased her mother into their apartment, forcing his way through the door, Detective Danny Hill said Tuesday. . . . The girl saw Fox choking her mother, grabbed her mother's pistol and fired a single shot into his chest, Hill said. The county coroner said Fox, 25, died of a single gunshot wound to the chest Saturday at an area hospital. Fox had been arrested for domestic violence against the girl's mother, his on-and-off girlfriend, at least twice, Hill said. A youth court

judge ruled the shooting self-defense, Hill said. The girl's
name was withheld because of her age.[83]

The first two stories represent one side in the gun debate, and the
third represents the other. One event generated 88 separate news stories worldwide from Australia to Ireland and received coverage in
many large newspapers from the *New York Times* to the *Chicago Tribune;* another resulted in 24 separate articles; and the other was covered in three papers, the largest of which was the *Seattle Times.* Can
you guess which story received which coverage? By now it should be
pretty obvious that the stories of the children getting shot received
the most attention, with the child shot on his birthday receiving the
greatest attention. If anything, the most unusual aspect of the news
coverage regarding the twelve-year-old who protected her mother was
that it even received as much as three separate mentions. Defensive
gun use virtually always results at most in one news story.

On occasion reporters have called me to discuss the risks of having
a gun in the home and inevitably the issue turns to accidental gun
deaths of children. As I have learned, the article that they are writing
and the focus of their story is virtually always based on some incident
in which a child has died from an accidental gun death. In response,
I have begun asking reporters why these stories get the news coverage that they do. After all, I now have five children, and I can't imagine what life would be like losing any of them for any reason, let
alone a gunshot. But it's not clear to me why this particular type of
death gets so much more news coverage when there are so many
other ways children die—and in much greater numbers. The response
that members of the media usually give me is that stories about children dying by guns get coverage precisely because they are so rare.
Often they will cite the old adage that "Man Bites Dog" stories are
much more newsworthy than "Dog Bites Man" stories.

However, I don't find their answer particularly satisfying for two
reasons. First, there are lots of other equally rare and tragic ways that
children die that don't get the same attention as gun deaths. Second,
even if these events attract coverage because they are so rare, that is
not the impression that people come away with after watching the
news. People see these broadcasts and become very concerned about

the risks of guns in the home. Fear of these tragedies has driven many to keep guns out of their homes, and the disproportionate coverage given to the bad events while ignoring the good ones undoubtedly bears some responsibility for this change.

News stories about airline crashes often try to soothe readers' or viewer's fears by reporting that air travel is safer than cars.[84] But the media don't try to soothe readers' or viewers' fears about guns by reminding them how important they are to self-defense. While gun ownership was increasing after September 11, reporters felt more compelled than usual to mention the risks of having guns in the home, particularly the risk for children.

Recently, ABC's *20/20* conducted an experiment, placing children under the age of ten alone in a room with toys.[85] Real guns were hidden among the toys. Some children treated the real guns as toys and played with them. Audiences were probably horrified by this, but subtle issues, such as whether a child would have known or been capable of pulling back the slide on a semi-automatic pistol or known how to turn off a safety were never addressed. Or, as George Will later commented, "As a controlled social science experiment, that little clip from ABC leaves something to be desired. I mean, the voice 'it wasn't long before the shooting began.' There was no shooting. There was make-believe play, which children do."[86]

But the show lacked any notion of context. The bottom line is: How often do children actually use guns improperly? The year the show aired was 1999, that same year thirty-one children under the age of ten in the country died from accidental gun deaths. And few of those actually involved a child firing the gun. There are about 40 million children under age ten in the U.S. While every child's life is important, it is also important for the media to give a realistic report of the unlikelihood that a child will die by a gun. It is hard to think of any other way children die that is treated by the press with the same level of alarm.

CHAPTER 3

How the Government Works Against Gun Ownership

The Limitation of Government Research on Guns

Just as the media tend to cover the bad events involving guns—while ignoring the benefits—so too do government studies on gun crime. However, while much of the media coverage is understandable, the government bias is harder to explain. Given how hard-fought national elections are over the gun issue, one might expect government research to take a careful, moderate path when measuring the costs and benefits of guns. A more cynical person might assume that the tone government research takes on guns depends on whether Republicans or Democrats are in office.

Surprisingly, however, neither the National Institute of Justice nor the Bureau of Justice Statistics has published anything on the benefits of gun ownership, regardless of whether Democrats or Republicans are in office. Take a few recent examples of government research over the last decade:

Firearm Injury and Death from Crime, 1993–97[1]
Reducing Illegal Firearms Trafficking: Promising Practices and Lessons Learned[2]
Guns Used in Crime: Firearms, Crime, and Criminal Justice[3]
Weapons Offenses and Offenders—Firearms, Crime, and Criminal Justice: Selected Findings[4]
Kids and Guns[5]

Some studies systematically list the number of bad events that happen with guns (but not the good events). Others contain purely anecdotal discussions. *Guns Used in Crime* lists the top ten guns used for committing crime, but does not correspondingly list the top ten guns used defensively. The bias here is obvious: There will always be a top ten list of guns preferred by criminals, and gun control organizations argue that since a gun is on that list, it should be banned. But frequently the very characteristics that make a gun attractive to criminals (e.g., lightweight, stopping power) also benefit potential victims of crime.

Reducing Illegal Firearms Trafficking is a ninety-six-page monograph that attempts to justify the tracing of guns obtained from crimes back to their original owners—simply by listing the harm done with guns in general. Other than a few anecdotal stories, no evidence is provided that tracing programs even reduce crime, let alone evidence that tracing is the most cost-effective method in reducing crime. There ought to be evidence one way or the other, considering that hundreds of millions of dollars have been spent on tracing, and the program had been in place for seven years when the study was released in 2000.

Kids and Guns goes into great detail on gun-related homicides, accidents, and suicides of children under the age of fifteen. The introduction states: "Guns kill. In many cases, guns kill our children," a message repeated throughout the report. There is no discussion of whether the presence of guns saves children's lives or whether children use guns defensively to save lives. Not once does the report mention a benefit from gun ownership. *Kids and Guns* also misinforms readers by giving many false impressions, such as equating "acquaintance murders" with murders by "friends." Readers may fear that a friendly acquaintance is likely to use a gun in a crime against them, because they are not informed by the report that the term "acquaintance" is defined by the FBI to include rival gang members.[6]

Flawed, biased studies like these endanger lives. Concentrating on only one side of the issue makes it impossible to truly evaluate any policy. Imagine if my research (presented in the second part of this book) based evaluations of gun storage or gun show regulations only on reductions in harm, and having found at least one life saved by the law, I stopped the analysis and concluded that the law was beneficial. While that approach would surely simplify research, the problem is more complicated. Laws requiring that guns be locked up may well leave victims defenseless when they need quick access to a weapon, but government's concern should be whether laws or policies save more lives than they cost.

How the Government Should Conduct Gun Research

Different approaches exist on how to investigate the costs and benefits of guns. For the future, it would be simple to reform the massive National Crime Victimization Survey, which surveys some 100,000 people each year. It should ask whether people used a gun defensively (or anything else) when they were confronted by a criminal. While the survey now directly asks people how they acted only if they have been a victim of a crime, many who have used a gun defensively may have stopped the crime before they ever became a victim. Thus, the survey never records that a person avoided becoming a victim through using a weapon defensively. Other survey data indicate that defensive gun use is highly successful and usually stops crimes at the gate.

The Bureau of Justice Statistics, which conducts the National Crime Victimization Survey, could then use these new data to advise victims on how to behave when confronted by a criminal. Publishing a top ten list of guns used defensively would be just as useful as the top ten list of guns used in crime. It would help law-abiding people decide what guns might be good for them. If there is a benefit to listing the top ten crime guns, there must be a benefit to listing the top ten defensive guns.

The government must also do more to get the data right. Many crime myths persist due to incomplete or inaccurate data reporting. Hundreds of "justifiable homicides" are reported each year by the FBI, but many more homicides might fall into that category. Since many jurisdictions do not report data on "justifiable homicide," this makes the FBI's "total" essentially meaningless. If the number is to be reported, effort has to be made to obtain an accurate total.

"Murders by acquaintances" is given a lot of attention. As discussed in detail in *More Guns, Less Crime*, the way these numbers are usually reported gives people a false impression that murders are disproportionately committed by people who are emotionally close to each other.[7] An improvement in presenting the statistics would be to separate out murders by non-friends (e.g., rival gang members or murders of cab drivers killed by fares or prostitutes killed by johns or pimps). While it is true that members of rival gangs may be acquaintances, those aren't the types of relationships that most people think about when they hear the term.

Another potentially more important improvement would be to report information on the criminal background of the killer. As nearly ninety percent of adult murderers have adult criminal records, it is an important identifying characteristic. We could then answer questions such as: Do murders committed against women by male acquaintances primarily involve males who have extensive criminal records? My guess is that the answer is "yes," but nobody really knows because no data exists. When women hear of murders committed by "male acquaintances" against women, some undoubtedly become fearful. If indeed it turns out that virtually all of these killers had extensive criminal records, women might be able to relax when dealing with men who have clear backgrounds.

GOVERNMENT-FUNDED RESEARCH ON GUNS: WHAT ARE YOU PAYING FOR?

Many people think that the government should fund academic research. Yet as clear as the benefits are, there is also a downside: Government officials simply cannot resist injecting politics into supposedly objective science.

On some scientific issues, such as astronomy or particle physics, one would think politics could play little role in determining funding. But in 1988, there was a major national debate on where to locate a giant particle accelerator. As politicians realized that the accelerator would not be located in their home state, many lost interest in the project. By 1993 funding for the project was terminated, even though construction had been underway for four years. Denying that science can be politicized is like denying that politics plays a role in determining which weapons systems are developed by the military.

Surely the academics who stand to gain the research funds, whether for stem cell or AIDS research, are also prone to exaggerate what they hope to accomplish. And perhaps more insidiously, politicians want research studies produced that support their already taken positions. Therefore only certain types of questions are permitted to be studied, with funding restricted to select, pre-approved researchers or institutions.

Take the recent National Academy of Sciences panel on firearms research. The panel began work during the last days of the pro–gun control Clinton administration. Its report is scheduled for release right before the 2004 elections, and its findings could hurt politicians who support gun ownership. The project scope set out by the Clinton administration was carefully planned to examine only the negative side of guns. Rather than comparing how firearms facilitate both harm and self-defense, the panel was only asked to examine "firearm violence" or how "firearms may become embedded in community."

It is difficult to see how these researchers could be looking at the positive side of guns if they are using terms such as "embedded." For President Clinton, who could never bring himself to mention that guns could be used for self-defense, it is not too surprising that the project scope never mentions defensive use. But if one knows about the academic and private surveys showing two million defensive gun uses a year, such an omission makes it difficult for any panel to seriously "evaluate various prevention, intervention and control strategies."

Moreover, the members selected to sit on the panel are as key to the report's outcome as the questions they study. While only half of the members on the committee have taken a public stand on firearms, almost all of them have extensively-formed views supportive of gun control. I know from private discussions over the years that other members support gun control. Some of those who have made public comments on gun control include:

— Benjamin Civiletti, attorney general under President Carter, believes that "The nation can no longer afford to let the gun lobby's distortion of the Constitution cripple every reasonable attempt to implement an effective national policy towards guns and crime."[8]

— Richard Rosenfeld, criminologist, University of Missouri, St. Louis. Despite his inability to cite any research showing that the Brady Act had reduced crime or total suicides, he wrote: "There may be reasons to repeal the Brady Act, but they rest on normative and political premises immune to scientific assessment."[9]

— Another panel member, Steve Levitt, an economist, has been described in media reports as being "rabidly anti-gun."[10]

— Peter Reuter, a criminologist at the University of Maryland, has written a pro–gun control paper entitled "Preventing Crime Through Gun Control: An Assessment of the Australian Buyback."[11] The paper claimed that the Australian government's buying back of guns in 1997 reduced homicides with guns. The results were obtained by comparing the average firearm homicide rate after 1996 with the rate prior to that. The problem is that the rate was actually lower for almost the entire period from 1990 to 1996 than it was in 1997 and 1998. The only reason that he was able to claim that there had been a decline was the higher rates of firearm homicide prior to 1990. No other factors were accounted for.

Amazingly, $900,000 is being spent on this panel: $600,000 of it is from the federal government, and $300,000 comes from three antigun private foundations. Crime reduction is a noble cause, but not much is being produced with this money. The money goes primarily towards assembling a book and uses data which is already provided by other scholars. Lois Mock, who supervises the money given out by the National Institute of Justice for firearms research and provides half of the $600,000 given out by the federal government, estimated that the meetings attended by the panel could cost nearly $50,000. When I asked her how they could possibly spend the other $850,000 in putting together their report, she replied that she didn't know but that it took a lot of time to put together a report the length of a book. Jokingly, I told her that I would be happy to put together a book for her for *only* $100,000.

Unfortunately, this is not the only stacked National Academy of Sciences panel. During August 2002, I was asked to participate in a National Academy of Sciences daylong workshop on "Children, Youth, and Gun Violence." I was one of the last people invited for the September 18 meeting. Despite my concerns that I was being included simply so that they could claim that they had a "balanced panel," I was assured by the staff person who invited me, Mary Ellen O'Connell, that the workshop would be balanced. I only attended my session, and at the beginning of my talk I asked the audience of over a hundred people: "How many people here are presenters?" About twenty-five people raised their hands. I then asked of those who were presenters: "How many of you think that it might be possible, not for sure but just possible, that existing gun control produces more problems than benefits?" All the hands went down. Not one of the presenters was even willing to acknowledge the possibility. Even worse than the bias, the problem was that the academy was unwilling to even acknowledge their biases and were unwilling to engage in a balanced debate. As in the panel on firearms regulation, the academy accepted funding from an anti-gun private foundation, the Packard Foundation, to fund this workshop.

Others have raised concerns about the integrity and competence of the academy. A devastating critique by Henry Miller of the Hoover Institution at Stanford described how when different government agencies asked the academy to study the same question, the academy provided reports that were "internally inconsistent, incompatible," but that each report supported the government agency that had funded it.[12]

Unfortunately, it will be hard to keep the National Academy of Sciences out of the gun control debate. There are strong political pressures to have the academy in the process, including the benefits of a national registry of the ballistic fingerprints for all new guns.[13]

SEPARATING ADVICE FROM POLITICAL AGENDAS

The following radio and television ads were distributed by the U.S. Department of Justice:[14]

Male Announcer: Every day ten children are killed by gunfire. It's time we said "enough is enough." Find out what you can do. Call 1-800-WE-PREVENT. Not one more lost life. Not one more grieving family. NOT ONE MORE.

Screen shots (emphasis in the advertisement): Newspaper covers "6-YR-OLD GUNNED DOWN"; "DRUG WAR SHOOT-OUT KILLS CHILD," and "TODDLER SLAIN IN CROSS FIRE." Picture of person dialing telephone to call "1-800-WE-PREVENT." "NOT ONE MORE." "NOT," "ONE," "MORE."

Television ad from 1996

Girl: Kalie was my baby sister. She loved pink. We were playing with her dolls. I found a gun in the drawer. It went off. I make Kalie go away. I hate me.

Voice-over: An unlocked gun can be the death of your family. Please lock up your gun.

Screen shots (emphasis in the advertisement): Opens with a crayoned sketch of a smiling baby girl in a pink dress. The camera pans from another drawing of Kalie, this time with her dolls and with her older sister. The hand-drawn pictures now show Kalie being shot, then lying on the floor, with blood on her pink dress. Then follows a drawing showing the older sister alone and her image nearly obliterated by scrawls of black crayon. Final screen shows that the ad is sponsored by the U.S. Department of Justice, the Ad Council, and the National Crime Prevention Council and invites people to visit unloadandlock.com.

Television ad from 2000

Boy: My brother Omar was eight years old when he died. He had a hole in his tummy. A bullet hit him. The gun came from the garage. I was just playing. I didn't mean to shoot Daddy's gun.

Voice-over: An unlocked gun could be the death of your family. Please lock up your gun. A message from the Ad Council and the National Crime Prevention Council. Visit unloadandlock.com.

Radio ad from 2000

Alicia: We were all out there having a good time, laughin' and jokin' around. I danced...(LAUGHS) When, all of a sudden, we heard gunshots. Three shots (GUNSHOT). Three shots fired...It was a boy laying on the floor dying—he was killed. That somebody that you knew was now gone—it really hurts. That was the last dance that we ever had.

President Clinton: Unfortunately, Alicia's story is all too common. Too many children have had their childhood taken from them. Fear of violence is robbing our nation's children of their future. We must take away that fear and give them hope. As a parent, I want this violence to stop. And, as your president, I'm committed to ending it. We must give Alicia, and all our children, back their childhood. Working together, we can.

Announcer: Call 1-800-WE-PREVENT now, to find out what you can do. 1-800-WE-PREVENT. A public service message of this station, the Crime Prevention Council, the Justice Department, and the Ad Council.

Radio ad from 1995

From 1993 to 2000, the federal government aired a dozen different antigun ads, some running many thousands of times. The ads constantly focused on the risks that guns pose to children. The advertisements and accompanying websites contain a staggering number of inaccurate statistics, all designed to exaggerate people's fear of guns.

The newspaper headlines in the first television advertisement clearly imply that the ten deaths a day involve young children: all the references are to a "six-year-old," a "toddler," and a "child." Yet, in 1995, the year before the ads appeared, 126 children under the age of ten were murdered with firearms, and an additional fifty-two deaths were accidental. This translates into a total rate of less than 0.5 a day, a far cry from the ten per day claimed in the ads. The "ten deaths a day" was obtained only by including murders, accidental deaths, and suicides for *all* ages under twenty. Murders of children under ten only account for only 4.5 percent of all murder victims for people under age twenty. Seventeen-, eighteen-, and nineteen-year-olds account for about two-thirds of all firearm deaths for those under twenty.

Can this misrepresentation be an accident? I seriously doubt it. The Justice Department ad misleadingly links the images of young children to the ten-deaths-a-day claim for a purpose. Deaths of young innocent children are much more likely to motivate legislative changes than gang-related deaths of eighteen- and nineteen-year-olds. It also fits in with the agenda to encourage people to lock up their guns in their home, even though that can endanger their lives, as Chapter 7 will show.

The second television ad with "Kalie" and the first radio ad with "Omar" create similar misimpressions. The accidental gun deaths involve a "baby" and an eight-year-old. Yet, in 1999, the year before these ads appeared, not a single child under the age of one died from an accidental gunshot. And the five years from 1995 to 1999 saw a total of 12 babies under the age of one who died from accidental gunshots. For the older age group over the same five years, an average of 48 children under ten years of age died from accidental gunshots. As shown in later data, only 5 to 8 children a year were shot by another child or themselves.

What other product with that number of accidental deaths elicited such ads from the federal government? Even such seemingly harmless household items, such as adult beds, take more children's lives. From 1999 to 2001, 41 children age five and under died from adult beds, when children were wedged between the mattress and adjoining wall or the headboard.[15]

The "Kalie" and "Omar" ads were produced by the advertising agency Foote, Cone & Belding, which did a great deal of research. Two employees, Sandy Greenberg and Terri Meyer, traveled to such cities as Atlanta, Pittsburgh, St. Louis, and Portland and interviewed families so "we could figure out how to get our message through to them."[16] They found that:

> In focus groups with gun owners, the spots struck a responsive chord. Defensiveness was replaced with the attitude that, if you didn't lock up your gun, it was child abuse. When asked who was sponsoring this work, the prevalent guess was a grass-roots group analogous to Mothers Against Drunk Driving. Some even conjectured that it was the National Rifle Association. [Terri] Meyer described the NRA reference as

"fascinating in that they felt the message was coming from
more of a friend to gun owners."

Obviously, the ad could have taken an opposite tack by emphasizing
the small number of accidental gun deaths that actually take place
each year, and contrasting it with the benefits of using a gun in self-
defense. Instead of the message that an unlocked gun represents child
abuse, the more accurate message would be that not providing access
to a gun increases the risk of harm to your family.

Almost every "fact" in the websites promoted in these ads is inaccurate. For example, in 2002 the National Crime Prevention Council
claimed that "A child between ten and nineteen years old commits
suicide with a handgun every six hours."[17] During 1999 the Centers
for Disease Control identified exactly two hundred handgun suicides
for this age group, a rate of one every forty-four hours.[18] When I asked
Jean O'Neil of the council to explain these differences, she was unable
to do so, but simply repeated the claim that the information was
obtained from the CDC. No sources were even cited for other statements, such as the claim that "Eighty-eight percent of the children
who are injured or killed in unintentional shootings are shot in their
own homes or in the homes of relatives or friends."[19]

Much of the advice is absurd. Take the unloadandlock.com website referenced in the ads. Under advice for "Building Safer Neighborhoods," the first recommendation is: "Do not be reluctant to ask
whether the parents of your children's friends have guns and if they
are properly secured."[20]

Advice offered on gun storage is more likely to endanger lives than
save them, as we shall see in the subsequent chapters. The small
number of accidental gun deaths is never discussed, and self-defense
is never mentioned either. Undoubtedly, "Most experts agree that a
gun safe is the most secure storage," but that doesn't make it the wis-
est course of action. Suggestions such as putting keys for a safe "in an
envelope and give it to a trusted friend, emphasizing that it's for your
use only" completely rules out any notion of defensive gun use.[21]

As U.S. attorney general, Janet Reno sent cover letters to the media
along with the advertisements noting: "The media greatly influences

the messages that motivate civic and individual action on important problems." She is quite correct. Yet this very influence can be dangerous when misused: The government's apparent inability to separate politics from responsibly informing the public makes this a dangerous combination.

The issue here is not the importance of the number of children who die, but the accuracy of the government information and the eagerness of the government to affect the debate in a biased, potentially dangerous way. Ultimately we have to ask whether government can divorce political pressures from its responsibility to inform the public. If the government can't, perhaps it should stay out of issue advertising altogether.

CHAPTER 4

THE SHIFTING DEBATE: TERRORISM, GUN CONTROL ABROAD, AND CHILDREN

SEPTEMBER 11 AND THE SHIFTING POSITIONS ON GUN CONTROL

> This started out as a documentary on gun violence in America, but the largest mass murder in our history was just committed—without the use of a single gun! Not a single bullet fired! No bomb was set off, no missile was fired, no weapon (i.e., a device that was solely and specifically manufactured to kill humans) was used. A boxcutter!—I can't stop thinking about this. A thousand gun control laws would not have prevented this massacre. What am I doing?
>
> *Michael Moore, a left-wing comedian directing a*
> *movie lobbying for additional gun control*[1]

September 11 changed the views of many people on guns, at least temporarily. The Capitol Hill newspaper *Roll Call* reported that after September 11 some of the strongest, though unnamed, supporters of gun control in Congress bought guns and sought training.[2] Anti-gun members of state legislatures, such as in Massachusetts, also behaved similarly.[3]

Politicians and celebrities clearly understand the benefits of guns for their own protection. This is nothing new. Congress certainly sees the benefits of firearms for its own safety since representatives and senators have long been allowed to legally carry guns around the Capitol grounds.[4] Even states with relatively strict gun control, such as Rhode Island, allow legislators to carry guns wherever they go.[5]

Chicago mayor Richard Daley surrounds himself with armed guards
even when he visits low-crime areas, but he refuses to issue handgun
licenses for people to keep a gun at home—even in the most dangerous parts of the city.[6]

Celebrity advice often runs counter to celebrity actions. Talk show
host Rosie O'Donnell had her bodyguards apply for concealed handgun permits, while at the same time publicly opposing concealed
handgun laws—even saying that "I also think that you should not buy
a gun anywhere."[7] A spokeswoman for Rosie justified the use of guns
for her protection because she was threatened with violence. Yet, how
does Rosie's concern for her own safety differ from what motivates
anyone who gets a gun for self-defense? Rosie's explanation—that she
still does not "personally own a gun"—misses the whole point. Of
course, she does not need one when she can pay her bodyguards to
own and carry guns.

Since September 11 the idea of remaining passive when confronted
by criminals appears to have been discredited—at least for airline passengers who risk certain death if they don't confront their hijackers.
But despite this change in attitude, despite the many politicians and
celebrities who embrace guns when their own lives are at risk, and
despite scholarly research proving otherwise, the press still recommends that people behave passively when confronted by criminals.

As Michael Moore noted in the quote opening this chapter, the
September 11 attack was committed with knives and box cutters, not
one single gun. For that matter, no guns were used in the Islamic fun-
damentalist bombing of the World Trade Center in 1993 or in the
2001 anthrax attacks on Washington, D.C. Yet, within months of September 11, there were calls for new gun control laws. The stretches
of logic and facts became farcical, with legislation pushed to ban certain guns, such as those firing .50-caliber bullets. These guns are
labeled the "terrorist weapon of choice" simply because the U.S. government sold twenty-five of them to Afghanis resisting the Soviet
occupation in the 1980s.[8] Not one of these guns has ever been used in
a murder or a wounding in the United States, yet this imaginary link
to terrorism creates calls for legislation.

Senators John McCain of Arizona, Joe Lieberman of Connecticut,
and Mike DeWine of Ohio used the terrorist threat to promise that

they would fix the mythical "gun show loophole."[9] In fact, the rules for selling guns at a gun show are identical to those for selling guns anywhere else. Dealers who sell guns at a show must perform the same background checks and obey the same rules as when they sell guns at their stores. But in most states, private sales—sales between individuals—are unregulated whether they occur at a gun show or not. A law regulating private sales at gun shows could be circumvented by an individual walking outside the show and selling the gun off the show's premises. To have any hope of regulating private sales, the government would have to register all guns, a point we will revisit shortly.

Senator Dick Durbin of Illinois claims that thousands of terrorists are buying weapons at gun shows, but he only provides three anecdotal cases from over multiple years.[10] Disappointingly, the major media uniformly accepted and reprinted gun control organizations' misleading claims about these three cases and exaggerated the risks. Editorials and news stories repeated the organizations' press releases in the *New York Times*, the *Washington Post*, *USA Today*, and numerous other publications.[11] None involved a terrorist threat to Americans. In one case, two shotguns were purchased by a naturalized American, the brother of the accused.[12] The transaction was reported as follows: "Thanks to the political clout of the U.S. gun lobby, a member of the terrorist group Hezbollah, Ali Boumelhem, was able to buy weapons at Michigan gun shows without undergoing a police background check."[13]

In the second case, a jury explicitly rejected allegations that four people who purchased guns in Florida were linked to the Irish Republican Army, though the media failed to report this and instead continually talked about someone "accused of being a member of the Irish Republican Army."[14]

In the third case, an illegal immigrant from Pakistan who had been in the U.S. for twenty years, was convicted for the possession of fifty bullets. In the aftermath of September 11, the press reported that police were "investigating whether [the Pakistani] may be linked to al-Qaeda terrorists."[15] Although the police quickly discredited this suspicion by September 20, 2001, months later the press was still reporting this claim.[16]

Whatever the exaggerations behind these three cases, the real issue for everyone is whether closing the so-called gun show loophole reduces violent crime rates. Few would argue against making private sales at gun shows subject to background checks if this proved a successful method of reducing criminals' and terrorists' access to guns. Yet, while Americans for Guns Safety claims that eighteen states currently have these laws for handguns and thirteen states have them for long guns, there has been no evidence on what effect the rules have on crime rates. This book will provide the first evidence that has been offered on this issue.

Little attention is given to the cost of these laws: For example, do they reduce the number of gun shows that take place? Do they make it more difficult for law-abiding citizens to obtain guns?

ISRAEL AND TERRORISM

How weird is it that in the post–Sept. 11 atmosphere, when the Justice Department itself is in the forefront of the effort to narrow potential threats to security, the attorney general decides it would be a good idea to throw open the doors to a wholesale increase in gun ownership?

Bob Herbert, New York Times *columnist*[17]

America is safer when steps are taken to prevent terrorists from getting weapons in the first place, not when citizens are engaged in gunfights on airplanes or on our streets.

Million Mom March website[18]

[W]e should worry about the fallout from 9/11 on gun ownership. Already, since the beginning of September, more than four times as many Americans have fallen to guns as to terrorism, but quietly, one by one, with no one noticing. . . . It's not terrorism, but it should be terrifying.

Nicholas Kristof, New York Times *columnist*[19]

Media figures reacted with disdain to the jump in gun sales that took place after September 11.[20] A different attitude prevails in Israel, which has had to deal with terrorism for decades and has encouraged ordinary, responsible citizens to carry guns.

Israelis have come to accept the unfortunate fact that the police and military simply can not always be there to protect people when terrorists attack; there are simply too many vulnerable targets. (Even when the police or military are nearby, terrorists wait until they leave before striking.) And when terrorists strike, their first targets include anyone carrying an *unconcealed* gun, such as the military or police.

That's why Israelis have found it helpful in thwarting terrorist attacks to allow law-abiding, trained citizens to carry concealed handguns. Over 10 percent of Jewish adults in Israel are now allowed to carry concealed handguns.[21] In large public gatherings, the odds are good that at least some citizens will be able to shoot at terrorists during an attack, because the terrorists won't know which civilians have guns. During waves of terror attacks, Israel's police inspector general has called on all concealed handgun permit holders to make sure they carry firearms at all times and he has said that "there's no question that weapons in the hands of the public have prevented acts of terror or stopped them while they were in progress. Chance passers-by have killed terrorists in the midst of gun attacks."[22] A couple of cases from the very end of 2001 illustrate his claim:[23]

> Witnesses said the gunman opened fire on the No. 25 city bus at an intersection in the French Hill section of northeastern Jerusalem, which is near several Palestinian villages and neighborhoods.... "He was standing there and shooting [into the right side of the bus]," the civilian shooter, who identified himself only as Marcus, told Israeli radio. "I got out of the car. I fired. I emptied an entire clip. He fell...."[24]

> Israel Radio reported that the Israeli, who is a resident of the Karni Shomron settlement, had been shot five times, but managed to fire his weapon and kill one of his assailants, causing the other two attackers to flee.[25]

With terrorist violence in Israel from the Intifada continuing unabated in 2002, Israel has done something that many Americans would find unthinkable: The country's rabbis have agreed to allow some armed worshippers in every synagogue during the Passover holidays.[26] Except in emergencies, Orthodox Jews are otherwise banned from even touching guns on holidays and during the Sabbath. But everyone recognizes that synagogues could be targets of terror attacks, and that it is important either to deter or to limit the harm from the attacks with armed citizens in the congregations.

Similar drama occurs in the United States, where concealed handgun holders stopped multiple victim attacks. In one case during 2001, a mentally disturbed man yelled that President George W. Bush was going to have him killed, and started firing at people in passing cars. A permit holder at the scene fired shots, making the attacker stop shooting and run away. The attacker barricaded himself in an empty apartment, fired at arriving police officers, and ultimately committed suicide.[27]

Americans have concealed handgun permits at only a fraction of the rate of Israelis. To be at the same level, we would have to increase the number from the current level of 3.5 million permits to almost 21 million.

Thirty-three states now have "right-to-carry" laws, which let law-abiding citizens above a certain age obtain a permit for a fee. (About half of these states also require some training in gun use.) Another eleven states have so-called "may issue" laws requiring people to demonstrate a need to a public official before they are issued a permit. As a result, a much smaller fraction of the population obtains permits. If more states pass right-to-carry laws, or if states with existing laws lower their fees or change training requirements, the U.S. could significantly expand the number of law-abiding citizens carrying guns. The media might shudder at such an idea, but then they ignore the benefits of an armed public.

The fact is states that pass concealed handgun laws experience drops in murder rates and other violent crime. Could terrorism also be reduced if more citizens carried guns? Would the Israeli experience work equally well here? A Zogby poll conducted after the September 11 attack shows 66 percent of Americans support right-to-carry laws, so the question is not merely one of academic curiosity.[28] This book will present the first statistical work on what types of government policies can help prevent multiple victim public shootings and bombings.

The passage of concealed handgun laws is only one opportunity for guns to help fight terrorism. President Bush's revival of the federal marshals' program on airplanes is another example. This program for domestic flights started in 1970, but ended in the early 1990s,[29] despite evidence suggesting that it did indeed work well. There were thirty-eight hijackings in America in 1969, but in 1970—as the marshals were employed—the number of hijackings fell to the twenties for each of the next three years, before finally declining to low single digits. Empirical research by Bill Landes at the University of Chicago found that between a third and a half of the drop in airplane hijackings during the 1970s could be attributed to a combination of two factors: the introduction of armed U.S. marshals on planes and our generally increased ability to catch and punish hijackers.[30]

Since terrorists will always find some way to smuggle a weapon on board, guns in the right hands aboard planes provide a last line of defense. It will never be possible to perfectly prevent any weapon from getting on board. For instance, terrorists can evade metal detectors with knives made of plastic or ceramics. Long thin metal blades can be difficult to notice with X-rays and hidden as part of a metal box. Even checking all carry-on baggage by hand does not prevent weapons from getting onboard, as some security workers and baggage handlers could be bribed. Moles can be planted in these professions.

In December 2001, Richard Reid successfully hid a small amount of the military plastic explosive C-4, a clay-like substance that is easy to mold and shape, in the heel of his shoes. The amount was apparently enough to bring down his American Airlines flight.[31] X-raying shoes will help if wires are connected to the explosive, but this small amount of explosives, like knives, can be hidden in many other places.

Inspections are important, but they cannot constitute our entire defense. Ironically, the same week in January 2002 that the British government quietly announced it would not place armed guards on planes and that its airline security efforts would concentrate "on making sure that nothing dangerous gets onto our aircraft," British journalists successfully smuggled an assortment of weapons onto a British

Airways flight.[32] Security and X-ray machines missed a stiletto, a cleaver, and a four-inch dagger.

September 11, however, changed the rules for American hijackings. If anything, more than one gun is needed on a plane to keep it safe. During the 1970s, a hijacker acting alone or with one accomplice usually tried to take the plane to Cuba. But bin Laden's organization was capable of putting a whole group of hijackers on the same plane. While a plainclothes marshal possesses an advantage (terrorists don't know which passenger is armed), having only one marshal on each plane creates the potential for hijackers to disclose their presence in stages. Only after the marshal reveals himself would the remaining hijackers attack.

Though President Bush reacted coolly to proposals to arm pilots, legislation allowing pilots to carry guns was signed by the end of 2002. Most pilots have had military experience and understand their planes even better than the marshals. All the pilot unions supported making guns available to pilots.[33] Over 70 percent of the pilots at commercial passenger airlines have military training, and the military requires its pilots to carry guns with them when they are flying on missions outside of U.S. territory. Arming pilots is not new. Pilots were required from the 1920s until the early 1960s to carry handguns on their aircraft to protect first class mail, and some were routinely armed until 1987. During the nearly seven decades that pilots were authorized—and sometimes required—to carry firearms, there was never a documented incident of firearm misuse, despite the fact no federal training was required. Strangely enough, many government officials seem to prefer the idea of a pilot initiating dangerous emergency dives and rolls to throw hijackers (and innocent passengers) against the ceiling over the idea of a pilot carrying a gun.[34]

President Bush's rules strengthening cockpit doors don't eliminate the need to arm pilots. Doors can still be blown open. Security can be breached and terrorists may obtain the key or code used to open the door. Israel's El Al airline has strengthened cockpit doors, yet it still arms its pilots.[35] According to the Airline Pilots' Security Alliance, Luftansa and another European airline also arm their pilots.[36] I have confirmed that information in meetings with the air marshals and the Transportation Security Administration.

As of 2002, few flights actually had marshals on them, and it will take years for the FAA to cover a noticeable fraction of flights with them. The numbers six months after the September 11 attack are instructive.[37] While the exact number of marshals has not been made public, eight months after the attacks there were still fewer than one thousand marshals across the nation, and only a fraction of those were available on any given day. That means that even if marshals worked the same hours as pilots, fewer than 1 percent of commercial flights operating in the U.S. were under marshal protection.[38] Despite repeated promises that marshals would be present on all flights into Reagan National Airport in Washington, D.C.— an airport located in a target-rich environment for terrorists—pilots' union officials tell me only a third of flights out of Reagan are covered.[39] With the exception of flights bound for Salt Lake during the 2002 Winter Olympics, union officials claim there have not been marshals on other flights.[40]

The whole process of recruiting marshals has been slow and expensive. A marshal program covering all flights would cost well over $20 billion per year and require a force twice the size of the U.S. Marine Corps to implement this policy for all commercial passenger flights.[41] Even covering a third or a quarter of flights will be very difficult and costly. Not only does it take a long time to attract and train new marshals, but the program has had serious problems with retention. According to the Federal Aviation Administration, boredom is a major detraction, as marshals must fly back and forth across the country, merely waiting for something to happen.[42]

So, what to do if things go wrong and terrorists make it into the cockpit? Few were happy with the FAA's official guidelines issued during 2002 that suggested pilots use their "fists and feet" against terrorists.[43] Pilot unions weren't asking for guns to police the airplane— just to protect the cockpit.[44] Their task of defending a single entrance is relatively simple. Terrorists have only one narrow door that they can pass through to get to the cockpit.

Proposals to provide pilots with Tasers (stun guns) ignored their limitations. Not only are there well-known cases such as Rodney King who "fought off tasers" twice,[45] but thick clothing can also foil their effectiveness.[46] The New York City police department reports that "Even Taser guns—which the department uses to administer electric shocks to people—fail about a third of the time."[47] Because of these problems, even the Taser manufacturer recommends lethal weapons as a back up.[48]

The fears of having guns on planes are exaggerated.[49] As Ron Hinderberger, director of Aviation Safety at Boeing, noted in testimony before the U.S. House of Representatives:

> Boeing commercial service history contains cases where guns were fired on board in service airplanes, all of which landed safely. Commercial airplane structures are designed with sufficient strength, redundancy and damage tolerance that a single or even multiple handgun holes would not result in loss of an aircraft. A bullet hole in the fuselage skin would have little effect on cabin pressurization. Aircraft are designed to withstand much larger impacts whether intentional or unintentional. For instance, on fourteen occasions Boeing commercial airplanes have survived, and landed, after an in flight bomb blast.[50]

While Hinderberger's statement addressed the impact of standard bullets, special ammunition is available for pilots (high-velocity handgun ammunition containing birdshot or "dust shot") that packs quite a wallop but does not penetrate the aluminum skin of the plane. But as Hinderberger notes, even with regular bullets, which could penetrate a plane's skin, a change in cabin pressure would be hardly noticeable: the air outlet at the back of the plane (which draws the air through the cabin) would automatically shrink to a smaller size to compensate.[51]

Pilots also face a much less difficult job in defending the cockpit than marshals do in securing the cabin. An armed marshal in the cabin can be attacked from any direction. He must be able quickly to distinguish innocent civilians from terrorists. An armed pilot only needs to concern himself with the people trying to force their way into the cockpit. It is also much easier to defend a position such as the cockpit, as a pilot would, than to have to pursue the terrorist and physically subdue them, as a marshal would. The terrorists can only enter the cockpit through one narrow entrance, and armed pilots have time to prepare themselves while hijackers try to penetrate the strengthened cockpit doors. Pilots must also fly the airplane, but with two pilots, one pilot could continue flying the plane while the other defends the entrance. In any case, if terrorists make it into the cockpit, one must assume pilot concentration on flying the plane will be diminished, whether or not a gun is present.

An oft-repeated concern over arming pilots is that they will hurt themselves with their weapons or hijackers will take the guns from them, since "21 percent of [police] officers killed with a handgun were shot by their own service weapon."[52] (Similar concerns are frequently raised when discussing civilians using guns for their personal protection.) But the FBI's Uniform Crime Report paints a quite different picture. In 2000, 47 police officers were killed with a gun, out of which 33 cases involved a handgun, and only one of these firearm deaths involved the police officer's gun.[53] It is really not that easy to grab an officer's gun and shoot him. Assaults on police are not that rare, but only in a minuscule fraction of the cases do officers end up being shot with their own gun. Statistics from 1996 to 2000 show that only 0.008 percent of assaults on police resulted in them being killed with their own weapon.[54] Therefore, the risk to pilots would probably be even smaller. Unlike police who have to come into physical contact with criminals while arresting them, pilots will use guns to keep attackers as far away as possible.

Besides planes, there are still plenty of other vulnerable targets in the U.S. There are plenty of crimes stopped by armed off-duty or retired police. For example, a 2001 public school shooting at Santana High School near San Diego, California, was stopped by an off-duty police officer. Officer Robert Clark just happened to be registering his daughter at the school.[55] He saw the chaos unfolding and was able instantly to run over and force the killer to take cover, preventing him from doing more harm. As one law enforcement organization put it: "Were it not for the valiant intervention of off-duty police officer Robert Clark, the shooting at Santana High School likely would have been worse—perhaps horribly worse."[56]

Unfortunately some states such as Illinois and Missouri forbid police to carry their guns off duty. And state laws forbid police to carry guns across state lines unless the officer has a concealed handgun permit and the two states have concealed handgun reciprocity agreements.[57] Proposed legislation in Congress would allow police officers to carry their guns with them wherever they travel, but gun opponents prevented the bill from getting out of the House Judiciary Committee during the 2001–2002 session, and the legislation has never received a hearing in the Senate.[58] Some states, such as California, are passing similar legislation that would let police in their states carry their guns anywhere in the state.[59]

OTHER COUNTRIES' GUN LAWS

Gun control advocates in the U.S. often point to Europe's strict gun laws as the example for the U.S. to follow. Yet, the three very worst public shootings during 2001 and the first half of 2002 all occurred in Europe. Around the world, from Australia to England, countries that have recently strengthened gun control laws have seen violent crime soar. Ironically, the gun laws are passed because politicians promise they will reduce these types of crime.

Sixteen people were killed during an April 2002 public school shooting in Germany. The United States seems peaceful by comparison: Though the U.S. has almost five times as many students as Germany, thirty-two students and four teachers were killed from all types of gun death at elementary and secondary schools over almost five school years (August 1997 to June 2002).

Recent public school shootings have also occurred in France and Belgium, but shootings have not been limited to schools. The other two worst public shootings were the killing of fourteen regional legislators in Zug, a Swiss canton (September 2001), and the massacre of eight city council members in a Paris suburb (March 2002).

European gun laws are very strict. Indeed, they contain everything that American gun control advocates have been lobbying for. Germans who wish to acquire a hunting rifle must undergo checks that can last a year, while those wanting a gun for sport must be a member of a club and obtain a license from the police. And the French must apply for gun permits, which are granted only after an exhaustive background and medical record check and after the applicant proves a need deemed acceptable to the state. Once granted a permit, the applicant must reapply for renewal in three years.

Even Switzerland's once famously liberal laws have become tighter. In 1999 Switzerland's federation ended policies that left concealed handguns unregulated. Such policies had been in effect in as many as half of the cantons, and the rest of the cantons had relatively minor restrictions. Even in many cantons where regulations had previously existed, the restrictions were not terribly strong. But Swiss federal law now limits permits to only those who can demonstrate in advance a need for a weapon to protect themselves or others against a specified danger.

All three European killing sprees share one thing in common: They took place in so-called gun-free "safe zones." That criminals are attracted to gun-free zones is hardly surprising. Guns surely make it easier to kill people, but guns also make it much easier for people to defend themselves. As with many other gun laws, it is law-abiding citizens, not would-be criminals, who obey gun-free zones. Hence, "gun free" zones turn the law-abiding into sitting ducks.

In two of the European cases, the killers also managed to evade extensive laws on gun ownership. The killer of eight city council members in Paris was a psychiatric patient and did not have the required gun license.[60] The killer of fourteen people in the canton parliament in Zug also had a history of mental illness. He falsified records to obtain a license for a military rifle.[61]

After a long flirtation with gun free "safe zones," many Americans have learned their lesson the hard way. The U.S. has seen a gradual but significant change from 1985, when just eight states had right-to-carry laws. Today the number is thirty-three. And, as this book will show, deaths and injuries from multiple victim public shootings fell on average by 78 percent in states that passed such laws. The drop in the number of attacks—while not as large as the deaths and injuries resulting from those attacks—was still substantial.

This book has also tried to extend the lesson more broadly. Violent crime is becoming a major problem in Europe.[62] While many factors, such as law enforcement, drug gangs, and immigration affect crime, the lofty promises of gun controllers can no longer be taken seriously.

Indeed, countries such as the U.K. and Australia have seen violent crime soar after the passage of strict gun prohibitions and even penalties for defensive gun use. Yet, both the U.K. and Australia have ideal conditions for gun control to work, as both countries are surrounded by water, making gun smuggling relatively difficult.

Of course, advocates of gun control look for ways to get around the new evidence. Publications such as the *New York Times* and the *Los Angeles Times* blame Europe's increasing crime problems on a seemingly unstoppable black market that "has undercut...strict gun-control laws."[63]

Assume the black market is to blame for gun control's failure in these countries. Wouldn't smuggling be the natural consequence of these gun control laws? In the U.K. "gang and drug activity have propelled an influx of guns," but it is not obvious why governments expect to be any more successful controlling the black market in guns than they have been in controlling the black market in drugs.[64] It is hardly surprising that drug gangs will smuggle in guns along with their drugs if only to help them protect their illegal drug markets.

Another inconvenient fact frequently ignored by gun control advocates is that many countries with very high homicide rates have either complete or virtually complete gun bans. Major countries such as Russia and Brazil have homicide rates several times that of the U.S. After decades of severe restrictions on gun ownership, Brazil temporarily tried to ban guns, but its supreme court eventually threw out the law. Other countries such as Colombia and Venezuela have even much higher homicide rates, but there are other obvious explanations (such as the drug trade).

The 2002 shooting in Germany was followed by the passage of even stricter gun laws, but increased crime in Europe is causing new center-right governments to rethink their reflexive support for more anti-gun laws. At the same time Germany was moving against guns, Italian defense minister Antonio Martino suggested that Italy model its laws after the U.S. Constitution's Second Amendment, which protects the right of citizens to bear arms.[65]

The growing fears of crime may have been responsible for Jean-Marie Le Pen's upset second place showing in France's presidential elections in 2002. As a fifty-eight-year-old mother of two in France said: "My son was last week mugged—just for a cigarette! I've never done this before and you may not like to hear it, but I'm voting for Le Pen."[66]

Many French politicians complained during their 2002 presidential election that the shooting in Paris meant "It's getting like in America, and we don't want to see that here."[67] Americans may draw a different lesson from the evidence and hope that they don't become more like the Europeans.

THE UN'S EFFORTS

The 2001 United Nations conference on small arms, which ended in controversy, had an admirable enough goal: to save lives. Some conference attendees claimed that guns used in armed conflicts cause 300,000 deaths worldwide every year.[68] The international community's proposed solution? Prevent rebels from getting guns by requiring that "member states complete a registry of all small arms within their borders" and by "limiting the sale of such weapons only to governments."

This may be an understandable solution from governments that don't trust their citizens. But it also dangerously disregards their citizens' safety and freedom. For that reason, the Bush administration should be thanked, not scolded as it was by many, for effectively squelching the accord. Why? First, and most obviously, because not all insurgencies are bad. It is hardly surprising that infamous regimes such as those in Syria, Cuba, Rwanda, Vietnam, Zimbabwe, and Sierra Leone support these antigun provisions. Banning guns for rebels in totalitarian countries—because guns cause killings—is like arguing that wars are never justified.

In hindsight, would the international community really have preferred that Hitler's takeover of Europe go unresisted? Should the French or Norwegian resistance movements simply have given up? Surely this might have minimized war casualities.

Many countries today already totally ban private gun ownership, with Rwanda and Sierra Leone as two notable examples. With more than a million people hacked to death with knives and cleavers over the last seven years, were the citizens of Rwanda and Sierra Leone better off without guns to defend themselves?

What about the massacres of civilians in Bosnia? If Bosnians had possessed guns, would the massacres have taken place? And what about the Jews in the Warsaw ghetto during World War II? Would it not have been better if they had had more guns to defend themselves? With all the well-deserved publicity for the movie *Schindler's List*, the movie left out how Schindler, an avid gun collector, stockpiled guns and hand grenades in case the Jews he was protecting needed to defend themselves. More recently, the proposed rules would have prevented the American government from assisting the Afghanis in their fight against the Soviet Union. When the Taliban took over during the mid-1990s, one of their first actions was to disarm the citizens. While people apparently complied without much resistance at the time, with hindsight it is not so obvious that this was really in their best interest.

There is a second important reason mentioned earlier for allowing citizens to keep small arms: Even in free countries, with little risk of a totalitarian regime, gun bans all but invariably result in higher crime. In the U.S., the states with the highest gun ownership rates also have by far the lowest violent crime rates. And similarly, over time, states with the largest increases in gun ownership have experienced the biggest drops in violent crime.

Jeff Miron at Boston University recently examined homicide rates across forty-four countries and found that the countries with the strictest gun control laws also had the highest homicide rates, though the higher rate was only statistically significant in half of his estimates. Miron does an excellent job accounting for different factors not previously accounted for in cross-country comparisons, and he uses data for a large set of countries (rather than subjectively selecting a half-dozen or a dozen as is normally done).

One particularly dramatic comparison was recently provided by William Pridemore on the historical homicide rates in the U.S. and the former USSR. Using the actual homicide rate data for the Soviet Union and not the data that had been released for propaganda purposes, Pridemore shows that the USSR's homicide rate "has been comparable to or higher than the U.S. rate for at least the past 35 years."[69] Indeed, during the entire decade from 1976 to 1985, the USSR's homicide rate was between 21 and 41 percent higher than that of the United States. By 1989, two years before the collapse of the

Soviet Union, their homicide rate rose 48 percent above ours. Neither the ban on private ownership of guns nor the ruthless totalitarian-communist system that enforced this ban was able to produce a low homicide rate.

"Time-series" evidence that examines how crime rates change in only one particular area over time also provides some interesting relationships. In 1996, Britain banned handguns. Prior to that time, over 54,000 Britons owned handguns.[70] The ban was so tight that even shooters training for the Olympics were forced to travel to Switzerland or other countries to practice. Four years have elapsed since the ban was introduced, and gun crimes have risen by an astounding 40 percent.[71,72] The United Kingdom now leads the United States by an almost two-to-one margin in violent crime.[73] Although murder and rape rates are still higher in the United States, the difference has been shrinking.[74] A recent Associated Press Report notes "Dave Rogers, vice chairman of the [London] Metropolitan Police Federation, said the ban made little difference to the number of guns in the hands of criminals.... The underground supply of guns does not seem to have dried up at all."[75]

Australia also passed severe gun restrictions in 1996, banning most guns and making it a crime to use a gun defensively. In the next four years, armed robberies there rose by 51 percent, unarmed robberies by 37 percent, assaults by 24 percent, and kidnappings by 43 percent.[76] While murders fell by 3 percent, manslaughter rose by 16 percent. In Sydney, handgun crime rose by an incredible 440 percent from 1995 to 2001.[77] Again, both Britain and Australia are "ideal" places for gun control as they are surrounded by water, making gun smuggling relatively difficult. The bottom line, though, is that these gun laws clearly did not deliver the promised reductions in crime.

Finally, one can't avoid mentioning a certain irony. At the same time members of the United Nations, with the notable exception of the United States, were advocating broad extensions of gun regulation, the UN itself was disobeying federal U.S. gun control laws and import regulations. Among other weapons, the UN apparently imported machine guns into the U.S. and did not register any of the weapons.[78] The UN had also put together its own security force that carried these machine guns in New York City in violation of numerous other city and state gun laws. UN Secretary-General Kofi Annan, who oversees this security force, has been a particularly strong proponent of small arms restrictions.

Organizations on both sides of the U.S. gun control debate have been harshly critical of the UN's inconsistency. On the Right, a spokesman for Gun Owners of America noted, "The UN wants to regulate small arms world-wide, but apparently, that doesn't apply to them."[79] On the Left, the Violence Policy Center accused the UN of "flouting" the laws and "sending a terrible message to the average citizen."[80]

WHO BENEFITS THE MOST FROM OWNING GUNS?

One of the more searing images during the 2000 presidential campaign was the dragging death of James Byrd, an African-American man in Texas. No one could avoid the graphic NAACP ads and the calls for greater penalties. But Texas already had the stiffest penalty—the death penalty—and two of the killers were sentenced to death. A third received life in prison.

Compare this scenario to a recent case in Bremerton, a city in western Washington State. An African-American man, waiting for his girlfriend to get off work, was "insulted and challenged" by three drunk young white men who "used racial epithets." One of the young men ordered his pit bull to attack. The African-American "pulled a handgun from his car" and fired it to defend himself against the dog. "By the time deputies arrived, things had calmed down, the black man was found to have a permit to carry the gun," and he declined to press charges against his attackers. Fortunately, no one was injured.[81]

Without a gun, it is not obvious what else the African-American man could have done. He was outnumbered three to one and attacked by a pit bull, and there were no police nearby to help.

Criminal penalties are important in reducing crime and so are the police, but there are limits. Obviously, James Byrd was murdered despite the death penalty. Likewise, despite research showing that the police are the single most important factor in stopping crime, police simply can't be everyplace all the time. As in the Byrd case, they virtually always arrive on the crime scene only after the crime has been committed.

The typical advice in the media—to behave passively—could have gotten the Bremerton man killed or seriously injured. Indeed, passive behavior is not usually the safest course of action. Men who behave passively are 1.4 times more likely to end up seriously injured than men who have a gun. For women, passive behavior is even more dangerous, making them 2.5 times more likely to wind up seriously injured than if they resist with a gun. In contrast, the probability of women being seriously injured was almost 4 times greater when resisting without a gun than when resisting with a gun.[82] The survey that I conducted found that while 30 percent of those who felt threatened with physical violence but did not use a gun to defend themselves ended up being harmed, none of those who used a gun to defend themselves were harmed.

An additional woman carrying a concealed handgun in a given population reduces the murder rate for women by about three to four times more than an additional man carrying a concealed handgun reduces the murder rate for men. The bottom line: Those who are most likely to be the victims of crime or those who are relatively weaker physically benefit the most from being able to protect themselves. It's important for women to carry a gun because attackers are almost always males, and there is a large strength differential. It is still important for men to carry a gun because men are generally more likely to be victims of crime than women.

African-Americans living in high crime urban areas benefit the most from either carrying or owning a gun for protection. For example, while allowing people to carry concealed handguns reduces violent crime rates across the board, the annual drop in violent crime is 4 percentage points faster in the counties that are 40 percent African-American than in counties that are only 5 percent African-American. The drop in murder rates for the heavily African-American counties was eight times larger than in the counties with few African-Americans. The NAACP unfortunately ignores the importance that guns play in self-defense for African-Americans and rather puts all its emphasis behind strengthening existing hate crime laws.

WHAT ABOUT THE RISKS OF GUNS IN THE HOME?

The Bethlehem YWCA's sixth annual Week Without Violence wrapped up Thursday.... During the exchange, volunteers collected about 25 toy guns in 90 minutes and passed out crayons, candies and a choice of a nonviolent toy. There were also stickers, bookmarks and other literature about stopping violence. "This is a little lower than last year," said Peggy Leith, coordinator of the event. "We had four or five different sites last year, and only two this year...."

"The toy guns collected will be thrown out," Leith said. Leith thinks children cleaned out most of their toy guns last year, so there were not that many to exchange this year.[83]

Called "Kids Need Toys, Not Guns," the event was organized by Parents for Better Beginnings and 51 Division police in hopes that by replacing toy guns with educational toys, kids will stop playing with guns.[84]

A common concern is that guns kept in the home are more likely to harm residents of the home than to kill an intruder. Some suggest that we go so far as asking neighbors if they own a gun. They point to the public school shootings—where shooters took guns from the home—as a major reason for these concerns. Some elementary and secondary schools have even "quizzed [students] on whether their families owned guns."[85] Fears have become so intense that toy retailers such as eToys and Toys "R" Us stopped selling toy guns in 2001.[86] Target Department Stores "removed realistic toy guns from their shelves years ago."[87] Other companies, such as Kmart, agreed to stop selling handgun ammunition.[88]

This antigun climate is relatively new. Until 1969 virtually every public high school—even in New York City—had a shooting club. High school students in New York City carried their guns to school on the subways in the morning, turned them over to their home-room teacher or the gym coach during the day, and retrieved them after school for target practice. Club members were given their rifles and ammunition by the federal government. Students regularly competed in citywide shooting contests for university scholarships. As late as 1968, it was possible for children to walk into a hardware store—virtually anywhere in the United States—and buy a rifle. Few states even had age restrictions for buying handguns. Buying a rifle through the mail was easy.

The reaction to children and guns today is typified by this response to Mel Gibson's movie *The Patriot* when it appeared during the summer of 2000:

> It takes a lot to shock today's jaded movie audiences, especially those attending a Hollywood preview. Yet, Mel Gibson's new movie about America's Revolutionary War, *The Patriot*, drew loud gasps at a recent screening. The outrageous scene? Mr. Gibson's character handing over guns to his 10- and 13-year-old sons to help fight off British soldiers. Few critics were soothed by the screenwriter replying that the scenes accurately portrayed the complexities of war—or Mr. Gibson's assurance that he would let his own children use guns in self-defense.[89]

Against this backdrop, a massive advertising and letter-writing campaign in 2001 tried to persuade parents to ask neighbors whether they owned guns. It was sponsored by ASK (Asking Saves Kids), an umbrella organization comprising groups such as the National Education Association, the Children's Defense Fund, and Physicians for Social Responsibility. The campaign's eye-catching ads pictured a young girl wearing a flak jacket, and it warned parents against letting children play in the homes of gun owners. In a pitch reminiscent of the National Crime Prevention Council, parents are advised to question their neighbors about gun ownership.

Should neighbors object to such questions about guns, ASK's literature tells how to respond to comments such as, "This is not any of your business."[90] Given the risks of young children being "naturally curious," eliminating or locking up guns is presented as part of child-proofing a home. Sarah Brady, chairwoman of the Brady Center to Prevent Gun Violence (formerly Handgun Control, Inc.), made similar comments after September 11, pleading, "If you must keep a gun in the home, we urge you to keep it locked up and stored out of the reach of children."[91]

Unfortunately, not only gun control organizations offer this potentially dangerous advice. The National Shooting Sports Foundation advises people to "keep all firearms locked in a safe place" and to "store ammunition under lock and key, separately from firearms."[92] With a $5 million grant from the federal government in 2001, the council prepared to give out 3.5 million gun locks.[93] Their literature warns of the risks that guns pose for children, but provides no numbers and no discussion of potential problems that might arise with these programs.[94] The Bush administration even sought and received $40 million from Congress to distribute gun locks nationwide.

Especially given all the negative coverage in the media, the general fear of guns is understandable. But as the evidence provided in Chapter 7 shows, persuading owners either to give up their guns or lock them up makes victims more vulnerable and emboldens criminals. Indeed, locking up guns reduces safety and, on net, results in a loss of lives.

I have come across this hysteria myself. For example, my wife and I first took our four boys to the Yale University Health Service for medical checkups during 1999. Prominently displayed posters on the walls warned against keeping handguns in the home. Along with the normal questions about medical histories, the nurse practitioner asked us whether we owned guns and whether they were locked up or loaded. Her tone made it clear she disapproved of my answers, and she was unmoved by any numbers showing that guns saved lives or were much less of a risk than other common household items.[95] (My wife, worried that I was antagonizing our children's health care providers, forcefully ground her heel into my foot to signal me to stop pursuing the issue.)

With the American Medical Association recommending in 2001 that physicians ask patients about gun ownership during office visits, this type of experience is likely to become more and more common for others.[96] A coalition of doctor organizations, which claims to represent two-thirds of all doctors, has made similar recommendations, and they propose making these questions part of the training given in medical school.[97]

But the evidence suggests that their energies are being wasted. Accidental gun deaths among children are fortunately much rarer than most people believe. As noted earlier, in 1999, the last year for which a detailed breakdown is available, thirty-one children younger than age ten died from accidental shootings in the United States, slightly more than one for every two states.[98] The Centers for Disease Control could only identify four children under age ten dying from accidental handgun deaths. With some 94 million gun owners and almost 40 million children younger than ten,[99] it is hard to find any item in American homes that is potentially lethal that has as low an accidental death rate as guns. With preliminary estimates for 2000 indicating that there were 600 accidental gun deaths for all ages combined, accidental gun deaths for any age are rare.[100]

Few gun-owning Americans are in danger of accidentally shooting someone. As discussed in Chapter 7, accidental shooters are overwhelmingly adult males with long histories of arrests for violent crimes, alcoholism, suspended or revoked drivers licenses, and involvement in automobile crashes. I will show that nationally the number of accidental gun deaths in recent years involving children under ten either accidentally shooting themselves or other children under ten is consistently fewer than ten a year. While gun locks could theoretically prevent the very few children who abuse a gun from doing so, gun locks cannot possibly stop adults from firing their own guns. Most accidental gun deaths of children have little to do with "naturally curious" children shooting other children, as the shooters themselves tend to be quite old. No more than nine cases in recent years involve a child younger than ten shooting another child. This should come as no surprise to those who are familiar with guns, for few children are strong enough to cock a pistol, let alone know how to do it.

The dangers of children getting into guns pale in comparison to many other risks. Over 1,260 children under ten died as a result of motor vehicles in 1999, and almost another 370 died as pedestrians killed by cars.[101] Accidents involving residential fires took 484 children's lives in 1999. Bicycles are also much more likely to result in accidental deaths than guns.[102] Ninety-three children under ten drowned in bathtubs; another thirty-six children under age five drowned in five-gallon plastic water buckets.[103] More children under five drown in this one type of water bucket than children under ten die from any type of accidental gunshot. Strangely, none of our doctors asked questions about whether we kept our buckets stored away or our bathroom doors locked.

Chapter 3 illustrated how the Clinton administration made accidental gun deaths of children a major issue during the 1990s, with, among other things, public service ads showing the voices and pictures of six-, seven- and eight-year-old children juxtaposed to the claim that during the mid-1990s, ten children a day died from guns. The ads surely gave the impression that these deaths involved young children and that these deaths resulted from accidents. President Clinton frequently linked gun deaths of children to gun locks.[104] Yet, the vast majority of these deaths did not occur as the Clinton administration implied. Seventy percent of those deaths involved "children" between the ages of seventeen and nineteen, and the vast majority of those were homicides—primarily involving gang fights.[105]

Advocates of gun locks frequently say: "If this saves one child's life, it's worth it."[106,107] But it makes no more sense to say "we should lock up guns if they save one life," than it makes sense to say that "guns shouldn't be locked if their ready availability will save one live." Ultimately, it is an empirical question—and not a sentimental one—whether, on net, lives are saved or lost. To answer this, Chapter 7 examines juvenile accidental gun deaths and suicides for all states from 1977 to 1996, analyzing what happens when people either stop owning guns or lock them up. Using surveys on the rate at which people in different states claim to lock up their guns helps establish whether there is a link between how people store their guns and criminal attacks in people's homes.

GUNS IN SCHOOLS

Much of the momentum for gun control during recent years has arisen from the public school shootings and the desire to "do something" about them. As noted earlier, thirty-two students have been killed by any type of gun death at elementary and secondary schools between the fall of 1997 and the spring of 2002.[108] This total includes gang fights, robberies, and accidents, as well as the much publicized public school shootings, and corresponds to an annual rate of one death per 4 million students. During the same period, four teachers were shot to death at elementary or secondary schools, an annual rate of one per 3.3 million teachers.[109] The National Education Association made national headlines during 2001 with an offer to its members of a free $150,000 insurance policy, payable if they are shot to death on school grounds.[110] By any measure, deaths from any type of school shooting are exceedingly rare. For example, compare it to the 53 students who died playing high school football over the same period of time,[111] deaths that went completely unnoticed by the national media.

Schools have reacted to these shooting horrors with a "zero tolerance" approach to aggression, even banning dodge ball and tag because the games encourage "violent behavior."[112] Some schools are removing any references to the military from their libraries, and some high schools are banning military recruiters.[113] Elementary students in Texas and Louisiana have been suspended for pointing pencils and saying "Pow" or drawing pictures of soldiers. Students in Mississippi were held in jail for trivial infractions, such as throwing peanuts at one another. And a fifth-grader in St. Petersburg, Florida, was arrested for drawing pictures of "weapons."[114]

Recent students caught in the zero tolerance policy include an exemplary high-school student, a National Merit Scholar, jailed in Fort Myers, Florida, because school authorities found a kitchen knife under her car seat. The knife had accidentally fallen there during a move between apartments. And "terrorist threat" criminal charges were filed against two eight-year-olds in Irvington, New Jersey, for "playing cops and robbers with a paper gun." A seven-year-old in Ann Arbor, Michigan, who pointed a toy gun at three other youngsters, was charged with three counts of felonious assault.[115] Second-graders have been arrested for bringing toy guns to school. And while some juvenile records can be expunged, other records last a lifetime. Those can, for instance, trigger the Brady law background checks and prevent individuals with trivial infractions of irrational rules like these from ever possessing a gun.

Banning guns to create "safety" zones surely seems like an obvious approach to problems of violence, but ironically even standard schooling tools—such as pencils—have apparently been used in felony stabbings.[116] The real question is whether the 1995 Safe Schools Act that banned guns within 1,000 feet of schools has really made things safer. As Chapter 6 will show, it hasn't.

PART II

EXAMINING THE EVIDENCE

CHAPTER 5

EVALUATING EVIDENCE ON GUNS: HOW AND HOW NOT TO DO IT

THE DIFFERENT TYPES OF EVIDENCE

As we will extensively rely on empirical evidence in this book, as opposed to subjective feelings about the rightness or wrongness of gun use, it is useful to review the difficulties with relying solely on either cross-sectional or time-series analyses.

First, the cross-sectional studies: Suppose for the sake of argument that high-crime countries are the ones that most frequently adopt the most stringent gun control laws. Suppose further, for the sake of argument, that gun control indeed lowers crime, but not by enough to reduce rates to the same low levels prevailing in the majority of countries that did not adopt the laws. Looking across countries, it would then falsely appear that stricter gun control resulted in higher crime. Economists refer to this as an "endogeniety" problem. The adoption of the policy is a reaction to other events (that is, "endogenous")—in this case, crime.[1] To resolve this, one must examine how the high-crime areas that chose to adopt the controls changed over time—not only relative to their own past levels but also relative to areas that did not institute such controls.

Unfortunately, many contemporary discussions rely on misinterpretations of cross-sectional data. The *New York Times* recently conducted a cross-sectional study of murder rates in states with and without the death penalty,[2] and found that "Indeed, 10 of the 12 states without capital punishment have homicide rates below the national average, Federal Bureau of Investigation data shows, while half the states with the death penalty have homicide rates above the national average." However, they erroneously concluded that the death penalty did not deter murder. The problem is that the states without the death penalty (Alaska, Hawaii, Iowa, Maine, Massachusetts, Michigan, Minnesota, North Dakota, Rhode Island, West Virginia, Wisconsin, and Vermont) have long enjoyed relatively low murder rates, something that might well have more to do with other factors than the death penalty. Instead one must compare, over time, how murder rates change in the two groups—those adopting the death penalty and those not.

For time-series data, relying on only one jurisdiction involves other equally severe problems. For example, while the ideal study accounts for other factors that may help explain changing crime rates, a pure time-series study of one area makes such a task difficult. Many factors usually fluctuate simultaneously, making it very difficult to separate out the ones responsible for changes in crime. In other words, if two or more events occur precisely at the same time in a particular jurisdiction, a study of only that one jurisdiction cannot possibly help us distinguish which event triggered the change in crime. Only if a law has changed in many different places and at different times can one have a chance of disentangling the different factors and find good evidence as to whether a similar crime pattern exists before and after the law.

Unfortunately, there are some problems for which only time-series data are available. Take, for example, the 1966 U.S. Supreme Court decision in *Miranda v. Arizona*. Most people are familiar with the *Miranda*-rights warning that police must provide before interrogating criminal suspects. ("You have the right to remain silent, etc.") Paul Cassell, a law professor at the University of Utah, argues that as many as 28,000 violent felons go free each year because of the *Miranda* warning. According to him, criminals who otherwise would have confessed clam up, or confessions that are blurted out are thrown out due to technical violations of the *Miranda* ruling.[3] Cassell may be correct, but his case is difficult to prove since one cannot separate out the effect of *Miranda* from the effects of other Supreme Court decisions or from other changes in society during the mid-1960s. Unlike state law changes, which essentially provide us with fifty different "laboratories" (fifty-one including Washington, D.C.), the Supreme Court decision simultaneously affected all the different states.

Fortunately, for some problems, it is possible to use changes in different state laws to combine time-series and cross-sectional evidence into what is called a "panel" data set. Panel data track many different jurisdictions over many years. One can then introduce separate variables, so that for each year the national (or regional) changes in crime rates are accounted for. These trends are then subtracted from changes in the crime rates for places within those geographic areas.[4] For example, crime fell nationally between 1991 and 1992. The panel data can tell us, for each state or county, whether there is an additional decline over and above that national drop. Then the states that adopted a particular law, such as safe storage provisions for guns, can be compared to the other states. Using data for fifty states and the District of Columbia also allows us to separate out many different factors that affect everything from crime to accidental gun deaths. States may pass multiple laws at the same time or may increase the number of police officers, but if we have enough different experiments (as long as not all the states pass the identical set of laws at the same time), we can sort out which policy changes were important. I will use a set of measures that account for the average differences in crime rates across places even after demographics, income, and other factors have been accounted for. It has only been since 1997 that gun-control studies have taken this approach.[5]

The typically larger size of panel data sets helps us to account for many more factors than are possible with either cross-sectional or time-series data alone. Studying crime rates in one state over twenty years generates only twenty observations. By contrast, studying all fifty states and the District of Columbia over twenty years yields 1,050 observations. If you collect data on all 3,140 counties in the United States over twenty years, that yields over 62,000 observations. Most high-quality crime data are available for only a few decades at most. Thus the only way to generate enough information is to simultaneously study many different jurisdictions. This is important because you cannot try to account for many factors if you don't have plenty of observations.

To take a simple example, suppose the murder rate in a state fell from one year to the next. If two different factors changed, either one could potentially explain it. But there is no way to know which one accounted for the drop or whether both factors could explain the drop. Even if we were convinced that one factor alone could be credited with the lower crime rate, a mere two observations would hardly provide much confidence in testing that effect. It would be like flipping a coin just once to see if it was "fair." Getting "heads" once is not that difficult, as there is a 50 percent chance with a fair coin. But there is only a 3 percent chance of getting heads five straight times with a fair coin. Getting ten straight heads is very unlikely with a fair coin: It should happen less than 0.1 percent of the time. Thus, certainty increases with more observations.

The same holds true with any statistical test. But unfortunately, most controversies are more complicated than simply determining whether a coin is fair. If there is more than one question that needs to be answered, the number of observations we need increases proportionately. There may also be numerous alternative explanations for each question. Thus, a large set of observations is crucial.

Combining cross-sectional and time-series as panel data allows us to account for many factors that are not possible with either one separately. Of special importance is the recent nationwide decline in crime rates. Crime started falling nationally in 1991. Crime in some states fell more or less quickly than others, but it is evident that there must have been something happening nationally to explain the drop. Hence, if one tries to evaluate laws passed during the 1990s, it is crucial not only to distinguish the drop in crime in the states with the law compared to those without the law but also to disentangle the influences in these states from those on the national level. It is impossible to disentangle these differences when looking at a single jurisdiction and you risk falsely attributing the national decline in crime to what is happening in the individual state. As indicated above, the solution is to study simultaneously many different states over time. Thus, what I have done in the next few chapters is examine whether the states that adopted a particular law had crime rates that fell more or less quickly than the rates in those states that didn't adopt the law.

Crime rates are different in many states or counties for many different reasons. As noted earlier in our discussion on the death penalty, it is necessary to make sure whether the differences in crime rates are due to the particular policies or simply whether high or low crime rate states adopted a law. Again, simultaneously examining many different jurisdictions over time provides a simple solution in the form of so-called "geographic fixed effects." Any effect of the policy is then relative to whatever crime rate existed before the policy.

THE PROBLEM WITH RELYING ON ONLY BEFORE-AND-AFTER AVERAGES

There are lots of pitfalls in evaluating empirical evidence. Most empirical work—such as the research on *Miranda* discussed earlier in this chapter, or the death penalty, or other work on gun control—compares the average crime rate with and without some policy change. Cross-sectional evidence such as that for the *New York Times*'s death penalty discussion almost always relies on a simple comparison of averages. While this has obvious intuitive appeal and can serve as a useful first glance, the results can also occasionally be very misleading.

Take the simple hypothetical case where crime rates were already rising prior to *Miranda*. If the increase continued at the same rate after the Supreme Court decision so that someone looking at the crime rate saw it rising on the same perfectly straight line before and after the court decision, it would be obvious that the average crime rate was higher after the decision than it was before it, but it would also be equally clear that the decision did not affect the rise in crime.

Neglecting this point can also make it look like a law or a court decision has no effect on crime when the effect is actually very large. Suppose that crime rates were falling before a law went into effect, but then rose afterward. Simply comparing the before-and-after averages could produce any number of results. If the pre-law decline roughly equaled the post-law increase, the before-and-after averages would be the same even though there had been a clear change in trends. However, if the pre-law decline had been very large relative to the post-law increase, examining only the before-and-after averages could make it look as if the law caused the crime rates to decline. The reverse is also true. These might seem like simple points, but relatively few studies disentangle differences in averages from differences in trends.

CORRELATION AND CAUSATION

It is important to find out whether or not crime systematically goes up or down with different law enforcement actions or different laws. Not only would this help legislators select effective policies, but it can also help evaluate other theories about crime. Unfortunately, correlation between a given policy and a given crime trend does not, in itself, imply causation. There is always the possibility of multiple explanations for any given result. The key is to construct many completely different types of tests for the various possible explanations. The greater number of different tests you have, the more you can narrow down the number of alternative explanations.

Take my evidence on allowing law-abiding citizens to carry concealed handguns. Violent crime rates fell after the laws were passed, but there is still more evidence of a causal relationship. For instance, those states that issued the most permits also had the biggest drops in crime, and violent crime declined further over time as more permits were issued. In addition, crimes involving direct contact between victims and criminals fell relative to crimes such as property theft where there is no direct contact. When looking at counties that border each other on the opposite sides of state lines, counties located in a state with the concealed carry law tended to experience a drop in violent crime—while the counties on the other side of the state line were experiencing a sudden, though smaller, increase.

It is important to account for as many of the other factors as possible that affect crime. For example, one might incorrectly obtain a statistically significant relationship between two events when important factors are excluded that affect the variable that one is studying. In other words, one might wrongly conclude that just because B followed A, A must have caused B. On the other hand, factors that should not be included can also cause problems. For example, it might prevent the discovery of statistically significant results, even when those effects are really there. The matter is more complicated than it may at first seem, since there are essentially an infinite number of variables. And so in order to ensure that a study is as accurate as possible, one must carefully examine and account for as many variables as are truly relevant.

CHAPTER 6

ACTS OF TERROR WITH GUNS: MULTIPLE VICTIM SHOOTINGS

(coauthored with William M. Landes*)

When the bullets started flying at the Seafood Market disco in Tel Aviv, shoe salesman William Hazan's first instinct was to duck under a table.

His second was to open his wife's purse and grab a gun to confront the attacker—a move that probably saved many lives.

"I didn't lose my cool," Hazan told Israel Radio from his hospital bed a few hours after the violence.

"Thank God I had my pistol with me."

Hazan and his wife were eating with friends at the nightclub when a Palestinian suicide shooter opened fire with an automatic rifle.

After Hazan pulled out the gun he's been carrying around for years, he crawled under the tables toward the exit and dashed outside.

There, he saw a tall man hitting a shorter man with a knife and jumped to conclusions.

"I thought the small man was the terrorist," Hazan said.

"I was going to hit him with the butt of my pistol, but then I got a knife in my belly," he said.

"I realized I was looking at the wrong man, so I turned my gun and shot the other one."

---

*Clifton R. Musser Professor of Law and Economics at the University of Chicago Law School

Because of his quick action, the killer—who had already
shot dead three people and wounded more than two dozen
others—never got the chance to detonate the explosives
strapped to his body.

*Uri Dan, "Hero Grabs Pistol from Wife's Purse and Guns
Down Terrorist," New York Post, Tuesday, March 5, 2002*[1]

At about 8:30 A.M., an Arab infiltrator managed to open fire
and throw at least one grenade at the Shavei Shomron kinder-
garten before setting off on a shooting spree through the town.
He opened fire at several residents and homes before David
Elbaz, owner of the local mini-market, gave chase and killed
him with gunshots. In addition to several grenades and the
weapon the terrorist carried on him, security sweeps revealed
several explosive devices that he had intended to detonate
during the thwarted attack.

Reported in Israel's Arutz Sheva, Friday, May 31, 2002[2]

I. INTRODUCTION

Few events generate as much national and worldwide news coverage
as when several people are shot and killed in a public place. Some
highly publicized examples come readily to mind. Colin Ferguson
killed six people in a shooting rampage on the Long Island Rail Road
in 1993. A single gunman indiscriminately killed twenty-two
lunchtime patrons at a Luby's Cafeteria in Texas in 1991. An out-of-
work security guard killed twenty-one people at a California McDonald's in 1984. Two students shot and killed thirteen people at
Columbine High School in Littleton, Colorado, in 1999. In another
vein, shootings by disgruntled post office employees have made the
phrase "going postal" part of our language.

It is widely thought that the way to prevent multiple public shootings (the term used here to describe shootings in public places where
two or more individuals are killed or injured) is to enact new and
tougher laws that make it more difficult for individuals to obtain
guns. For example, the 1996 public shootings in Australia and Scot-

land were followed by strict gun prohibitions in those countries. In the United States, public shootings have led to demands for national licensing of guns, laws requiring that guns be kept locked, and minimum waiting or "cooling-off" periods before a purchaser actually takes possession of a gun. By making it more difficult or costly for individuals to gain access to guns, these laws aim to reduce the likelihood that individuals will be able to carry out shooting sprees.

The legislative response to public shootings, however, has not been uniform. In Texas and several other states, multiple victim public shootings have been followed by the passage of concealed handgun laws that permit law-abiding citizens to carry firearms. Likewise, terrorist shootings in Israel have led to wider licensing of Israeli citizens to carry concealed handguns.

Those opposed to right-to-carry laws reason that these laws will make it easier for criminals to gain access to guns and that "if you introduce a gun into a violent encounter, it increases the chance that someone will die."[3] Consider the school shootings that took place from 1997 to 2000. The perpetrators obtained their guns a variety of ways: from relatives, neighbors, people at work, other acquaintances, or theft. Had guns been less available or not purchased in the first place, these acts may not have been committed. This argument is reinforced by the belief that shootings in public places often arise from temporary fits of rage that are later regretted. If this argument is sound, enacting laws that make handguns less accessible (even temporarily) should prevent many deaths.[4]

But there is another side, one rarely mentioned in the media. Concealed weapons in the hands of good people can be used to save lives and stop attacks. The prospect of a criminal encountering a victim who may be armed will deter some attacks in the first place.[5] Carrying a gun is also the safest course of action when one is confronted by a criminal.[6]

The most comprehensive empirical study of concealed handgun laws finds that they reduce murder rates by about 1.5 percent for each additional year a law has been in effect, with similar declines in other violent crimes.[7] And contrary to a popular misconception, permit holders are virtually never involved in the commission of any crime, let alone murder.[8]

Just as one can find examples of public shootings that support the desirability of more gun control, one can find other examples that support the desirability of less gun control. Consider the shooting spree at a public school in Pearl, Mississippi, in 1997. An assistant principal retrieved his gun from his car and physically immobilized the shooter before he caused further harm.[9] (The assistant principal had to park his car away from school property to obey the 1,000-foot "gun-free zone" around schools.)

Or take the 1998 public school–related shooting in Edinboro, Pennsylvania, which left one teacher dead. A local restaurant owner, hearing the attack, ran over and pointed his shotgun at the offender, preventing him from creating additional harm.[10] The police did not arrive for another ten minutes. Law-abiding citizens have also used guns to stop gun-toting attackers at restaurants, businesses, government offices, stores, and churches.

Similar examples can be found internationally. Referring to the 1984 massacre at a McDonald's restaurant in California, Israeli criminologist Abraham Tennenbaum wrote that something:

> [...]occurred at a [crowded venue in] Jerusalem some weeks before the California McDonald's massacre: three terrorists who attempted to machine-gun the throng managed to kill only one victim before being shot down by handgun-carrying Israelis. Presented to the press the next day, the surviving terrorist complained that his group had not realized that Israeli civilians were armed. The terrorists had planned to machine-gun a succession of crowded spots, thinking that they would be able to escape before the police or army could arrive to deal with them.[11]

Obviously allowing Israeli citizens to carry concealed handguns has not eliminated terrorist attacks. Indeed, terrorists may well have reacted to this change by substituting bombs for machine guns, which allow potential victims little chance to respond and thus are not as affected by people carrying guns to protect themselves. But there is the question of why terrorists preferred machine guns over bombs when they had the choice between the two. Presumably, since terrorists picked machine guns when they had a choice of either, they must have thought that bombs were not as well suited to their gruesome tasks.

While concealed handguns are more useful in stopping machine gun attacks, there are still plenty of stories where guns have also been used to stop bombings from occurring:

> An alert customer shot dead a terrorist who tried to set off an explosive device in a supermarket a few minutes ago in Efrat. The town is in Gush Etzion, a block of Jewish communities in Judea, south of Bethlehem.
>
> At least one small explosion did take place, leaving one customer lightly wounded but causing no casualties, said *Jerusalem Post* reporter Margot Dudkevitch. Nails from one of the explosions littered the floor.
>
> Further tragedy was averted when a woman shopping in the packed supermarket apparently saw the terrorist trying to set off a second explosion and shot him twice in the head from close range.
>
> A police source told Israel Radio the terrorist apparently intended to detonate a small bomb in the supermarket and then blow himself up with the explosive belt when police forces came to the scene.
>
> *The* Jerusalem Post *Internet Staff, "Alert Customer Shoots Terrorist in Efrat Supermarket," Friday, February 22, 2002*[12]

A heroic security guard saved hundreds of Tel Aviv partygoers from death at the hands of a homicide bomber last night.

Nobody was seriously hurt in the blast, one of two terror bomb attacks in Israel yesterday.

Near midnight, security guard Eli Federman was outside the Studio 49 disco in Tel Aviv when he saw the bomber's car pull up.

"I suspected the car because it came in at such a high speed," Federman told Israeli radio.

"I was afraid he wanted to run over the people lining up at the discotheque. And there were about 200 people inside.

"So I pulled out my pistol and I opened fire. And the moment I shot, the car exploded."

The bomber died instantly, authorities said.

Uri Dan, "Israeli Hero Kills Bomber," New York Post,
May 24, 2002[13]

Anecdotal evidence cannot resolve the question of whether laws allowing law-abiding persons to carry concealed handguns will save or cost lives. This study attempts to answer this question with respect to multiple victim public shootings and bombings. Our empirical analysis focuses primarily on right-to-carry (or "shall-issue") laws, which allow law-abiding citizens to carry concealed handguns. This chapter also examines the effects on public shootings of (1) laws that restrict access to handguns, including mandatory waiting periods, one-gun-a-month purchase limitations, and safe storage gun laws; and (2) statutes that impose additional penalties on individuals who use guns in the commission of a crime.[14]

There are a few remarks about why we should study shootings in public places. There is, of course, the widespread interest and curiosity that people have in these kinds of shootings. The more important reason, however, is that these shootings allow us to test the economic model (that if you make something more difficult people do less of it) in an area far outside the usual domain of economics. Perpetrators of multiple victim shootings are often thought to be psychotic, deranged, or irrational, and hence not responsive to costs and benefits. Indeed, the series in the *New York Times* mentioned earlier concluded: "About half [the 100 multiple victim public killers that they studied] had received formal diagnosis of mental illness, often schizophrenia" and the killings were described as "impulsive acts."[15] One could assume that legal sanctions, or, as in this case, the prospect of encountering an armed individual during a shooting spree, would have no deterrent effect on such irrational individuals. Consequences would not deter them. Indeed, a shooting spree itself is cited as powerful evidence of irrational or psychotic behavior since a sane person would never kill helpless victims in a public place where he could be caught or killed.

From this, the claim is made that a law permitting individuals to carry concealed weapons would not deter shooting sprees in public places because the criminally insane don't care about the consequences of their actions. Moreover, since concealed handgun laws might well increase the availability of guns to potential perpetrators, the combination of criminal irrationality and greater availability of guns should increase the number of multiple victim public shooting incidents.

In contrast, the economic model of crime predicts that a right-to-carry law will both raise the potential perpetrator's cost (e.g., he is more likely to be apprehended, wounded, or killed if he acts) and lower his expected benefit (e.g., he will be able to cause less damage if he encounters armed resistance). Although not all offenders will alter their behavior in response to the law, some individuals will refrain from a shooting spree because their net gain is now negative. Economics predicts, therefore, that right-to-carry laws will reduce the number of mass shootings—though the magnitude of this effect is uncertain.

One important qualification should be noted. If a right-to-carry law also decreases the potential perpetrator's difficulty in obtaining or gaining access to a gun—say because there are more guns on the secondary market or it becomes easier to steal a gun because more people own them—the net effect of the law may be weaker or may even increase the number of public shootings.

There is good reason to expect that a right-to-carry law will do more to deter multiple victim public shootings than more typical murders or other crimes. This greater deterrent effect may appear surprising in light of the claimed irrationality of individuals who go on shooting sprees. But another consideration points in the opposite direction. Suppose that a right-to-carry law deters crime primarily by raising the probability that a perpetrator will encounter a potential victim who is armed. In a single-victim crime, this probability is likely to be very low. Hence the deterrent effect of the law—though negative—might be relatively small. Now consider a shooting spree in a public place. The likelihood that one or more potential victims or bystanders are armed would be very large even though the probability that any particular individual is armed is very low.[16] This suggests a testable hypothesis: A right-to-carry law will have a bigger deterrent effect on shooting sprees in public places than on more conventional crimes.

Finally, economists have long recognized that deterrence can impact not only whether a crime occurs, but also its severity.[17] However, there are no empirical studies on severity. The data collected here make it possible for the first time to examine both how many attacks are deterred as well as reductions in the severity of each attack.

II. MULTIPLE VICTIM PUBLIC SHOOTINGS: A FIRST LOOK

This chapter examines all the multiple public shootings in the United States in the time period 1977 to 1997 (and, in some cases, through 1999).[18] As noted earlier, a multiple victim public shooting is defined as one in which two or more people are killed or wounded in a church, business, bar, street, government building, school, place of public transit, place of employment, park, health care facility, mall, or restaurant. The main advantage of restricting the analysis to the United States is that we can compare states with and without right-to-carry laws at different points in time (holding other factors constant), and therefore estimate the effects of a state changing its law during the sample period. In contrast, time-series data for a single country face the problem that many different events may occur at approximately the same time, which can make it difficult to disentangle the impact of a change in the law from other factors. Similarly, the alternative of conducting an international cross-country study was ruled out because of difficulty finding comparable data on gun laws, crime rates, and gun ownership.

The data on multiple victim public shootings are from articles in a computerized database of news stories from 1977 to 1997 (the Lexis-Nexis database). In analyzing shooting data, we excluded multiple victim public shootings that were byproducts of other crimes (e.g., a robbery or drug deal) or that involved gang activity (e.g., drive-by shootings), professional hits or organized crime. We also did not count serial killings or killings that took place over a span of more than one day.[19]

There are two reasons for excluding these types of multiple victim public shootings.[20] First, since shall-issue laws permit law-abiding citizens to carry guns, they should have little impact on killings related to gang activity, drug deals and organized crime. Criminals involved in gangs, drugs and organized crime are already engaged in unlawful activities that often require them to carry guns. Their behavior will be largely independent of whether a law on the books permits or prohibits citizens from carrying concealed handguns. Hence a "right-to-carry" law should not impact whether gang members or drug dealers are armed or kill each other.

Second, economic theory suggests a reason why a right-to-carry law will have a greater effect on multiple victim public shootings in public places than on other types of shootings.[21] Say 5 percent of the adult population is carrying a concealed handgun. That indeed represents some risk to a criminal who might attack a lone victim late at night in a dark parking lot or an alley, so some crime ought to be deterred. But for attacks in public places where many adults are present, the risks to the criminal and the deterrent effect on him are both much higher. For a restaurant with a hundred people (even if there is only a 5 percent chance that any one adult will be armed) the probability that at least one of the adults will be armed (a person unknown to the attacker) will be near 100 percent. The latter circumstance is unlikely for public places unless there are separate prohibitions on carrying guns in certain places (e.g., near schools). In short, a right-to-carry law should increase the likelihood that an offender will encounter a potential victim or bystander in a public place who is armed.[22]

Tables 6.1 and 6.2 present data on multiple victim public shootings for the United States as a whole, and for states with and without right-to-carry laws. Overall, the states without right-to-carry laws had more deaths and injuries from multiple victim public shootings per year (both in absolute numbers and on a per capita basis) during the 1977 to 1997 period. Note also that the number of states with right-to-carry laws increased from eight to thirty-one and the percentage of the U.S. population living in these states rose from 8.5 to 50 percent in this period. But states without right-to-carry laws still account for the large majority (often around 90 percent) of deaths and injuries.

Table 6.2 shows that the per capita rates of shootings and injuries are greater in states without right-to-carry laws in thirty-four of the forty-two comparisons. (See the last two columns in Table 6.2.) The annual differences are significantly different. The likelihood of getting this result accidentally is roughly equivalent to flipping a coin and getting five heads in a row.[23]

Table 6.1
The Number of Multiple Victim Murders and Injuries in Public Shootings by Year and by the Presence of a Concealed Handgun Law

	All States			States Without Right-to-Carry Handgun Law (Including the District of Columbia)						
Year	# of Murders in Public Shootings	# of Injuries in Public Shootings	# of Public Shootings	# of States Without Right-to-Carry Concealed Handgun Law	# of Murders in Public Shootings	# of Injuries in Public Shootings	# of Shootings	% of Total Deaths (Column 5/Column 1)	% of Total Injuries (Column 6/Column 2)	% of Total Shootings (Column 7/Column 3)
	(1)	(2)	(3)	(4)	(5)	(6)	(7)	(8)	(9)	(10)
1977	19	46	7	43	19	46	7	100%	100%	100%
1978	14	12	8	43	14	12	8	100%	100%	100%
1979	23	77	13	43	20	74	12	87%	96%	92%
1980	30	51	11	43	22	46	8	73%	90%	73%
1981	44	60	30	43	37	50	27	84%	83%	90%
1982	32	92	20	43	28	92	19	87%	100%	95%
1983	19	36	18	43	16	22	14	84%	61%	78%
1984	56	76	26	43	53	73	24	95%	96%	92%
1985	38	45	24	43	34	37	21	89%	82%	88%
1986	41	54	21	42	41	52	20	100%	96%	95%
1987	44	73	36	42	41	69	34	93%	95%	94%
1988	49	90	35	41	47	85	32	96%	94%	91%
1989	49	84	31	40	39	79	24	80%	94%	77%
1990	29	53	22	37	20	43	20	69%	81%	91%
1991	58	68	22	34	53	58	18	91%	85%	82%
1992	31	55	18	33	29	54	17	94%	98%	94%
1993	87	83	33	33	83	76	30	95%	92%	91%
1994	15	20	10	33	13	19	9	87%	95%	90%
1995	26	11	11	29	23	11	10	88%	100%	91%
1996	128	291	136	23	82	234	107	64%	80%	79%
1997	99	144	71	20	55	94	41	56%	65%	58%

Table 6.2: The Rate of Multiple Victim Murders and Injuries in Public Shootings by Year and by the Presence of a Concealed Handgun Law (Population-Weighted Averages)

Year	States Without Right-to-Carry Law			States With Right-to-Carry Law			Comparison of Rates Between Two Types of States	
	# of States Without Right-to-Carry Law (Including D.C.)	Murders and Injuries in Public Shootings Per 100,000 People	# of Shootings Per 100,000 People	# of States With Right-to-Carry Law	Murders and Injuries in Public Shootings Per 100,000 People	# of Shootings Per 100,000 People	Does the Murder and Injury Rate in States Without Laws Exceed the Rate in States with Laws?[1]	Does the Shooting Rate in States Without Laws Exceed the Rate in States with Laws?[2]
	(1)	(2)	(3)	(4)	(5)	(6)	(7)	(8)
1977	43	0.033	0.005	8	0	0	Yes	Yes
1978	43	0.013	0.006	8	0	0	Yes	Yes
1979	43	0.046	0.008	8	0.031	0.002	Yes	Yes
1980	43	0.033	0.006	8	0.067	0.006	No	No
1981	43	0.041	0.019	8	0.087	0.006	No	Yes
1982	43	0.057	0.013	8	0.020	0.002	Yes	Yes
1983	43	0.018	0.010	8	0.086	0.008	No	Yes
1984	43	0.058	0.017	8	0.030	0.004	Yes	Yes
1985	43	0.032	0.014	8	0.060	0.006	No	Yes
1986	42	0.042	0.014	9	0.009	0.002	Yes	Yes
1987	42	0.050	0.023	9	0.033	0.003	Yes	Yes
1988	41	0.063	0.022	10	0.021	0.005	Yes	Yes
1989	40	0.057	0.017	11	0.037	0.010	Yes	Yes
1990	37	0.034	0.014	14	0.031	0.002	Yes	Yes
1991	34	0.061	0.012	17	0.022	0.004	Yes	Yes
1992	33	0.045	0.012	18	0.004	0.001	Yes	Yes
1993	33	0.085	0.021	18	0.002	0.003	Yes	Yes
1994	33	0.017	0.006	18	0.004	0.001	Yes	Yes
1995	29	0.046	0.007	22	0.004	0.001	Yes	Yes
1996	23	0.218	0.074	28	0.079	0.024	Yes	Yes
1997	20	0.103	0.028	31	0.069	0.024	Yes	Yes
Average	38	0.055	0.0166	13	0.033	0.005	Yes	Yes

[1]Testing whether the difference in annual means is not equal to zero t=2.269 P>|t| = 0.0345
[2]Testing whether the difference in annual means is not equal to zero t=20.000 P>|t| = 0.0000

One interesting finding is the sharp increase in multiple victim public shootings in the year 1996. While the numbers decline substantially for 1997, they are still high relative to other years. For example, the number of murders in 1996 is 47 percent higher than the previous high in 1993. While the share of multiple victim killings in nonright-to-carry states fell in 1996 and 1997 [columns (8)–(10) in Table 6.1], the number of states and the population in states without right-to-carry laws fell so much faster, the per capita rates were still higher in non-right-to-carry states (Table 6.2).[24] While all the years of the data will be examined, the results that are shown later are not sensitive to the particular years examined. Limiting the sample from 1977 to 1992 or from 1977 to 1994 produces similar results to what will be shown in the rest of the chapter.[25] Section VI of this chapter also shows that the increased share during 1996 and 1997 shown in Table 6.1 arose because the nine states in their first full year with right-to-carry laws had much more restrictive stipulations on the law than earlier adopters.

It is also useful to focus on the changes over time in just the twenty-three states that adopted right-to-carry laws between 1977 and 1997 (Tables 6.3 and 6.4).[26] (No state has ever repealed this law.) Although there is an upward national trend in multiple victim shooting murders and injuries from 1977 to 1997 [see columns (1)–(3) in Table 6.1], Table 6.3 shows large declines in crime after states adopted right-to-carry laws. Murders fell by about 43 percent and injuries by 30 percent.[27] Breaking down the crime rates on a year by year basis around the time that the laws are passed indicates that the biggest drop occurred largely during the first full year after a state enacted its law (Year "1" in the first column of Table 6.4). Overall, the decline is so large that we observe zero multiple victim killings in two of the six years for all states with right-to-carry laws, an event that did not occur during any year before passage of the law.[28]

Another point worth noting is that the decline in shootings between the pre-law and post-law periods in Table 6.4 is not the result of a few shooting incidents in the former period. The last two columns in Table 6.4 show that the two worst attacks accounted for 55 percent of the average annual deaths in the years before the right-to-carry laws were adopted, compared to 64 percent after (excluding years in which there were no multiple victim murders).

Table 6.3
The Twenty-three States That Adopted Right-to-Carry Concealed Handgun Laws
Sometime Between 1977 and 1997 (Each value shows the mean.)

Twenty-three States That Went from Not Having to Having a Right-to-Carry Concealed Handgun Law	Murders in Multiple Victim Public Shootings Per 100,000 People (1)	Injuries in Multiple Victim Public Shootings Per 100,000 People (2)	Murders and Injuries in Multiple Victim Public Shootings Per 100,000 People (3)	# of Shootings Per 100,000 People (4)
(1) Years During Which These States Did Not Have Right-to-Carry Concealed Handgun Laws (Observations = 374)	0.021	0.028	0.050	0.0119
(2) Years During Which They Did Have Right-to-Carry Concealed Handgun Laws (Observations = 109)	0.012	0.020	0.0326	0.009
(3) Years During Which They Did Have Right-to-Carry Concealed Handgun Laws—Excluding cases involving school and government buildings where permitted concealed handguns were obviously forbidden (Observations = 109)	0.0099	0.0137	0.0236	0.0076

Twenty-three States That Went from Not Having to Having a Right-to-Carry Concealed Handgun Law	Actual and Attempted Bombings Per 100,000 People (5)	Actual and Attempted Incendiary Bombings Per 100,000 People (6)	Other Bomb-Related Incidents Per 100,000 People (7)	Total Explosive Incidents Per 100,000 People (8)
(1) Years During Which These States Did Not Have Right-to-Carry Concealed Handgun Laws (Observations = 374)	0.584	0.135	0.961	1.681
(2) Years During Which They Did Have Right-to-Carry Concealed Handgun Laws (Observations = 109)	0.721	0.1395	0.954	1.8079

Table 6.4
Examining the Means for States That Adopted Right-to-Carry Concealed Handgun
Laws During the 1977 to 1997 Period (Based on years before and after the adoption of right-to-
carry laws in which at least ten states have the law in place)

		States That Adopted Right-to-Carry Concealed Handgun Laws During the 1977–1997 Period: Using State Averages to Compute Rates			
Years Before and After the Adoption of the Law	*Number of States That Fall into That Category*	*Murders in Multiple Victim Public Shootings* Per 100,000 People	*Injuries in Multiple Victim Public Shootings* Per 100,000 People	*Murders and Injuries in Multiple Victim Public Shootings* Per 100,000 People	*The Number of Shootings* Per 100,000 People
(1)	(2)	(3)	(4)	(5)	(6)
-8	23	0.010	0.041	0.051	0.010
-7	23	0.020	0.047	0.067	0.014
-6	23	0.037	0.022	0.059	0.019
-5	23	0.003	0.002	0.005	0.001
-4	23	0.016	0.022	0.038	0.011
-3	23	0.008	0.015	0.022	0.005
-2	23	0.014	0.016	0.030	0.009
-1	23	0.035	0.055	0.089	0.028
0	23	0.024	0.061	0.085	0.030
1	23	0.010	0.013	0.023	0.008
2	20	0.007	0.007	0.014	0.008
3	14	0.017	0.040	0.057	0.015
4	10	0	0.002	0.002	0.001
5	10	0	0	0	0
6	10	0.011	0.023	0.034	0.012

States That Adopted Right-to-Carry Concealed Handgun Laws During the 1977–1997 Period: Using State Averages to Compute Rates

Total Number of Murders in Multiple Victim Public Shootings for All States in This Category (7)	Total Number of Injuries in Multiple Victim Public Shootings for All States in This Category (8)	Worst Attack in Terms of Number of Murders (9)	Worst Attack in Terms of Number of Injuries (10)
11	48	Arkansas (2), South Carolina (2)	North Carolina, South Carolina (9), Pennsylvania (7)
19	50	Kentucky (8), North Carolina (4)	Kentucky (12), North Carolina (5)
16	14	Idaho (5), Florida, Texas (2)	Florida (3), Texas (2)
8	5	Florida (8)	Florida (3), Pennsylvania (2)
41	39	Texas (23), Pennsylvania (4)	Texas (18), Pennsylvania (7)
10	25	Texas (2), Florida (1)	Arizona, Texas (6)
12	13	Virginia (3), Texas (2)	Arkansas (7), Georgia (2)
13	17	Florida (6), Virginia, Texas (2)	Georgia, Wyoming (4)
40	69	Florida (6), Texas (5)	Florida (10), Louisiana (6)
18	25	Texas (5), Kentucky (3)	Texas (6), Georgia, Louisiana (4)
14	14	Arizona, Texas (3)	Pennsylvania (2), North Carolina (3)
10	10	Florida (8), Alaska, Tennessee (1)	Florida (6), Alaska (3)
0	2	none	Pennsylvania (2)
0	0	none	none
9	19	Mississippi (4), Florida (3)	Mississippi (10), Florida (3)

Finally, consider the possibility that right-to-carry laws lead criminals to substitute bombings for shootings as mentioned earlier in the section on Israel and terrorism. Data on bombings show that after the passage of right-to-carry laws, actual and attempted bombings increased slightly, while incendiary bombings and other bomb-related incidents (involving stolen explosives, threats to treasury facilities, and hoax devices) declined (see Table 6.3).[29]

III. Accounting for Other Factors

Although the above tables suggest that right-to-carry laws reduce mass shootings, other factors may explain these changes. To take account of this possibility, we examined the impact of right-to-carry laws after accounting for: the arrest rate for murder; the probability of execution (equal to the number of executions per murder in a given year); real per capita personal income; real per capita government payments for income maintenance; unemployment insurance and retirement payments; the unemployment rate; the poverty rate; state population and population squared; and demographic information on the sizes of thirty-six different race, sex, and age groups in a state.[30] Besides factors to pick up the average differences across states and years,[31] we also included information for other gun control laws in states—such as whether a state has a waiting period before one can take delivery of a gun, the length of the waiting period in days and days squared, whether a state limits an individual's gun purchases to one per month, the Brady Act, whether a state requires that a gun be safely stored, and whether a state imposes enhanced penalties for using guns in the commission of crime.[32]

The analysis here also accounts for the average differences across years or across states.[33] This implies, for example, that if the multiple victim public shooting rate declines nationally between two years, the estimated impact of the law shows whether the decline is significantly larger in states that adopted laws during the two year period.[34] It also ensures that low crime states such as Idaho or Montana that adopted the law are not driving the results. Because we are accounting for the average difference across states, the estimates are measuring the change in crime rates that a state has experienced before and after the law.

Table 6.5: The Impact of Right-to-Carry Concealed Handgun Laws on the Average Rate of Public Shootings and Bombings

Exogenous Variables	Endogenous Variables			
	Murders in Multiple Victim Public Shootings	Injuries in Multiple Victim Public Shootings	Murders and Injuries in Multiple Victim Public Shootings	Number of Shootings
	(1)	(2)	(3)	(4)
Right-to-Carry Law's Impact	-75%*	-81%*	-78%*	-67%*

Exogenous Variables	Endogenous Variables			
	Attempted or Actual Bombings	Attempted or Actual Incendiary	Other Bombing Incidents	Total Bombing Incidents
	(5)	(6)	(7)	(8)
Right-to-Carry Law's Impact	-4%	19%	-2%	-1%

* z-statistic significant at least at the 1 percent level for a two-tailed t-test.
The regressions use the Poisson procedure, and the incidence rate ratios are reported. The regressions include the following independent variables: detailed demographic information by sex, race, and age; population and population squared; state unemployment rate; state poverty rate; real per capita personal income, unemployment payments, income maintenance, and retirement payments per capita; arrest rate for murder; the execution rate; waiting period dummy, and length of waiting period in days and days squared; one-gun-a-month law; safe storage gun law; penalties for using guns in the commission of crime; and state and year fixed effects.

Table 6.5 presents estimates for eight different dependent variables (four for multiple victim public shootings and four for bombings) using a very simple specification of the right-to-carry law that just measures whether the law is in effect.[35] The analysis contains 1,045 observations (50 states and the District of Columbia for 21 years minus 26 observations for various states and years in which we lacked data on the arrest rate).[36] To simplify the table, the text presents only the percent change in murders, injuries, or shootings from the passage of the right-to-carry law.

Table 6.5 indicates that concealed handgun laws significantly reduce multiple victim public shootings in public places (but have no systematic effects on bombings). For example, right-to-carry laws appear to lower the combined number of killings and injuries [equation (3)] in a state by 78 percent and the number of shootings [equation (4)] by 67 percent. The estimates imply that the average state passing these laws reduces its average total number of murders and injuries per year from 1.91 to 0.42 and its average number of shootings from 0.42 to 0.14. Although we might expect large deterrent effects from these laws, because of the high probability that one or more potential victims or bystanders will be armed, the drop in murders and injuries is surprisingly large. And as we shall see, alternative measures of shootings and adding other factors that might explain the drop do not seem to reduce the magnitude of the law's effect.[37]

We find that while arrest rates for murder lower between the number of people harmed and the number of attacks in a state, higher income maintenance payments and unemployment rates raise both numbers.[38] The compilation of cases by the *New York Times* that was discussed in Chapter 2 also found that so-called "rampage killers" were much more likely than other murderers to be unemployed.[39] Higher execution rates reduce the number of attacks and the number of people killed or injured, but these effects are not statistically significant.[40] Finally, none of the other gun laws produce significant changes in the number of multiple victim shooting incidents or the number of injuries and deaths caused by them.

Turning to the bombing estimates in Table 6.5, we observe that bombings are not systematically related to right-to-carry laws. After the passage of a law, some types of bombings appear to rise very slightly, others fall slightly, and the changes often depend on whether bombings are expressed as a rate or an absolute number. These small changes are not statistically significant. In short, there appears to be no significant substitution between shootings and bombings in states enacting right-to-carry laws.

While looking at the average rate of shootings or bombings before and after right-to-carry laws are adopted provides some valuable information, the previous chapter pointed out how these results can sometimes be quite misleading. Table 6.6 replaces the before-and-after average measure with a measure of two crime trends for those states that passed laws between 1985 and 1996. (No state passed a right-to-carry law between the years 1977 to 1984.) The first time trend measures the annual change in crime rates before passage of the law, and the second time trend measures the annual change after the law.[41] This specification enables us to test whether the impact of a right-to-carry law increases over time as more people obtain permits. It usually takes many years after enacting a handgun law for states to reach their long run level of handgun permits. For states in which data on handgun permits are available, the share of the population with permits is still increasing a decade after the passage of the law.[42,43]

The trends indicate that the number of deaths or injuries from multiple victim shootings remains fairly constant over time before the right-to-carry law is passed, and then falls afterwards. The difference in these trends is always quite statistically significant. The likelihood of accidentally getting this result is roughly equivalent to flipping a coin and getting heads nine times in a row.[44] As expected, therefore, the longer a right-to-carry law had been in effect in any of the twenty-three states that passed such laws in 1985 or later, the greater the decline in murders and injuries from mass public shootings. The results imply about a 15 to 22 percent annual decline in these different measures of crime after concealed handguns are legalized.

The other gun law–related variables generally produce no consistent significant impact on mass shootings. One exception is the impact of laws limiting a purchaser to no more than one gun a month. All the estimates imply that limitations on purchases *increase* multiple victim public shootings, though the statistical significance of this variable is driven solely by its impact on the number of injuries.

Waiting periods on gun purchases yield inconsistent impacts on crime. In some equations a longer waiting period suggests an increase in the risk of mass public shootings, and in others it suggests a decrease. In only one equation is the variable statistically significant.

Safe storage laws never significantly change crime rates.

The imposition of additional penalties for using a gun in a crime significantly reduces the number of murders, but the impact on injuries and the number of attacks is not statistically significant. Nor were any of the other non-right-to-carry gun control laws taken as a whole statistically significant. In sum, there is no evidence that these laws systematically reduce multiple victim public shootings.[45]

Although higher death penalty execution rates imply both fewer attacks and fewer people harmed, any statistical significance on the

Table 6.6: Examining the Average Annual Change in Multiple Victim
Crimes Before and After the Adoption of Right-to-Carry Laws

	Variables Being Explained			
Explanatory Variables	*Murders in Multiple Victim Public Shootings* (1)	*Injuries in Multiple Victim Public Shootings* (2)	*Total Murders and Injuries in Multiple Victim Public Shootings* * (3)	*Number of Shootings* (4)
Annual Average Change in Years Before the Right-to-Carry Law Went into Effect	3.5%	-3.4%	-0.3%	7.2%
Annual Average Change in Years After the Right-to-Carry Law Went into Effect	-17.6%*	-22.1%*	-20.3%*	-15.5%*
Are the Differences in Crime Trends Before and After Right-to-carry Laws Statistically Different from Each Other[†]	Yes	Yes	Yes	Yes
Waiting Period Dummy	65.7%***	-26.6%	20.5%	11.0%
Length of Waiting Period in Days	-35.3%	1.5%	-9.3%	-24.0%
Length of Waiting Period Squared	1.7%	-1.2%	-0.4%	1.1%
One-Gun-a-Month Purchase Rules	119.3%	697.0%*	302.2%*	263.8%
Safe Storage Gun Laws	-16.8%	-20.2%	-20.1%	-35.2%
Additional Penalty for Using Gun in the Commission of a Crime Dummy	-40.8%**	26.5%	-3.5%	-34.7%
Death Penalty Execution Rate	-1.1%	-3.7%*	-2.1%*	-0.2%

*z-statistic significant at least at the 1 percent level for a two-tailed t-test.

**z-statistic significant at least at the 5 percent level for a two-tailed t-test.

***z-statistic significant at least at the 10 percent level for a two-tailed t-test.

[†]All those that are significant are so at greater than the one percent level. Those that are not statistically significant are significant at less than the 20 percent level.

Variables Being Explained

Attempted or Actual Bombings (5)	Attempted or Actual Incendiary (6)	Other Bombing Incidents (7)	Total Bombing Incidents (8)
-1.0%	0.4%	0.1%	-0.4%
2.3%	3.1%	5.4%	4.4%
No	No	No	No
31.2%	-11.1%	16.2%	25.2%
-8.9%	-2.3%	-11.6%	-10.2%
0.6%	0.2%	0.9%	0.7%
-46.4%	-67.9%	7.0%	-44.7%
20.2%	44.3%	26.5%	23.8%
-2.6%	-15.8%	7.0%	-1.3%
-0.3%	-1.3%	-0.6%	-0.6%

The table shows the percent change in crimes from different laws. The regressions include the following independent variables: detailed demographic information by sex, race, and age; population and population squared; state unemployment rate; state poverty rate; real per capita personal income, unemployment payments, income maintenance, and retirement payments per capita; arrest rate for murder; the execution rate; waiting period dummy, and length of waiting period in days and days squared; one-gun-a-month law; safe storage gun law; penalties for using guns in the commission of crime; and state and year fixed effects.

number of people harmed is through its impact on the number injured, not killed.[46] Interestingly, the death penalty is less consistently significant in deterring multiple victim killings than it is in deterring "normal" murders. Using state and county level murder data for the whole U.S., a one percentage point increase in the execution rate is associated with a 4 to 7 percent decline in the overall murder rate, and the effect is quite statistically significant.[47] For multiple victim shootings, a one percentage point increase in the execution rate is associated with about a 10 percent reduction in the number of murders from multiple victim shootings, but it is never statistically significant for either the number of murders or shootings.

The remaining specifications in Table 6.6 [columns (5) through (8)] indicate that the passage of concealed handgun laws has no significant effects on the number of bombings. There is no significant trend in any type of bombing category, either before or after the passage of the law. Indeed, none of the gun control laws have any statistically significant effect on bombings.

It is possible to break down these results even further. Instead of relying on either a simple before-and-after comparison of averages or trends, it is possible to view the year-by-year variations in the differences between states with and without right-to-carry laws. Figure 6.1 looks at the case of murders and injuries. Values below zero mean that the rate of injuries and murders from multiple victim public shootings is lower for right-to-carry states in that year than for non-right-to-carry states. Values of –100 percent mean that the rate in right-to-carry states is 100 percent lower (i.e., that the rate is zero). When the estimates are above zero, the reverse is true. A value of +100 percent would mean that the rate of crimes was 100 percent greater—in other words, twice as high. The graph also tracks the right-to-carry states before, and after, they adopt the law. Year Zero is the year the law is passed, Year –1 is the year before passage, Year –2 is the second year before passage, and so forth. Similarly, Year 1 is the first year after passage, and so on.

What is clear from the figure is that the rate of murders and injuries from multiple victim public shootings was lower in the right-to-carry states even before the right-to-carry laws were adopted, but that after the right-to-carry laws were adopted that gap became even

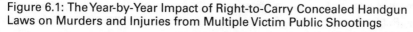

Figure 6.1: The Year-by-Year Impact of Right-to-Carry Concealed Handgun Laws on Murders and Injuries from Multiple Victim Public Shootings

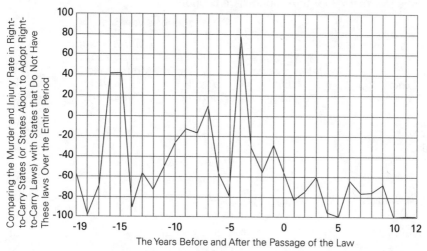

larger. Only five of the nineteen years before the right-to-carry laws were adopted had lower murder and injury rates than the highest rates during the twelve years after the laws were adopted.

Because of the relatively large number of shootings that occur in the years that the right-to-carry laws are enacted, and in the years immediately prior to adoption, there is a concern that the results simply reflect what is called "a regression to the mean." Suppose that there is a mass murder that prompts a state legislature to adopt a right-to-carry law. There might be a noticeably large drop in the number of people killed after the law is passed, but the drop is a result of the unusually deadly event that caused the law to be adopted in the first place, and is not reflective of the benefits of the law itself.

To account for the possibility that a regression to the mean is at play, Table 6.7 reexamines the analysis in Tables 6.5 and 6.6, removing observations for the year of passage and the two years prior to passage. Removing these three years means that only unusual events more than three years prior to the law going into effect could motivate the legislature. The new results confirm the previous ones. The impact of right-to-carry laws is statistically significant, with one exception. The change in before-and-after trends for injury rates remained slightly negative, but was no longer statistically significant.

Table 6.7: The Impact of Right-to-Carry Concealed Handgun Laws on the Rate of Public Shootings and Bombings When the Data for the Year of Adoption and the Two Years Prior to Adoption Are Dropped

Exogenous Variables	Endogenous Variables			
	Murders in Multiple Victim Public Shootings (1)	*Injuries in Multiple Victim Public Shootings* (2)	*Murders and Injuries in Multiple Victim Public Shootings* (3)	*Number of Shootings* (4)
Right-to-Carry Law's Impact	-73%*	-74%*	-73%*	-53%***
	(5)	(6)	(7)	(8)
Annual Average Change in Years Before the Right-to-Carry Law Went into Effect	3%	-7%*	-5%**	5%
Annual Average Change in Years After the Right-to-Carry Law Went into Effect	-10%****	-8%	-13%*	-7%
F-test for Differences in Time Trends (probability in parentheses)	(9%) significant	(87%) not significant	(9%) significant	(22%) not significant

*z-statistic significant at least at the 1 percent level for a two-tailed t-test.
**z-statistic significant at least at the 5 percent level for a two-tailed t-test.
***z-statistic significant at least at the 10 percent level for a two-tailed t-test.
****z-statistic significant at least at the 10 percent level for a one-tailed t-test.
†All those that are significant are so at greater than the 10 percent level.

The regressions use the Poisson procedure, and the incidence rate ratios are reported. The regressions include the following independent variables: detailed demographic information by sex, race, and age; population and population squared; state unemployment rate; state poverty rate; real per capita personal income, unemployment payments, income maintenance, and retirement payments per capita; arrest rate for murder; the execution rate; waiting period dummy, and length of waiting period in days and days squared; one-gun-a-month law; safe storage gun law; penalties for using guns in the commission of crime; and state and year fixed effects. The absolute z-statistics are shown in parentheses. Number of observations is 976 for all specifications.

In another set of estimates, we included the murder and total bombing rates as factors that could explain the rate that multiple victim public shootings occur. The rationale is pretty simple: the same factors that explain murders and bombings may also explain public shootings as well. Adding the murder and bombing variables to the specifications in Tables 6.5, 6.6, and 6.7, however, yields results similar to those shown earlier without these variables. In thirteen of the sixteen estimates, the right-to-carry laws statistically reduce the number of multiple victim public shootings.[48]

But perhaps the finding that right-to-carry laws reduce the number of mass public shootings is just spurious, an artifact of some other factors that shouldn't really be controlled for. Some may believe that certain factors are more likely to affect multiple victim attacks than other ones. For example, some may consider the death penalty to be important, while others believe it to be irrelevant. Since people probably differ in their beliefs about which precise combination of factors should be included, we tested the sensitivity of our results by breaking the control variables into six categories. They are: all other gun laws, the execution rate, population measures, the five measures of income and transfer payments, state unemployment and poverty rates, and thirty-six different demographic variables. We then examined all possible combinations of these six categories.[49]

The range of estimates is reported in Figure 6.2, which shows both the maximum and minimum percent changes as well as the point where half the estimates are greater and half are lower (the median percent change). For all the multiple victim public shooting estimates, passage of concealed handgun laws causes the percent annual change in crime rates to decline. The annual percentage of declines in murders ranges from 9 to 25 percent, injuries from 1.2 to 22 percent, and shootings from 12 to 25 percent. The median estimate always implies an annual decline of at least 12 percent. By contrast, the bombing results are erratic, with positive and negative values for both the extreme values. The estimated median annual percent change is never greater than 1.3 percent.[50]

Figure 6.2: Sensitivity of the Relationship Between Right-to-Carry Laws
and Annual Change in Crime Rates

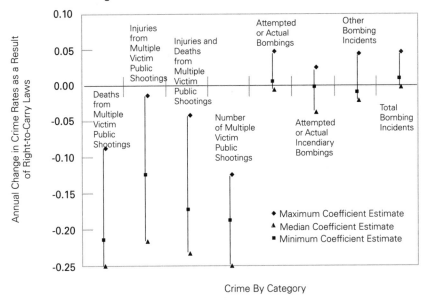

Crime By Category

IV. THE NUMBER OF PEOPLE KILLED
OR INJURED PER SHOOTING

The preceding evidence indicates that right-to-carry laws reduce both
the number of public shootings and the total number of people killed
or injured. As mentioned at the beginning of the chapter, however,
there are also good reasons to expect the amount of harm per incident
to decline. Numerous examples in this book have shown that shooters are stopped by armed citizens, and thus are presumably prevented
from doing more harm. One can also imagine circumstances where
right-to-carry laws increase the availability of guns to potential
offenders, or where guns used in self-defense lead to more, not fewer,
killings.[51] Yet, the results strongly indicate that these effects, if they
exist, are not sufficient to offset the overall negative impact of right-
to-carry laws on multiple victim public shootings.

Table 6.8 examines whether the number of people killed or injured
per shooting declines. These are the same estimates provided earlier
except that they now also account for the number of shootings in

Table 6.8: The Impact of Right-to-Carry Concealed Handgun Laws
on the Number of Deaths or Injuries From Each Shooting

	Murders in Multiple Victim Public Shootings	Injuries in Multiple Victim Public Shootings	Total Murders and Injuries in Multiple Victim Public Shootings
Specification Number	(1)	(2)	(3)
Right-to-Carry Dummy Variable	-52%*	-53%*	-53%*
Number of Shootings	40%*	34%*	36%*
Specification Number	(4)	(5)	(6)
Time Trend for Years Before the Right-to-Carry Law Went into Effect	0%	-4%	-2%
Time Trend for Years After the Right-to-Carry Law Went into Effect	-11%***	-13%*	-13%*
Number of Shootings	41%*	35%*	37%*
Differences in Time Trends (Are the Differences in Time Trends Before and After Right-to-Carry Laws Statistically Different from Each other†)	-11% (yes)	-8% (yes)	-10% (yes)

* z-statistic significant at least at the 1 percent level for a two-tailed t-test.
** z-statistic significant at least at the 5 percent level for a two-tailed t-test.
*** z-statistic significant at least at the 10 percent level for a two-tailed t-test.
†All those that are significant are so at greater than the 10 percent level.
The regressions use the Poisson procedure and incidence rate ratios are reported. The regressions include the following independent variables: detailed demographic information by sex, race, and age; population and population squared; state unemployment rate; state poverty rate; real per capita personal income, unemployment payments, income maintenance payments; retirement payments; arrest rate of murder; and regional and year fixed effects. Regional fixed effects were used because the specifications were otherwise unable to converge. The absolute z-statistics are shown in parentheses. The number of observations equals 1045.

explaining the number of people killed or injured. If right-to-carry laws allow citizens to limit the amount of harm caused by the attacks that still take place, the number of persons harmed should fall relative to the number of shootings (as the two school shooting examples suggest).[52,53] And indeed, that is what we find. The average number of people dying or becoming injured per attack declines by around 50 percent, and the average annual decline ranges from 11 to 13 percent.

V. Alternative Measures of Multiple Victim Public Shootings

Chapter 2 looked in depth at the *New York Times*'s major series on so-called "rampage killings." The *Times* collected data on one hundred killings that had taken place from 1949 to 1999.[54] Their definition of "rampage killing" had many similarities to our own definition of multiple victim public shootings. The *Times* identified cases where at least two people had been killed in a public place and excluded attacks that arose out of another crime, such as a robbery or gang activity. The two main differences between the two definitions are that the *Times* included non-gun killings and excluded politically motivated attacks. There is, however, as we discussed, a major problem with the *Times* data. They included all cases for the years 1995 to 1999, but included only "easily obtainable" cases for years prior to 1995.[55]

While the five-year period of 1995 to 1999 is fairly short, it still includes the spate of public school shootings that attracted so much media attention, as well as many other notorious mass public shootings. It is important to note, however, that public school shootings in right-to-carry states occurred in states where concealed handguns are prohibited because of "gun-free zones."

Of course, if we exclude such cases and only count attacks where people are allowed to defend themselves, our results would be dramatically stronger. Nonetheless, the estimates we report below include all shootings in right-to-carry states, whether or not they took place in "gun-free zones."

Table 6.9 (A) uses the *New York Times* data. The first four results in Table 6.9 (A) cover only the short period from 1995 to 1999. At the time we estimated these results, data on many of the factors we had accounted for were not available for 1999. So these estimates up through 1999 account for only a limited set of factors: state population, population squared, and variables to pick up the average differences across states and years. The second set of results covers the *Times* data from 1977 to 1998. Here we can account for all the factors used in our previous analysis.

The *Times* also lists eight "rampage killings" for the 1949 to 1976 period. While this small number of observations is of little use from

Table 6.9: Using the Data Collected from the *New York Times*

A) "Rampage Killings"

	Endogenous Variables			
Exogenous Variables	Murders from "Rampage Killings"	Injuries from "Rampage Killings"	Murders and Injuries from "Rampage Killings"	Number of Attacks
Using the *New York Times* Data from 1995 to 1999 and controlling for state population and population squared as well as state and year fixed effects	(1)	(2)	(3)	(4)
Impact of Right-to-Carry Law	-47%****	-74%*	-75%*	-61%****
Using the *New York Times* Data from 1977 to 1998 and controlling for all the variables used in the earlier regressions	(5)	(6)	(7)	(8)
Impact of Right-to-Carry Law	-97%*	-74%***	-94%*	-71%****

B) News Stories on Multiple Victim Public Shootings in the First Section of the *New York Times*

(Number of observations is 1045)

Exogenous Variables	Multiple Victim Public Shooting Stories Appearing in the First Section of the New York Times *for a State* (Poisson estimates)
Right-to-Carry Law Dummy Variable	-81%*

* z-statistic significant at least at the 1 percent level for a two-tailed t-test.
** z-statistic significant at least at the 5 percent level for a two-tailed t-test.
*** z-statistic significant at least at the 10 percent level for a two-tailed t-test.
**** z-statistic significant at least at the 10 percent level for a one-tailed t-test.
The regressions use the Poisson procedure and incidence rate ratios are reported. The first set of regressions account for state population and population squared as well as state and year fixed effects. The second set of regressions as well as the estimates in Section (B) include the following independent variables: detailed demographic information by sex, race, and age; population and population squared; state unemployment rate; state poverty rate; real per capita personal income, unemployment payments, income maintenance, and retirement payments per capita; arrest rate of murder; execution rate for the death penalty; waiting period dummy and length of waiting period in days and length squared; one-gun-a-month law; safe storage gun law; penalties for using guns in the commission of crime; and state and year fixed effects. Because the Poisson regressions with state specific effects did not converge, we substituted in regional dummy variables. The absolute z-statistics are shown in parentheses. The number of observations for estimates 1 through 4 is 253. The number of observations for estimates 5 through 8 is 1093.

a statistical point of view, it is still worth noting that all "rampage killings" occurred in states without right-to-carry laws.

For both the 1977–1998 and 1995–1999 periods, we find that the number of people killed in "rampage killings" declined by at least 47 percent after right-to-carry laws were passed. These results are statistically significant.[56] The decline in the number of attacks in states enacting right-to-carry laws ranges from 61 to 71 percent, but this result was not statistically significant.[57]

In Table 6.9 (B) we have constructed another measure of attacks from the number of multiple victim public shootings reported in the first section of the *New York Times* during the period 1977 to 1998. This measure proxies the seriousness, or at least the newsworthiness, of the multiple victim public shootings.[58] The drop in these stories after right-to-carry laws is quite large and statistically significant, with a decline in stories of 81 percent.

There is one other study that collects data on multiple victim murders. This study defines multiple victim murders as shootings in which four or more people are killed.[59] This way of defining the dependent variable greatly reduces the number of public shootings to thirty-six incidents over the entire 1977 to 1995 period. We attempted to explain both the per capita and absolute number of people killed in these shootings using the same specifications as in Tables 6.5 and 6.6.[60] The results are similar to our earlier ones, though not consistently significant for the case of four or more murders because of the much smaller sample size.[61] We find that right-to-carry laws reduce the number of deaths, and that these deaths were increasing before passage of the law and falling thereafter.[62]

VI. Explaining Permit Rates Using Differences in State Laws

There is one extremely notable time trend in the concealed handgun law results. The states that adopted the laws early on tend to be less restrictive: They have much lower fees, shorter training requirements, and fewer restrictions on where concealed handguns can be taken. For example, eight of the fourteen least restrictive states—with respect to where handguns may be carried—adopted their laws before

1961. By contrast, the first full year that the five most restrictive states had their laws was 1996 or 1997. The exact same breakdown is true for the length of training requirements. To put it differently, the nine states whose first full year with the law was 1996 or 1997 required twice as much training as the twenty-two earlier states, had 1.9 times higher fees, and had more than twice (2.6) the amount of restrictions on where one could carry the gun. The question this section examines is what impact these changes in rules have had, and how these rules have reduced the crime rate.

A. Relating the Differences in Training and Fees to the Number of Years That the Permit Rules Have Been in Effect

Central to much of the debate over right-to-carry is the relationship between the percent of the population with permits and the changes in crime rates. In the preceding sections, we used as a proxy the number of years that the law has been in effect. While the data on permits are limited, ten states provided data over at least a few years (permit data since enactment are available for Florida, Oregon, and Pennsylvania; more recent data for a few years are available for Alaska, Arizona, Oklahoma, South Carolina, Texas, Utah, and Wyoming). These data can be used to estimate how the percent of a state's adult population with permits has varied in other states. Four factors seem to have played important roles in explaining the percentage of the state's population with permits: the length of time that right-to-carry laws have been in effect, the training period required, permit fees, and the crime rate.

It takes at least a decade for a state to reach its long-run stationary percentage of the population with permits. Shorter training periods, lower fees, and higher crime rates are associated with a greater percentage of the population getting permits.[63] However, with everything else being equal, we expect more permits to create a greater level of deterrence. Changing the level of training or the amount of fees could affect the type of person who gets permits. Hypothetically, it is possible that shortening the required training period increases the number of permit holders, but still decreases deterrence, simply because permit holders will not be as prepared to deal with criminal attacks. The converse is also possible: Training may make each permit holder better able to deal with an attack, but at the same time so greatly reduce the number of permit holders that the net effect is to reduce deterrence.

There are two different ways of dealing with the differences in state laws and the rates at which permits are issued. We can estimate the relationship between the percent of the adult population with permits and changes in training, fees, the murder rate, and the length of time that the law has been in effect over the small sample of states with permit data. Then we can use the much more readily available data on how these rules vary across states to estimate the predicted permit rate across states. Alternatively, we could simply include the different state laws directly in the earlier estimates. We examined both approaches, and both support the hypothesis that more permits reduce the number of attacks.

As noted above, which exact permitting rules are in place in each state largely depends upon when the laws were first enacted. Once in place, the rules seldom change very much. States that adopted right-to-carry laws only recently tend to have more restrictive licensing requirements. For example, the three states requiring at least ten hours of training (Alaska, Arizona, and Texas) adopted their rules during the last few years of the sample period, with Arizona being the only right-to-carry state that requires additional training when permits are renewed. Six of the eight states with permitting fees of at least $100 have also enacted the law during the mid-1990s. Overall, permit fees range widely, from $6 in South Dakota to $140 in Texas. About half of the thirty-two right-to-carry states require no training, a quarter require three to five hours, and the remaining quarter between six to ten hours.

The results in Table 6.10 generally confirm that longer training periods, lower fees, and the number of years since adoption reduce the number of people harmed from multiple victim shootings, though neither the effects from training periods nor fees is statistically significant for murders. The increased deterrence from having a right-to-carry law in effect for additional years rapidly diminishes with virtually all (99 percent) the impact on murders occurring within the first eight years.

For some states we know the percentage of the population with permits, and for all the states we know the rules for obtaining the

Table 6.10: Examining the Differences in State Laws

A. Examining the Differences in Training, Fee, and the Number of Years That the Permit Rules Have Been in Effect

| | Endogenous Variables | | | |
Exogenous Variables	Murders in Multiple Victim Public Shootings (1)	Injuries in Multiple Victim Public Shootings (2)	Total Murders and Injuries in Multiple Victim Public Shootings (3)	Number of Multiple Victim Public Shootings (4)
Training Period in Hours	-3%	-74%	-7%	6%
Real Permit Fee	39%	291%	96%	25%
Years After the Adoption of the Right-to-Carry Law	-53%	-48%	-50%	-41%
Years After the Adoption of the Right-to-Carry Law Squared	9%	6%	7%	5%
Murder Rate	16%	13%	13%	10%

B. Examining the Areas Where Permitted Concealed Are Allowed

Index of Prohibited Places (The index ranges from 1 to 75, with 75 implying that the concealed handgun law has no prohibitions, and 1 equaling the most restrictive concealed handgun law)	-2%	-3%	-3%	-2%

* z-statistic significant at least at the 1 percent level for a two-tailed t-test.
** z-statistic significant at least at the 5 percent level for a two-tailed t-test.
*** z-statistic significant at least at the 10 percent level for a two-tailed t-test.
The regressions use the Poisson procedure and incidence rate ratios are reported. The regressions include the following independent variables: detailed demographic information by sex, race, and age; population and population squared; state unemployment rate; state poverty rate; real per capita personal income, unemployment payments, income maintenance, and retirement payments per capita; arrest rate of murder; execution rate for the death penalty; waiting period dummy and length of waiting period in days and length squared; one-gun-a-month law; safe storage gun law; penalties for using guns in the commission of crime; and state and year fixed effects. The absolute z-statistics are shown in parentheses. The number of observations equals 1045.

permits. We can thus use numbers from the states where we know the number of permits issued to see how the percentage of the population with permits varies with the permitting rules. We can then use this relationship to predict what the permit rate is in the states where we only have the data for the permitting rules. Using these predicted values implies a strong significant relationship between increasing the percentage of the population with permits and drops in multiple victim public shootings.

B. Examining the Impact of "Gun-free Zones"

The question of whether to allow permit holders to bring their guns onto school property starkly illustrates the opposing views on gun control. Some view with terror the very thought of guns on school property, while others see it as a way to stop terror.

Take the debate in Utah, which currently allows permitted concealed handguns on school property, and where many teachers and principals have taken concealed-weapon training courses.[64] University of Utah president J. Bernard Machen promised to expel students who carry a legally concealed handgun onto school property. (Machen's threat defies an opinion issued by Utah's state attorney general saying state law allows adults with concealed handgun permits to do that very thing.) But Machen says: "Classrooms, libraries, dormitories and cafeterias are no place for lethal weapons."[65] A law professor at the university has even threatened to resign and predicts that other faculty will do the same, because he claims that the presence of guns at the university would interfere with academic freedom.[66] At the time this book went to press, Utah's Gun Violence Prevention Center was working on a ballot initiative to ban permit holders from carrying their guns on school or church property.[67]

In other states there are similar debates. For example, in South Carolina, former governor Jim Hodges threatened to veto any legislation that allowed concealed weapons onto school grounds. Governor Hodges said in a statement, "As a parent with two children in public school, I don't buy the argument that guns make schools safer for our children. Schools and guns do not mix."[68]

Likewise, Florida barely passed a bill during the 2002 session allowing school boards discretion over whether students could have guns on school property if they were stored in locked cars.[69] While some Florida legislators raised the specter of the guns being used in school shootings, others noted, "Nothing would stop any student from running home, getting a gun and shooting somebody."

"Gun-free zone" advocates argue that guns lead to violence and surely escalate violence. In contrast, those who support permit holders carrying guns into these places, such as schools, respond that banning guns means that only the criminals—those intent on committing a crime—will be armed. Thus, most law-abiding citizens will obey the law and become sitting ducks.They argue that if the worst should occur, having a gun at the scene can limit the extent of the carnage.

Utah's attorney general Mark Shurtleff responded to critics: "I'm not saying we ought to arm the entire student body, but there is plenty of evidence to suggest that more guns equals less crime,"[70] and that "This would send a message to every maniac out there that they can come in our schools and wreak havoc without fear of anyone shooting back at them."[71,72]

Even if a concealed handgun law is on the books in a particular state, banning guns from specific locations such as schools or hospitals will defeat the law's ability to prevent an attack. (In some public school shooting cases—such as the ones in Pearl, Mississippi; Edinboro, Pennsylvania; and Santee, California—it was still possible for people to stop attacks with guns that were located nearby, away from school premises.) A recent study of state laws lists fifty different places where permitted concealed handguns can be prohibited.[73] A partial list of prohibited places in right-to-carry states includes bars, professional athletic events, school/college athletic events, casinos/gambling establishments, churches, banks and financial institutions, amusement parks, day care centers, school buildings, school parking lots, school buses, and hospitals and emergency rooms. Nine states allow private businesses to post whether permit holders are allowed to carry their weapons on the premises. Eleven states allow businesses to deny their employees the right to carry permitted handguns on the job. Unfortunately, there is no list of which businesses in a state exclude permitted concealed handguns. States also differ in what penalty is imposed for a violation. In some it is a felony and results in the immediate loss of the permit. In others, three violations are necessary before a permit is suspended for three years.

Greg Jeffrey has created a 75-point index measuring how restrictive different states are.[74] This index measures both whether a permitted concealed handgun is allowed and the penalty imposed for a violation. Two points are substracted for each place where there is a statutory prohibition without discretion; one point if there is discretion; and an additional point is substracted if the prohibition violation is a felony. Indiana is assigned a value of 75, because there are no restrictions. Pennsylvania is the next least restrictive, with a score of 73, because concealed handguns are banned only in courthouses, punishable only by a civil penalty. At the other extreme, six states have scores under 15. The most restrictive states are: Arkansas, Oklahoma, North Carolina, Texas, South Carolina, and Mississippi.

This index was not included in the first part of the table, since the weightings are somewhat arbitrary. For example, it is not obvious that all places where concealed handguns are restricted are equally important. Nor is it clear that permit holders view a felony as being twice as onerous as facing either a misdemeanor or no penalty at all. Yet, despite these concerns, the index probably constitutes a reasonable, though rough, measure of restrictiveness. To account for differences in restrictiveness as a possible factor that can help explain crime patterns across states, we reestimated the results reported in the first section of Table 6.10 with a new variable using Jeffrey's index.

The new estimates shown in Section B clearly indicate that the states with the fewest restrictions on where one can carry a gun have the greatest reductions in killings, injuries, and attacks. Each one-point increase in the index is associated with about a 2 percent further reduction in violent crimes. All the estimates are statistically very significant.[75] All the other explanatory variables show very similar results to what were reported earlier in Section A.[76]

VII. Do Shootings Produce More Shootings?

Does a public shooting lead others to imitate the behavior of the first gunman? Possibly, the notoriety a mass-shooter receives encourages others who crave the same attention. Possibly, the coverage given to attacks gives disgruntled people ideas on how to "solve" their perceived problems.

The notion of a crime "fad" or epidemic is not new. The increase and subsequent decrease in airline hijackings in Europe and the United States between 1961 and 1976 seemed like a reasonable example. However, on closer investigation, Bill Landes could find no support for that idea.[77] Instead, what he found was that this pattern could easily be explained by deterrence. At first, when the probability of apprehension and penalties were both low, hijackings surged. But as the problem increased, a tougher stance was taken. More hijackers were apprehended, and they faced stiffer penalties. As enforcement rose, further hijackings were discouraged.

What about mass public shootings? Is there any statistical evidence here for copycat behavior? It turns out that the evidence is not very strong here either for copycat effects. To test for imitative behavior, we examined the number of mass shootings that occurred any place by month. A total of 252 months were covered from 1977 to 1997. We wanted to see whether an attack occurring over the previous three months or an attack that received extensive news coverage (as measured by the number of attacks covered in the *New York Times*) increased the probability of another attack occurring. We accounted for the increase in the number of states with right-to-carry laws during this period by adding a variable denoting the percentage of the U.S. population covered by these laws. Because of our concern that passage of the late 1995 federal law banning guns within a thousand feet of a school might have encouraged attacks, a variable was included for when that law went into effect.[78] If this law is primarily obeyed by law-abiding citizens, it is plausible that it encourages attacks by making armed resistance less likely. We also included a variable for each month to pick up any seasonal differences in the rate at which these attacks occurred as well as a time trend to account for any general national changes in the rate that these attacks took place. Table 6.11 reports these estimates.

As shown in Table 6.11, the five sets of estimates give similar results for the percentage of the U.S. population covered by right-to-carry laws, a time trend variable, and the one month lags for the number of shootings and the number of *New York Times* stories.

Table 6.11: Do Shootings Encourage Yet More Shootings?

Exogenous Variables	Endogenous Variable: Number of Shootings Per Month				
	(1)	**(2)**	**(3)**	**(4)**	**(5)**
Number of Shootings in Previous Month	8%*	7%*	7%*	8%*	. . .
Number of Shootings Two Months Ago	. . .	2%	0%	. . .	. . .
Number of Shootings Three Months Ago	. . .	. . .	3%**	. . .	. . .
Number of New York Times Stories in the Front Section in Previous Month	-11%*	-11%*	-11%*	. . .	-8%
Number of New York Times Stories in the Front Section Two Months Ago	. . .	-4%	-4%	. . .	. . .
Number of New York Times Stories in the Front Section Three Months Ago	. . .	. . .	-7%	. . .	. . .
Percentage of the Nation's Population Covered by Right-to-Carry Laws	-96%*	-95%*	-94%**	-97%*	-97%*
Monthly Time Trend	1%*	1%*	1%*	1%*	1%*
Safe School Act	331%*	318%*	294%*	360%*	697%*

* z-statistic significant at least at the 1 percent level for a two-tailed t-test.
** z-statistic significant at least at the 5 percent level for a two-tailed t-test.
*** z-statistic significant at least at the 10 percent level for a two-tailed t-test.
Regressions use the Poisson procedure. The regression also includes monthly dummy variables. Incidence rate ratios are reported and the absolute z-statistics are shown in parentheses.

More past shootings seem to slightly increase the number of shootings later on. But past stories in the *New York Times* imply the opposite. If coverage in the *New York Times* measures the amount of national news coverage an attack receives, any fad effect should show up most strongly through this *New York Times* effect. But in fact it shows that news coverage reduces the number of attacks. In short, the evidence on fads is mixed.[79, 80]

A lot of anecdotal evidence suggests that the public school shooters have been motivated by previous attacks. It is not hard to find stories of students from Alabama to Kentucky to California who were apparently lured by the publicity resulting from the Columbine attack, and who tried to kill more people than the thirteen killed there.[81] It is quite possible that children are affected differently from adults, but shootings by juveniles are extremely rare and there are simply too few public school shootings to warrant any serious statistical analysis with them.

VIII. CONCLUSION

Right-to-carry laws reduce the number of people killed or wounded from multiple victim public shootings. Many attackers are completely deterred from attacking. For others, when attacks do occur, they are stopped before the police can arrive. We also demonstrate for the first time that the harm can be mitigated in those crimes that still occur in states with right-to-carry laws. Given that half the attackers in multiple victim public shootings have received formal diagnoses of mental illness, it's remarkable that our results indicate that concealed handgun laws *still* reduce the number of attacks by almost 70 percent.

Differences in state right-to-carry laws are also important. Limiting the places where permit holders are allowed to carry their guns increases the number of murders, injuries, and shootings. We found that increased training requirements reduce injuries but have no effect on murders or the number of attacks; and higher fees increase injuries and the number of attacks.

That right-to-carry laws deter multiple victim public shootings more than other crimes, such as murder, makes sense. It squares well with the rational assumption that when many citizens are present, the probability increases that someone will be able to defend the group against a multiple victim shooting.

The results are robust with respect to different specifications of the dependent variable, different specifications of the handgun law variable, and different control variables. Not only does the passage of a right-to-carry law have a substantial, statistically significant impact on multiple victim public shootings, but it is the only gun law that appears to have any real impact.

While other law enforcement efforts—from the arrest rate for murder and the death penalty—tend to reduce the number of people harmed from multiple victim public shootings, the effect is not as consistently significant. Finally, the data provide no evidence of substitution from shootings to bombings and little consistent evidence of "copycat" effects.

CHAPTER 7

GUNS AT HOME: TO LOCK OR NOT TO LOCK

Morley Safer: If a parent says, "Well, yes, we do keep a gun in the house," what do you tell them?

Dr. Danielle Laraque: I advise the family that I think the gun should be removed from the home, that absence of guns in the home really provides the safest environment for their child.

Dr. Tim Wheeler: Well, a gun in the home poses risks. There's no doubt about it. A bathtub in the home poses risks. Matches in the home pose a risk.

Safer: You talk about bathtubs and other household items in—in which, clearly, the benefits outweigh the risks of having a bathtub. Are you saying the same thing about guns?

Dr. Wheeler: Yes, I am. There is actually an enormous benefit to owning firearms—namely, that of self-defense.[1]

CBS's 60 Minutes, *May 12, 2002*

I. INTRODUCTION

The benefits of laws requiring that citizens store their guns safely seem undeniable. Presumably, such laws would lead to fewer juvenile accidental gun deaths and suicides. Some have argued that these restrictions might also reduce crime rates if criminals have a harder time stealing guns because they are locked away. Both congressional Democrats and Republicans tend to favor safe storage laws for guns.

Table 7.1: U.S. Accidental Deaths by Type and Age in 1999

	0 to 4 years old	5 to 9 years old	10 to 14 years old	15 to 19 years old	Age 20 and older
Population in millions	18.94	19.95	19.55	19.75	194.51
Types of Accidental Gun Deaths					
Handguns	2	2	12	29	85
Long Guns	1	3	18	20	70
Unknown/Other firearms	9	14	27	77	455
Other Types of Accidental Deaths					
Drowning/Submersion	558	192	177	359	2,209
Burns	352	171	92	88	2,764
Falls	67	25	28	112	12,926
Pedal Cycling	7	74	92	83	543
Motor Vehicles	834	802	969	5,198	34,568

Source: Centers for Disease Control and Prevention

Similar views were expressed by presidential candidates of both parties during the 2000 election, and the Clinton administration made it a major issue.[2]

Numerous states have considered laws mandating safe storage of guns. Illinois passed a law mandating that guns be kept locked or otherwise secured when a child under fourteen might have access to them, and New Jersey and California passed new laws requiring guns to be sold with locks.[3]

Concerns over accidental gun deaths and suicides are important in this debate. In 1999 Centers for Disease Control and Prevention data showed that thirty-one children under age ten died from accidental gun deaths. In cases where the weapon involved could be identified, four of these deaths involved handguns. One suicide with a gun was reported in this age group. When all children under age fifteen are examined, the total number of accidental gun deaths was eighty-eight, sixteen of which involved handguns. Over half the guns were unidentified or classified as "other." Of children under the age of fifteen, 103 died from gun suicides.[4]

Table 7.1 provides readers with some idea of how infrequently accidental gun deaths occur compared with accidental deaths from drownings, falls, cars, and so on. For children under twenty, accidental gun deaths involving all types of guns are about 16 percent as frequent as drownings, 30 percent as frequent as deaths from burns, and less than 3 percent as frequent as accidental car deaths.

A study by the General Accounting Office claims that mechanical locks—like those that fit over a trigger or in the barrel of a gun—only provide "reliable" protections for children under age seven.[5] So it is unclear what percentage of older children's deaths would have been prevented by the use of these locks. Nor would the locks even have been relevant in accidental gun deaths for cases where the gun is intended to be unloaded, such as hunting.

But gun locks have their own set of problems. Besides the actual cost of the locks, even more potentially discouraging is the reduced effectiveness of using the gun defensively.[6] Locked guns may not be as readily accessible for defensive gun uses. If criminals are deterred from attacking victims because of the fear that people might be able to defend themselves, gun locks may in turn reduce the cost to criminals committing crime, and thus increase crime. This problem is exacerbated because many mechanical locks (such as barrel or trigger locks) also require that the gun be stored unloaded.[7] The need to load a gun takes up yet more time in responding to a criminal.

One almost humorous example of the problems gun locks pose was provided by former Maryland governor Parris Glendening, who set up a press conference to generate support for his gun lock proposals. As the centerpiece of the press conference, the governor planned to demonstrate how easy it was to work a gun lock. Yet, the demonstration did not work as planned. One newspaper described the governor "struggling numerous times to remove it. He eventually got it after returning to the podium to try a few more times."[8] Indeed, he received the help of several police officers in removing the lock.

As one state legislator noted after the press conference: "Imagine what kind of trouble he'd have if he were staring down some intruder in the dark. Maybe we should be able to work the thing before we bring it out. Clearly it's not ready for prime time."

The costs of locks and the fear of accidental gun deaths, a fear that is highly publicized when these laws pass, could be expected to deter gun ownership. To the extent that gun ownership leaves people defenseless, a reduction in ownership may also further encourage crime.[9]

As demonstrated in the previous chapter on multiple victim shootings, there is evidence that restrictions on people's ability to defend themselves encourages criminals to attack. This is also proven by the different international rates of so-called "hot burglaries," where residents are at home when the criminals strike.[10] Fifty-nine percent of the burglaries in Britain, which has tough gun control laws, are "hot burglaries." By contrast, the U.S., which has fewer restrictions, has a "hot burglary" rate of only 13 percent. Consistent with this, surveys of convicted felons in America reveal that during burglaries they are much more worried about encountering armed victims than they are about running into the police. This fear of potentially armed victims causes American burglars to spend more time than their foreign counterparts "casing" a house to ensure that nobody is home. Felons frequently comment in these interviews that they avoid late-night burglaries because "that's the way to get shot."[11]

On the other hand, those who support safe storage laws claim that locking up guns can reduce crime by discouraging or preventing burglars from obtaining guns through theft.[12] Yet, given the General Accounting Office report that the types of trigger or barrel locks mandated by these laws can be removed by children over age six, the size of these benefits seems small if it exists at all.

Guns are not the first product governed by safe storage laws that economists have studied. Safety caps for medicines have been required for many years now and have been studied extensively. Surprisingly, economist Kip Viscusi found in 1984 that safe storage rules in this area actually lead to more poisonings due to a "lulling effect."[13] Because of the safety caps, he argued, families no longer take common sense precautions with children and medicine as they previously did. A similarly dangerous result could occur with guns if the General Accounting Office is correct that while mechanical gun locks are not very reliable, they lull parents into a false sense of security.[14]

Despite the active policy debate on guns, there has been surprisingly little research on the safe storage of guns compared with medicine safety caps. While one medical journal provides some preliminary evidence on safe storage laws and accidental gun deaths,[15] no evidence exists on any of the other possible effects of these laws.

No one has investigated the impact of these laws on suicides or on the possible costs of these laws, in particular whether the laws make it difficult for people to quickly access a gun for self-defense.

II. THE EXISTING LITERATURE

David Klein with several co-authors argued that accidental gun deaths and gun suicides are strongly linked to gun ownership for self-defense.[16] Studying all the fatal gun accidents involving persons under age sixteen in Michigan from 1970 to 1975, they concluded that guns used in fatal accidents were nearly always kept for self-protection. While they didn't have direct evidence to prove this point, Klein et al. claimed that "guns used for self-protection are more likely to be involved in accidental shootings because hunting or target guns are much less likely to be stored loaded or to be kept where they are readily accessible." In a later paper, Klein found that predominantly low-income urban families with child gunshot victims had "kept loaded guns within ready reach because they had no confidence that the police offered them protection against neighborhood crime."[17]

If Klein and his co-authors are correct in asserting guns stored primarily for self-defense are the ones that result in accidents, and if gun owners are correct that those guns help mitigate harm when an attack occurs, safe storage laws could reduce fatal gun accidents but also decrease one's ability to defend oneself. This would thus lower the cost to criminals, and increase crime. The empirical question is, then, whether the reduction in accidental gun deaths or suicides outweighs the costs from any increased crime. The tests carried out in this chapter will provide some additional evidence on the ability of guns to deter criminals.[18]

Half of all fatal gun accidents are self-inflicted. In cases where the fatal injury is inflicted on somebody else, the person firing the gun is on average 6.6 years older than the victim. Shooters tend to be between the ages of fifteen and twenty-four and come from low-income families. Data from 1980 indicate that the victim and shooter were of the same race in 96.5 percent of the cases, while the sex was the same in 75 percent of the cases. Shooters also tend to demonstrate

Table 7.2: Cases Where Children Under Ten Years of Age Were Killed By Other Children Under Ten

State	Victim	Age	Comments	# of News Articles on Incident
1999				
FL	Dymond Lee	2	Accidentally shot by 4-yr-old sister, handgun	7
AR	Jason Gacs	4	Accidentally shot by 2-yr-old brother, handgun	24
OR	Aaron Allen	2	Accidentally shot by 5-yr-old brother	4
LA	Darnell Simmons	4	Accidentally shot himself	7
WI	Bryant Welch Jr.	7	Accidentally shot himself	3
VA	Langston Murray	2	Accidentally shot himself	7
1998				
FL	Willie Hills Jr.	2	Accidentally shot by 3-yr-old playmate	19
VA	Hakeem Parson	3	Questionable whether or not gunshot was self-inflicted	4
IL	Dylan Drake	5	Accidentally shot himself	7
NC	Patrick Watkins	5	Accidentally shot by twin brother	9
NC	Linwood Martin	5	Accidentally shot while playing with guns with 6-yr-old brother	4
NC	Carlos Gilmer	6	Accidentally shot by 4-yr-old	88
VA	Carey Taylor Beaber	6	Accidentally shot while playing with 7-yr-old neighbor	13
KS	Darian D. Hinds	1	Accidentally shot by 6-yr-old cousin	7

Average 14.5

"poor aggression control, impulsiveness, alcoholism, willingness to take risks, and sensation seeking."[19] Others have found that accidental shooters were much more likely to have been arrested for violent acts and/or for alcohol-related offenses, and a disproportionate number had been involved in automobile crashes and traffic citations.[20] They were also much more likely to have had their driver's licenses suspended or revoked.

To obtain some rough information on whether more recent accidental gun deaths are similar to these older studies and to see how frequently children fatally shot other children, I conducted a search of news stories (a Nexis search, similar to that used in Chapter 6) that mentioned accidental gun deaths involving children under ten who shot other children under ten. Table 7.2 provides two striking pieces of information. First, these stories received extensive news coverage. On average, an accidental shooting of a child by another child receives 14.5 different mentions in the media (about 9 mentions when the death with the largest news coverage is not included). Second, it is interesting how relatively rare these accidental shootings are.[21] Of the fifty-six accidental gun deaths involving children under ten in 1998 and the thirty-one in 1999, only eight and six respectively were shot by another child or themselves. The same statistic for 1997 was only five.

Table 7.2 also provides some insight into why people have the perceptions that they do about the risks of having a gun in the home. While all of the bad stories about guns receive multiple mentions in the media, it is exceedingly rare to find any defensive gun use story that receives more than one mention. Even dramatic cases, such as the eleven-year-old mentioned in Chapter 1 who saved his grandmother's life, or the incidents of young children using guns to save lives that will be discussed later in this chapter, received only one mention in small local newspapers.

Passing safe storage laws that are largely unenforceable might result in only the most "law-abiding citizens" changing their behavior. But, if we consider the data, these are not likely to be the high-risk groups for accidental shootings. Because accidental shooters tend to be more likely to violate the laws anyway, it is possible that safe storage laws will raise the cost of deterring criminals where the benefit of reducing accidents is smallest.

The issue of suicide raises two questions: (1) whether safe storage or other gun control laws *prevent suicides involving guns* and (2) whether these *laws reduce total* suicides or merely change the method of suicide. However, the second question only becomes relevant if safe storage laws indeed have much of an effect on gun suicides. The few existing studies that test for the impact of gun control laws (but not safe storage laws) on total suicide rates (from both guns and through other means) use purely cross-sectional level data, and find no significant relationship.[22] Some other studies use proxies for gun ownership rates (e.g., the number of federally licensed firearms dealers or sub-scriptions to gun magazines), and analyze whether they are correlated with suicides.[23] Still other studies use surveys on individual suicide attempts, so as to describe various individual characteristics (such as impulsiveness) and examine whether suicides are more likely when guns are available.[24]

The normal assumption is that guns will almost by definition increase both accidental gun deaths and gun suicides, though as this discussion suggests, it is possible that the risks vary according to how law-abiding the household in question is. Indeed, this chapter and the appendix provide evidence that the link between gun ownership and either of these types of death is actually fairly difficult to establish. Survey data on gun ownership rates is never statistically related to accidental gun deaths or gun suicides, and using gun magazine sales as a proxy for gun ownership only implies a small relationship for one particular magazine.

III. THE RAW DATA

Sixteen states adopted safe-storage laws between October 1, 1989, and December 31, 1998, with the average law adopted in the middle of January 1993.[25] For the implementation dates of safe storage laws, I relied primarily on an article published in the *Journal of the American Medical Association*,[26] though this only contained laws passed through the end of 1993. The website for Handgun Control, Inc. provided information on the four states passing laws after this date and confirmed the information found in the medical journal for the earlier dates.[27] The laws share certain common features, such as penalizing those who store a firearm in such a way that a reasonable person could expect a child to gain use of the weapon. The primary differences involve exactly which penalties are imposed, and the age at which a child's access is permissible. While Connecticut, California, Florida, and Massachusetts classify such violations as felonies, other states classify them as misdemeanors. The age at which children's access is permitted also varies across states, ranging from twelve in Virginia to eighteen in North Carolina, Texas, and other states (see Table 7.3). Most state rules protect owners from liability only if

Table 7.3: Enactment Dates of Safe Storage Gun Control Laws

State	Date Law Went into Effect*	Access is Restricted for Children Under Age	Type of Crime
Florida	10/1/89	16	Felony
Iowa	4/5/90	14	Misdemeanor
Connecticut	10/1/90	16	Felony
Nevada	10/1/91	14	Misdemeanor
California	1/1/92	14	Felony
New Jersey	1/17/92	16	Misdemeanor
Wisconsin	4/16/92	14	Misdemeanor
Hawaii	6/29/92	16	Misdemeanor
Virginia	7/1/92	12	Misdemeanor
Maryland	10/1/92	16	Misdemeanor
Minnesota	8/1/93	14	Misdemeanor
North Carolina	12/1/93	18	Misdemeanor
Delaware	10/1/94	18	Misdemeanor
Rhode Island	9/15/95	16	Misdemeanor
Texas	1/1/96	18	Misdemeanor
Massachusetts	10/1/98	18	Felony
Illinois	1/1/00	14	Fine
New Hampshire	1/1/01	18	Misdemeanor

* Source for the enactment of safe storage laws through the end of 1993 is Peter Cummings, David C. Grossman, Frederick P. Rivara, and Thomas D. Koepsell, "State Gun Safe Storage Laws and Child Mortality Due to Firearms," *Journal of the American Medical Association*, October 1, 1997, pp. 1084–86. The other dates were obtained from the Handgun Control website at: http://www.handguncontrol.org/caplaws.htm and from a Nexis search to determine the effective dates and the rules involved in the law.

firearms are stored in a locked box, secured with a trigger lock, or obtained through unlawful entry.

The data for crime rates examined in this study range from 1977 to 1998, and from 1979 to 1998 for the accidental death and suicide rates. Most of the analysis is conducted at the state level because the county level data are not broken down by age. Only a tiny fraction of one percent of the counties will experience an accidental gun death or gun suicide by children under age fifteen in any given year.[28,29]

Not all states experience accidental gun deaths in any given year. In 1998, for example, 13 states experienced at least one death for children under the age of five; 21 states for children between five and nine; and 30 states for children between ten and fourteen. Suicides were more evenly distributed across the states for ten- to fourteen-year olds, with 40 states experiencing at least one suicide.

Figure 7.1: Ratio of Gun and Handgun Accidential Deaths in
Safe Storage States to States Without Safe Storage Laws

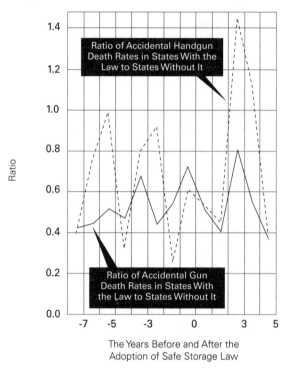

The Years Before and After the
Adoption of Safe Storage Law

One of the 16 states adopting the safe storage laws had the laws in
effect for only part of a year, 12 states for five full years, 6 states for
seven full years, and 3 states for eight or more years. Because the different states have such different crime, accidental death, and suicide
rates, the before-and-after rates need to be made comparable. Therefore, the simple graphs presented here will primarily compare the
before-and-after rates for only the twelve states that had their law in
effect for at least five full years, though the other groupings of states
produce similar results.

As a rough method to detect any effect from the passage of the law,
Figure 7.1 illustrates how accidental gun death rates changed over time
for states with safe storage laws applying to children under age fifteen,
relative to the thirty-four states without such laws. The diagram provides information on per capita accidental death rates from guns and
per capita accidental death rates from handguns. Handguns are exam-

ined separately because much of the public debate has focused on the possible risks of having handguns in the home as opposed to shotguns or rifles.[30] Unfortunately, most gun deaths (about 56 percent) are listed as "unclassified" as to the type of weapon. Yet, this does not pose a major problem for the comparisons presented here, as the share of unclassified cases remains fairly constant over the period.

To calculate the ratio of accidental deaths in states with safe storage laws relative to those without the law, the yearly accidental death rate in each individual state that adopted a safe storage law is divided by that same year's average accidental death rate in states that do not adopt the law. The figure reports the average of these ratios for the safe storage states. The comparison is made in this way because different states adopted safe storage laws in different years, and it is necessary to examine how the accidental deaths changed in the years before and after the law while making sure that national trends are accounted for.

Figure 7.1 shows how this ratio varies in states adopting safe storage laws relative to the ones that do not.[31] As in the diagrams in Chapter 6, Year 1 represents the first full year that the law is in effect, Year 2 is the second full year, and so on. While the states adopting safe storage laws tended to have lower accidental gun death rates than states without the law even before the laws were adopted, the figure indicates little systematic impact of safe storage laws on accidental deaths. The relative rate of accidental gun deaths in states passing the laws first falls after adoption, and then rises. The rate of total accidental gun deaths in the two sets of states ends up being virtually the same at the end of the period as when the law passed. The same holds for the subcategory of handgun deaths. Despite these laws' potential to stop accidental handgun deaths, there is no obvious decline. In fact, while relative accidental handgun deaths first fall, the relative accidental handgun death rate in states passing safe storage laws almost doubles four years afterward.[32,33]

The relative changes in suicide rates are shown in Figure 7.2, and they are calculated in the same way as in Figure 7.1. For suicides, no clear impact can be observed. The relative gun suicide rate ends up at almost the same level four years after adoption as the year that the law was adopted. Suicides from *all* non-gun methods (the middle curve)

Figure 7.2: Ratio of Gun and Non-gun Suicides in
Safe Storage States to States Without Safe Storage Laws

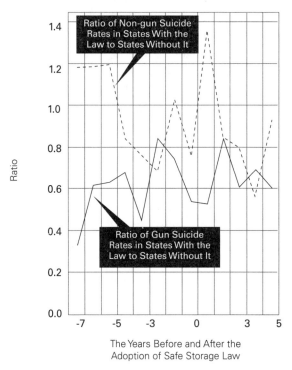

The Years Before and After the
Adoption of Safe Storage Law

actually rose slightly between Year Zero and Year 4, but it was due to
an increase in suicides by non-gun methods. If a relationship between
safe storage laws and suicides exists, it will have to be ferreted out by
more sophisticated estimates, such as the ones presented in Section V.

Figure 7.3 examines the relative violent crime rates, and it provides
the first indication that crime rates may have changed around the
time that safe storage laws were enacted. For the twelve states that
had their safe storage laws in effect for at least four years, the relative
violent crime stopped falling when these laws were adopted and then
ended up even higher at the end of the period.

IV. OTHER FACTORS

While very large changes can sometimes be seen in the raw data, patterns often emerge only once other factors are taken into account. As

Figure 7.3: Ratio of Violent Crimes in Safe Storage States
to States Without Safe Storage Laws

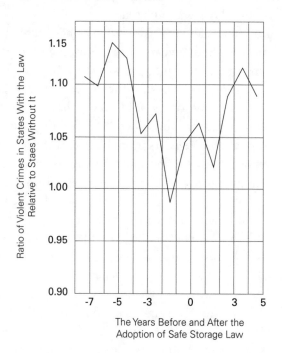

The Years Before and After the
Adoption of Safe Storage Law

with the preceding diagrams, probably the most obvious variables to account for in explaining accidental gun deaths for children are the rates at which other non-gun accidental deaths occur, as well as the rate at which other age groups in the population die from accidental gunshots. Since none of the safe storage restrictions apply to people older than seventeen, the per capita accidental gun death rate for people over age nineteen is used as a comparison. Accidental gun deaths for those outside the age group impacted by the safe storage law may also help measure not only the availability of guns in the home (since some of these deaths will involve parents or other adults), but also other risk factors that might vary by state. I also broke down the accidental gun death information for those over age nineteen into narrower age groupings under the assumption that those closest in age to the age group being studied would explain more of the variation. While there is some evidence for that hypothesis, and while these narrower age groupings for people over age nineteen help explain more of the variation in juvenile accidental gun deaths, none of the results for the safe storage laws was affected.

The accidential death data can be broken down by age (from one to four years of age, from five to nine years of age, from ten to fourteen years of age, and from fifteen to nineteen; see Appendix 2 for the descriptive statistics of these variables). If the desire to access guns were the same for all age groups, one would expect that safe storage laws—if they prevent access to guns—would have their biggest impact on the youngest children. As noted earlier, the General Accounting Office reported in 1991 that mechanical safety locks are unreliable in preventing children over six years of age from using a gun,[34] and there is probably little that can prevent an older teenager from doing what he wants with a gun. Yet, even if the benefits are smaller for older children, it is possible that children who are older than the ages for which the restrictions apply could experience a drop in accidental gun deaths.[35]

A similar approach will be used to explain how suicides by youngsters vary. Information on people in that age group who committed suicide by means other than guns, along with suicide rates for people older than nineteen years of age, will be used to account for other factors that can explain changes in gun suicide rates by juveniles. Whatever might cause youngsters to attempt to commit suicide by means other than guns might also help explain the rate at which they try to commit suicide *with* guns. In addition, factors that determine the general suicide rate for those over age nineteen might also be relevant for explaining the gun suicide rate for those under that age.

It is simply not possible to break down the data by age for suicides to the extent that I did for accidental deaths. For example, there were no gun suicides for children under age ten in 1998. The categories thus have a somewhat broader age range: one category with children under age fifteen, and one with adolescents from fifteen to nineteen.

To try to account for differences in accidental gun deaths or suicides, all the variables used in Chapter 6 other than safe storage laws are again used here. In addition to the normal average differences across states and years, this includes: real per capita income; poverty rates; unemployment; state population and state population squared (to account for population density); demographic information by age, sex, and race; as well as information on per capita unemployment insurance payments; income maintenance payments; and government retirement payments to those over age sixty-four. I also tried including information on the percentage of families with only one parent present to measure the ability of parents to supervise children, and the median education level.

Unfortunately, one variable that is not available is the rate at which people are arrested for violating these laws across different states, though it is possible to classify states by whether the violation is a felony or a misdemeanor. This difference in laws could explain why the accidental gun deaths, suicides, or crime rates vary across each of the sixteen states that passed safe storage laws. The consistency of these results across states provides some assurance the results do not arise simply because some states enforce the law while others do not. Even in the few cases where a significant effect is found for an individual state, that impact is not consistent across accidental gun deaths, suicides, and crime rates.

While much of the focus of other gun laws is on the crime rate, gun laws also control the accessibility and availability of guns, and hence might affect accidental gun deaths and suicides. Therefore, the results will also account for right-to-carry laws, one-gun-a-month purchase rules, states that border one-gun-a-month states, waiting periods, and mandatory prison penalties for using guns in the commission of a crime. I have previously examined the impact of right-to-carry laws on county-level accident and suicide rates and found no significant impact, but it is still possible that some specific age groups might be placed at greater risk. For instance, waiting periods might impact an adult's ability to obtain a gun to commit suicide, while it is less plausible that this would apply to suicides by people under eighteen.[36]

V. THE RESULTS

A. Accidental Gun Deaths

> John Doyle, a longtime hunter, had always treated firearms
> with care and respect. But about a year ago, with three children

at home, both he and his wife worried about the security of the locked storage area where he kept his hunting weapons. "Whenever I read or hear of a kid getting hurt because they got a hold of some firearm in the house, it just turns my stomach," Doyle said. "I've got a couple rifles and a shotgun for deer and bird hunting. But I was only using them a few weeks out of the year. The rest of the time, I kept them locked up in a safe." Doyle has an 8-year-old and 4-year-old twins.

Mike Martindale, "Police Store Residents' Guns: S. Lyon Plan is Rarity in Oakland," Detroit News, Sunday, January 27, 2002[37]

Do accidental death rates fall after safe storage laws are adopted?[38] The estimates shown in columns 1, 5, 9, and 13 in Table 7.4 account for only the average differences across states and years. The other specifications also account for all the other variables discussed in the preceding section with the exception of the other gun control laws. The estimates are broken down in two ways, by age category (from one to four, from five to nine, from ten to fourteen, and from fifteen to nineteen) and by what factors are accounted for (the rate of non-gun accidental deaths for people in that age group, or the accidental gun death rate for people over nineteen years of age).

Despite these different combinations, it is difficult to observe any systematic evidence of reduced accidental gun deaths from the safe storage law. Half of the sixteen estimates imply that the law lowers accidental gun deaths and half imply the reverse, though one of the four estimates for ten- to fourteen-year-olds indicates a statistically significant reduction in accidental gun deaths. The results imply about equally large percentage increases or decreases in accidental gun deaths for the three youngest groups, but the net effect on all four age groups added together is very small—resulting in between five to eight fewer accidental deaths when all the control variables are used. (Specifications 4, 8, 12, and 16 imply that six lives are saved for those from one to four years of age, 9 more lives are lost for those from ages five to nine, 12 lives are saved for those from ten to fourteen years of age, and 8 more lives are lost for those from fifteen to nineteen years of age.) An even smaller impact was implied by the estimates accounting for only the average differences across states and years. Since one expected the biggest drop in accidents to occur for the youngest children, the differential pattern for different age groups also seems inconsistent with what would be predicted of safe storage laws.[39]

While increases in the accidental death rate from non-gun methods for people in an age group are usually associated with more accidental gun deaths, the effect is only statistically significant for those under age five. The effect is also extremely small: increasing the number of non-gun accidental deaths by one hundred increases the number of accidental deaths by guns by at most 1, and the increase is often less than 0.05. The accidental gun death rate for people over age nineteen does a better job of explaining the accidental gun death rate for juveniles that are relatively closer in age, but the effect is still not large: increasing accidental gun deaths over age nineteen by 100 increases the number of accidental gun deaths for those under nineteen by 0.3.

To further investigate the impact of these laws, Table 7.5 reexamines the data in the same way Chapter 6 did for multiple victim shootings to see whether there was a change in accidental gun death trends before and after the law was adopted. It is possible that people gradually began to lock up their guns after enactment and that any benefit might thus have increased over time. If so, accidental gun deaths might begin to decline slowly after the law. So while Table 7.4 examined whether there was a lower average accidental death rate after the law, Table 7.5 estimates the trends in accidents before and after the law, as well as whether the trends are statistically different from each other.

The trend results show no impact of accidental gun deaths from safe storage laws. Only for ten to fourteen years was there a statistically significant downward trend in accidents after the law. But even in that case, there was a statistically significant downward trend before the law. While the decline afterward was slightly larger than the drop beforehand, the two trends were not statistically different from each other. Even ignoring statistical significance, the results imply an almost random relationship between accidental gun deaths and the law. For children under five and those from fifteen to nineteen years of age, the trend after the law tends to rise relative to the pre-law trend. The reverse is true for those from ages five to fourteen.

Table 7.4: The Averages in Accidental Gun Deaths Before and After
Safe Storage Laws from 1977 to 1998

Percent change in accidental gun deaths from:	UNDER AGE 5			
	Accounting for only the average differences between states and across years		All other control variables used	
Specification Number	**(1)**	**(2)**	**(3)**	**(4)**
Adopting safe storage law	-18%	-26%	-30%	-31%
An additional accidental death for people in age group from means other than guns			1%**	1%**
An additional accidental gun death for people over 19 years of age				1%**

Percent change in accidental gun deaths from:	FROM AGES 15 TO 19			
	Accounting for only the average differences between states and across years		All other control variables used	
Specification Number	**(13)**	**(14)**	**(15)**	**(16)**
Adopting storage law	4%	6%	6%	7%
An additional accidental death for people in age group from means other than guns			0.02%	0.05%
An additional accidental gun death for people over 19 years of age				0.5%***

*** The two-tailed t-test is significant at the 1 percent level.
** The two-tailed t-test is significant at the 5 percent level.
* The two-tailed t-test is significant at the 10 percent level.

FROM AGES 5 TO 9				FROM AGES 10 TO 14			
Accounting for only the average differences between states and across years	All other control variables used			Accounting for only the average differences between states and across years	All other control variables used		
(5)	**(6)**	**(7)**	**(8)**	**(9)**	**(10)**	**(11)**	**(12)**
17%	27%	27%	28%	-10%	-20%*	-20%	-19%
		0.03%	0.01%			-0.1%	-0.1%
			0.2%				0.2%

TOTAL EFFECT FOR ALL AGES UNDER 20			
Accounting for only the average differences between states and across years	All other control variables used		
(17)	**(18)**	**(19)**	**(20)**
-3%	-3%	-3%	-2%
		-0.02%	-0.03%
			0.3%***

Note: All regressions are Poisson and use state and year fixed effects. Not reported are the 36 demographic variables, state population and population squared, unemployment, poverty rate, income variables, or the fixed effects.

Table 7.5: The Trends in Accidental Gun Deaths Before and After
Safe Storage Laws from 1977 to 1998

Percent change in accidental gun deaths from:	UNDER AGE 5			
	Accounting for only the average differences between states and across years	All other control variables used		
Specification Number	(1)	(2)	(3)	(4)
Annual average change in accidental gun deaths before adopting safe storage law	2.4%	-3.1%	-2.6%	-3.6%
Annual average change in accidental gun deaths after adopting safe storage law	-3.7%	-0.15%	-0.6%	0.8%
Difference in annual before-and-after trends	-6.1%	3.0%	2.0%	4.4%
An additional accidental death for people in age group from means other than guns			0.6%*	0.7%**
An additional accidental gun death for people over 19 years of age				-0.8%**

Percent change in accidental gun deaths from:	FROM AGES 10 TO 14			
	Accounting for only the average differences between states and across years	All other control variables used		
Specification Number	(9)	(10)	(11)	(12)
Annual average change in accidental gun deaths before adopting safe storage law	-0.02%	-2.8%*	-2.8%*	-2.6%*
Annual average change in accidental gun deaths after adopting safe storage law	-3.5%	-6.4%*	-6.4%*	-6.6%*
Difference in annual before-and-after trends	-3.5%	-3.6%	-3.6%	-4.0%
An additional accidental death for people in age group from means other than guns			-0.1%	-0.1%
An additional accidental gun death for people over 19 years of age				-0.1%

FROM AGES 5 TO 9

Accounting for only the average differences between states and across years	All other control variables used		
(5)	**(6)**	**(7)**	**(8)**
1.9%	7%	7%	8%
-1.6%	-0.5%	-0.6%	-1.1%
-3.5%	-7.5%	-7.6%	-9.1%
		0.04%	0.02%
			0.3%

†† The f-test is significant at the 10 percent level.
† The f-test is significant at the 15 percent level.
*** The two-tailed t-test is significant at the 1 percent level.
** The two-tailed t-test is significant at the 5 percent level.
* The two-tailed t-test is significant at the 10 percent level.

Note: All regressions are Poisson and use state and year fixed effects. Not reported are the 36 demographic variables, state population and population squared, unemployment, poverty rate, income variables, or the fixed effects.

FROM AGES 15 TO 19

Accounting for only the average differences between states and across years	All other control variables used		
(13)	**(14)**	**(15)**	**(16)**
-0.8%	-1%	-1%	-0.1%
0.09%	1.6%	1.9%	-1.9%
0.9%	2.6%	2.6%	2.0%
		0%	0%
			0.5%***

Including information on other gun control laws showed that none of them was associated with any statistically significant reduction in accidental gun deaths for any specific age categories, nor for all those under twenty as a group.[40] Both of the only significant results imply that one-gun-a-month rules have some adverse effect on accidental gun deaths. Possibly one-gun-a-month rules result in homes threatened with attack leaving their sole gun out in the open so that it is more readily accessible and thus more likely to be used improperly by juveniles. But that is only speculation.

The results were also broken down in Table 7.6 by whether violating the safe storage law was a felony or misdemeanor and the age at which access to a gun is allowed. These results attempt to disentangle the aspects of the law that resulted in the net effects shown earlier in Table 7.5. If safe storage laws reduce accidental deaths, higher age restrictions and greater penalties should save more lives.[41] Yet, the results are not particularly encouraging. For two age groups (those between five and nine and between fifteen and nineteen), higher age limits are associated with significantly more accidental deaths. It seems hard to reconcile these significant results with the theory offered for the law. With respect to penalties, seven of the eight results imply a drop in accidental deaths, but only for five to nine year olds does imposing felonies reduce accidental deaths. However, as noted in Table 7.4, the laws for this age group are associated with a net increase in accidental deaths. Breaking down the results to look at the changes in accidents in individual states also doesn't provide consistent evidence of the law's benefits. The two states that experience the biggest drops in accidents are Delaware and Maryland, yet neither has particularly high penalties.

Taken together, these estimates provide no consistent evidence that safe storage laws reduce accidental gun deaths. The adverse consequences of safety caps for medicine or car safety regulations do not appear to be present here, but neither are there any benefits. The estimated changes in accidents are almost never statistically significant, and the pattern is essentially random. In any case, the effect (if it does indeed exist) is extremely small and suggests a very small number of additional deaths per year. As noted earlier, in the description of the previous research, one possible reason for these laws not having an

Table 7.6: Examining Whether Increasing the Age at Which Children Are
Allowed Access to Guns Decreases Accidential Deaths

	Under 5	Ages 5 to 9	Ages 10 to 14	Ages 15 to 19
Age at which access to gun is allowed—estimate indicates the percent change in the number of accidental gun deaths of children in the age category from increasing the access age by another year	-2.3%	4.9%*	0.8%	2.1%*
Felony penalty for violations	-53%	-62%**	-30%	-15%
Misdemeanor penalty for violations	32%	-12%	-26%	-20%

Note: Not reported are the 36 demographic variables, state population and population squared, unemployment, poverty rate, income variables, or the fixed effects. All regressions are Poisson and use state and year fixed effects.

*** The two-tailed t-test is significant at the 1 percent level.
** The two-tailed t-test is significant at the 5 percent level.
* The two-tailed t-test is significant at the 10 percent level.

effect is that accidental deaths primarily occur among the not-so-law-abiding segments of society, and these groups do not appear to care very much whether a law exists regarding the storage of guns.[42]

B. Suicides with Guns

The examination of suicide laws follows the set of specifications used to examine accidental gun deaths, but with two exceptions: (1) The age categories for children under five, from five to nine, and from ten to fourteen have been combined into one group—children under age fifteen—and (2) the variables on accidental deaths from other sources and for people over age nineteen have been replaced by the analogous variables for suicides.

The estimates in Table 7.7 correspond to the earlier results presented for accidental gun deaths in Table 7.4. These results show no significant change in gun or non-gun suicides for children under fifteen after safe storage laws are adopted, though there is some weak evidence that gun suicides decline slightly and non-gun suicides increase by almost the same percent. For fifteen- to nineteen-year-olds the data do show a significant 9 percent drop in gun suicides. In 1999, this would have been the equivalent of nine fewer gun suicides. But at the same time that gun suicides were falling, suicides without

Table 7.7: The Averages in Suicides Before and After Safe Storage Laws from 1977 to 1998

Children Under Age 15

	Suicides With Guns				Suicides Without Guns	All Methods
Percent change in accidental gun deaths from:	Accounting for Only the Average Differences Between States and Across Years	All Other Control Variables used				
	(1)	(2)	(3)	(4)	(5)	(6)
Adopting safe storage law	0.6%	3.8%	3.4%	3.3%	-3.5%	-1%
An additional accidental death for people in age group from means other than guns (except for columns 5 and 11, where it is with guns)			-0.7%	-0.6%	-0.8%	
An additional accidental gun death for people over 19 years old				0.03%	0.001%	0.01%

Note: All regressions are Poisson and use state and year fixed effects. Not reported are the 36 demographic variables, state population and population squared, unemployment, poverty rate, income variables, or the fixed effects.

guns were rising by almost 8 percent. The net effect is essentially a draw, with a small and statistically insignificant few percent decline in overall suicides. To the extent there is a benefit from the law, older teenagers appear merely to substitute other methods for guns to commit suicide.

15- to 19-Year-Olds

Percent change in accidental gun deaths from:	Suicides With Guns				Suicides Without Guns	All Methods
	Accounting for Only the Average Differences Between States and Across Years	All Other Control Variables used				
	(7)	(8)	(9)	(10)	(11)	(12)
Adopting safe storage law	-12.9%***	-9%**	-9.1%*	-9.4%**	7.7%*	-3%
An additional accidental death for people in age group from means other than guns (except for columns 5 and 11 where it is with guns)			-0.05%	-0.05%	-0.08%	
An additional accidental gun death for people over 19 years old			0.005%		0.02%**	0.01%**

*** The two-tailed t-test is significant at the 1 percent level.
** The two-tailed t-test is significant at the 5 percent level.
* The two-tailed t-test is significant at the 10 percent level.

Examining the trends in suicide rates before and after the safe storage law indicates that gun suicides for children under fifteen were rising slightly before the law and falling slightly afterward (see Table 7.8), but none of the trends was statistically significant. On the other hand, while total suicides were also rising before the law, they

Table 7.8: The Trends in Suicides Before and After Safe Storage Laws
from 1977 to 1998

Children Under Age 15

	Suicides With Guns				All Methods
	Accounting for Only the Average Differences Between States and Across Years	All Other Control Variables Used			
	(1)	(2)	(3)	(4)	(5)
Annual average change in accidental gun deaths before adopting safe storage law	0.3%	2.1%	2.1%	1.8%	0.4%
Annual average change in accidental gun deaths after adopting safe storage law	0.1%	-0.01%	-0.1%	0.5%	0.9%
Difference in annual before-and-after trends	-0.2%	-1.1%	-1.2%	-0.1%	0.11%
Suicide rate by people in age group committed by means other than guns			-0.7%	-0.5%	
Suicide rate by people over 19 years old				0.03%	0.01%

Note: All regressions are Poisson and use state and year fixed effects. Not reported are the 36 demographic variables, state population and population squared, unemployment, poverty rate, income variables, or the fixed effects.

were rising even faster afterward. Again, none of the results were statistically significant.

Table 7.9 shows essentially no change in suicides from increasing the access age to guns. The small, statistically insignificant changes are essentially random and difficult to reconcile with any possible

15- to 19-Year-Olds

	Suicides With Guns			All Methods
	Accounting for Only the Average Differences Between States and Across Years	All Other Control Variables Used		
	(6)	(7)	(8)	(9)	(10)
Annual average change in accidental gun deaths before adopting safe storage law	-1.1%***	-0.8%	-0.8%	-0.8%	-1%
Annual average change in accidental gun deaths after adopting safe storage law	-2%***	-1.7%*	-1.7%*	-1.6%	-0.04%
Difference in annual before-and-after trends	-0.9%	-0.8%	-0.8%	-0.5%	0.96%
Suicide rate by people in age group committed by means other than guns				0.01%	0.01%
Suicide rate by people over 19 years old				0.04%	0.01%

*** The two-tailed t-test is significant at the 1 percent level.
** The two-tailed t-test is significant at the 5 percent level.
* The two-tailed t-test is significant at the 10 percent level.
†† The F-test is significant at the 10 percent level.
† The F-test is significant at the 15 percent level.

impact from the law. One expects the greatest benefits to apply to the youngest children, but the results imply that suicides rise for those under fifteen and rise by the same amount for those between fifteen and nineteen. There is a similar lack of consistent results with respect to the severity of penalties. Examining the suicide rates in individual

Table 7.9: Examining Whether Increasing the Age at which Children Are
Allowed Access to Guns Decreases Suicides

	Gun Suicides		Total Suicides	
	Under 15	Ages 15 to 19	Under 15	Ages 15 to 19
Age at which access to gun is allowed—estimate indicates the percent change in the number of accidental gun deaths of children in the age category from increasing the access age by another year	0.3%	-0.3%	-0.1%	-0.2%
Felony penalty for violations	-16%	-8%	-6%	-0.4%
Misdemeanor penalty for violations	16%	-5%	2%	-2%

Note: All regressions are Poisson and use state and year fixed effects. Not reported are the 36 demographic variables, state population and population squared, unemployment, poverty rate, income variables, or the fixed effects.

*** The two-tailed t-test is significant at the 1 percent level.
** The two-tailed t-test is significant at the 5 percent level.
* The two-tailed t-test is significant at the 10 percent level.

states again shows consistent drops in Delaware and Maryland, while California—where violating the safe storage law is a felony—actually experiences a relative increase in juvenile gun suicides.

Unlike the estimates for accidental gun deaths, a couple of results indicated that gun suicides declined for older teenagers after the passage of the safe storage law. However, even in these cases, the total number of suicides, committed by all methods, essentially remains unchanged.

C. Crime Rates

> Florida, clearly, is easy picking for criminals—too easy. . . . If all Florida gun owners were required to secure unattended weapons—not just from children—fewer guns would be stolen and fewer innocents would become victims of foul play.
>
> *Editorial, "A Grip on Security,"* Orlando Sentinel, *July 21, 2002*[43]

A building contractor, on his way home from work, picked up three young hitchhikers. He fixed them a steak dinner at his house and was preparing to offer them jobs. But two of the men grabbed his kitchen knives and started stabbing him in the back, head and hands. The attackers only stopped when he told them that he could give them money. But instead of money, the contractor grabbed a pistol and shot one of the attackers. The contractor said, "If I'd had a trigger lock, I'd be dead. If my pistol had been in a gun safe, I'd be dead. If the bullets were stored separate, I'd be dead. They were going to kill me."

Ellen Miller, "Man Faces Suspects Accused of Attacking Him After Getting Ride," Denver Rocky Mountain News, *March 20, 2001*

Jessica Lynne Carpenter is 14-years-old. She knows how to shoot.... Under the new "safe storage" laws being enacted in California and elsewhere, parents can be held criminally liable unless they lock up their guns when their children are home alone...so that's just what law-abiding parents John and Stephanie Carpenter had done.... [The killer], who was armed with a pitchfork...had apparently cut the phone lines. So when he forced his way into the house and began stabbing the younger children in their beds, Jessica's attempts to dial 9-1-1 didn't do much good. Next, the sensible girl ran for where the family guns were stored. But they were locked up tight.... The children's great-uncle, the Rev. John Hilton, told reporters: "If only [Jessica] had a gun available to her, she could have stopped the whole thing. If she had been properly armed, she could have stopped him in his tracks." Maybe John William and Ashley would still be alive, Jessica's uncle said.

Vin Suprynowicz, Las Vegas Review-Journal, *September 24, 2000*

The lack of benefits from safe storage laws in the preceding sections of this chapter suggest two possible explanations: either the safe storage laws have no impact on people's behavior in storing or owning guns, or the laws alter the behavior of people for whom the risks of accidental gun deaths or suicides were already very low. This

Table 7.10: The Impact of Safe Storage Laws on Crime Rates: 1977 to 1998

	Violent Crime	Murder	Rape
Impact from adopting safe storage law	1.5%	5.2%*	11.5%***
Right-to-carry laws (annual rate of change after the law minus annual rate of change before the law)	-1.1%†	-2%††	-1.2%†
One-gun-a-month purchase rule (equals fraction of year that the law is first in effect and 1 thereafter)	5%	12.5%*	12.2%**
Neighbor's adoption of one-gun-a-month purchase rule (equals fraction of year that the law is first in effect and 1 thereafter)	25%***	23%***	17%***
Additional penalty for using a gun in the commission of a crime	2%	2.6%	2.5%
Waiting period in days	0.01%	0.4%*	-0.2%

Note: All regressions are weighted Tobits, where the weighting is each state's population, and use state and year fixed effects. Not reported are the 36 demographic variables, state population and population squared, unemployment, poverty rate, income variables, or the fixed effects. The variable being explained is the natural log of the crime rate.

second explanation is consistent with what is known about the types of people involved in accidental gun deaths, but additional information on changes in crime rates can help distinguish between these two hypotheses.

The specifications reported here are similar to those discussed in the preceding tables, though the crime-specific arrest rates and the execution rate for murder are now included. Table 7.10 finds that safe storage laws are significantly related to higher murder, rape, robbery, and burglary rates, and that these effects are quite large, at least for the first two categories—with rape and robbery rates rising by 11 percent and 14 percent respectively.[44,45] Specifications controlling for only the safe storage law and the average differences across states and years imply a similar pattern of results. These are surely very large changes in crime rates that occur when the safe storage laws are adopted. However, as the survey data in the next section show, the percentage changes in the rate at which people lock up their guns or

Robbery	Aggravated Assault	Property Crime	Burglary	Larceny	Auto Theft
13.9%***	-4%	2.5%	3.8%*	0.6%	-0.07%*
-2.5%††	-0.6%	-0.4%	-1.2%††	-0.4%	-3%††
10%	10%	-0.007%	-0.7%	-2.9%	20%***
7.3%	29.8%***	10%***	14%***	10%***	30%***
4.2%	-5.1%**	3%	1%	4%***	2%
0.1%**	0.06%	0.27%**	0.13%	0.3%***	0.7%

†† The f-test is significant at the 1 percent level.
† The f-test is significant at the 5 percent level.
*** The two-tailed t-test is significant at the 1 percent level.
** The two-tailed t-test is significant at the 5 percent level.
* The two-tailed t-test is significant at the 10 percent level.

no longer own guns after these laws are passed are much larger than the change in crime rates.

The statistically significant results from Table 7.10 predict that the fifteen states that had the safe storage law in effect for all of 1998 experienced 309 more murders, 4,649 more rapes, 24,884 more robberies, 35,814 more burglaries, but 28 fewer auto thefts.[46] Perhaps when criminals don't have to worry about readily accessible guns, burglaries become more attractive than auto theft. It is possible to put a rough dollar value on the losses that result from these safe storage laws. The National Institute of Justice has estimated the costs to victims of various types of crime, as a result of lost productivity, out-of-pocket expenses, medical bills, and property losses, as well as losses from fear, pain, suffering, and lost quality of life.[47] Using these estimates, the total annual loss to victims from safe storage laws is about $1.85 billion in 1998 dollars. If the rest of the country were to adopt similar safe storage laws, the most conservative estimates here imply that there would be 451 more murders; 6,290 more rapes; 22,531 more robberies; and 47,393 more burglaries; but 395 fewer auto thefts.

As expected, higher arrest rates and higher execution rates for murder deter violent crime, and the longer a right-to-carry law is in effect, the greater the drop in crime. Each one percentage point increase in execution rates is associated with a 4 percentage point drop in murder rates. One-gun-a-month regulations raise violent crime, though the effect on crimes other than murder is not statistically significant. It is also interesting to see that one-gun-a-month rules are frequently consistent with increased crime in neighboring states. At the very least, concerns about crime arising from straw purchasers exporting guns to neighboring states appear to be misplaced.

The preceding discussions examine only how the adoption of safe storage laws change the before-and-after average crime rates. Yet, as noted earlier, sometimes such simple averages can be quite misleading. Figure 7.4 graphs out the general trend in crime rates for the ten years before and after the law.[48] These results indicate that a variable that measures the before-and-after average underestimates the crime-increasing impact of safe storage laws. The simple variable in Table 7.10 actually found a very slight insignificant increase in violent crime. Looking at Figure 7.4 it is easy to see how the after-law average violent crime rates are only slightly greater than the pre-law average, yet it is also obvious that violent crime rates stopped declining and started rising at the time the safe storage law was passed. The simple before-and-after averages shown in Table 7.10 hide the change trends. In a country of 270 million people, this difference of 33 violent crimes per 100,000 people would amount to over 89,000 violent crimes. The patterns for the individual crime categories were similar, and the graphs are available from the authors upon request.[49]

Table 7.11 provides more refined estimates of the victimization costs of safe storage laws. The first part of the table calculates the difference in the number of crimes by year between the new trend as a result of the safe storage law and what the crime rates would have been if the pre-law trend had continued. The estimated impact from the law diminishes over time because not all the states have had the law in effect for all nine years. The fifteen states with safe storage

Figure 7.4: Violent Crime: Comparing the Change After the Adoption of Safe Storage Law With Pre-existing Trend

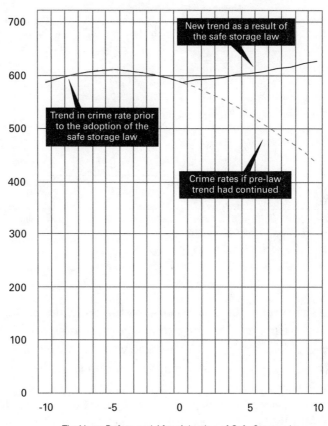

The Years Before and After Adoption of Safe Storage Law

laws in effect for at least one full year would be expected to experience 125 more murders in the first full year that the law is in effect. Despite a reduction in the number of states covered by the law, the number of murders peaks in the fifth full year at 387 murders. The number of rapes and robberies is still rising five full years after the law is in effect, with robberies peaking at more than 36,000. Of the property crimes, burglaries show by far the biggest increase over the period. Aggravated assaults and auto thefts provide a much more mixed picture here than indicated from the simple before-and-after averages, with inconsistent and small effects across the years.

Table 7.11: The Change in the Number of Crimes by Year After the Adoption of the Safe Storage Law

Number of Years After Passage	Number of States with Law in Effect That Long	Population Covered by Law in Millions	Change in Number of Murders	Change in Number of Rapes
1	15	109	125	1468
2	15	111	237	2830
3	15	112	334	4052
4	13	92	338	4160
5	12	92	387	4835
6	10	81	369	4676
7	5	55	262	3384
8	3	21	100	1314
9	1	15	69	936
Total change in crimes during the years that the law has been in effect			2,223	27,653
Change in Victimization Costs in 1998 dollars Using the National Institute of Justice's estimates			$7.69 billion	$2.9 billion

The total victimization costs using the National Institute of Justice's estimates continue rising over the period, reaching $2.3 billion during the sixth year. The average yearly cost to victims over the six years is $1.5 billion, of which $1.4 billion arises because of increased violent crimes.

Again, it is possible to break down the earlier before-and-after results by the two main components of the law: access age and whether the penalty is a felony or misdemeanor (see Table 7.12). Increasing the access-age requirement results in significant increases in all crime categories except rape. The results for penalties are much more mixed, with some penalties associated with increased crime rates and significantly more associated with declines. While the differences are not statistically significant, making violations a misdemeanor and not a felony tends to produce bigger drops in both violent and property crimes. Breaking down the results by individual states reveals that Florida had a large significant increase in both violent and property crimes, while Virginia and Wisconsin had statistically significant drops in violent crimes, and no state had a significant drop in property crimes.

Change in Number of Robberies	Change in Number of Aggravated Assaults	Change in Number of Burglaries	Change in Number of Larcenies	Change in Number of Auto Thefts
12429	-10156	15027	17034	58486
23484	-16251	34648	29901	88646
32755	-18281	58905	38339	85066
32509	-13183	71522	34337	38718
36208	-7955	98272	33377	-15385
33162	728	112533	24995	-74586
22384	8010	96856	11848	-96767
7939	6814	45057	1647	-53797
5000	8340	38828	-1475	-49669
205,871	-41,934	571,647	190,003	-19,286
$1.97 billion	-$1.1 billion	$ 905 million	$81 million	-$8.4 million

This last set of results is particularly interesting because many claim that Florida should have experienced the biggest benefit from the safe storage law because "Florida has made the biggest fuss, with stiff punishments and high-profile cases."[50] Yet, the results in these last three sections indicate that Florida did not experience a statistically significant reduction in either accidental gun deaths or gun suicides. Instead it experienced more crime. The results are consistent with the hypothesis advanced here: that it is only the law-abiding citizens who will change their behavior, and therefore there will be no significant change in accidental gun deaths or gun suicides. Instead there will be an increase in crime as law-abiding citizens are less able to defend themselves from attack.

There is one final prediction about the impact of safe storage laws on crime, and that is after the passage of safe storage laws, criminals should find it more attractive to commit crimes in residences—where guns are locked up—than in other places. Unfortunately, the FBI Uniform Crime Reports do not break down crimes in this manner. By contacting state law enforcement agencies I obtained yearly data from 1987 to 1999 for two states (California and Oregon) showing the

Table 7.12: Examining Whether Increasing the Age at Which Children Are Allowed Access to Guns Produces Additional Safety

	Violent Crime	Murder	Rape	Robbery	Aggravated Assault	Property Crime	Burglary	Larceny	Auto Theft
Age at which access to gun is allowed— estimate indicates the percent change in the crime rate from increasing the access age by another year	0.5%*	1.4%***	-0.24%	0.8%***	0.7%***	0.4%***	0.49%*	0.6%***	0.75%*
Felony penalty for violations	-6%	-9.8%*	7.9%*	-2%	-8.6%	-0.06%	4.9%	-2.9%	-12.6%*
Misdemeanor penalty for violations	-7%	-17%***	15%***	1.6%	-15%***	-5.8%	-7.3%	-9.7%***	-18.5%***

*** The two-tailed t-test is significant at the 1 percent level.
** The two-tailed t-test is significant at the 5 percent level.
* The two-tailed t-test is significant at the 10 percent level.

Note: All regressions are weighted tobibts, where the weighting is each state's population, and use state and year fixed effects. Not reported are the 36 demographic variables, state population and population squared, unemployment, poverty rate, income variables, or the fixed effects.

Figure 7.5: The Percent of Homicides and Robberies in Residences

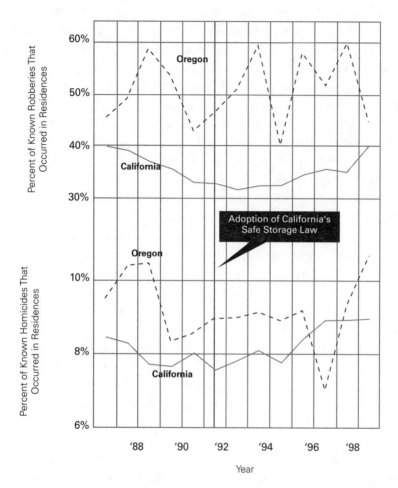

percentage of homicides and robberies that took place in residences. Keeping in mind that the data are very limited, Figure 7.5 suggests that California's safe storage law increased the rate at which crimes occurred in the home. While the percentage of homicides and robberies exhibit no observable pattern in Oregon (a state without the safe storage law), the California data indicate that these percentages obtained their lowest values in 1993 for robberies and 1992 for homicides, and there is a general upward trend after those dates. (California enacted its safe storage law in 1992.)[51]

— Angie, Louisiana: Last Friday, four men, ages 17 to 25, attempted robbing a woman dying of cancer at gun point. The woman, who weighs only 85 pounds, takes pain medication, including OxyContin, which the men reportedly wanted to steal. A small newspaper described the plan: "One guy [Brumfield] went in on a pretense to visit. He was to open the door, then the others were to rush in, put a gun on him and say 'get down'. The others were wearing ski masks." But the woman's 13-year-old son saw the masked men before they broke into the house and got the family's .20 gauge shotgun. He fired a shot, wounding one of the criminals, and causing the criminals to run away.[52]

— Clarksdale, Mississippi: A Clarksdale man was shot to death by a 12-year-old girl Saturday night as he allegedly attacked the girl's mother, police said. "She was sitting on the front porch with a friend when Mr. Fox came along and jumped on her. She went into the house, and he came in behind," said Fortenberry. "She tried to close the door behind her, but he forced his way on in." Coahoma County Coroner Scotty Meredith said the girl, whose name is being withheld because she is a juvenile, witnessed the attack, grabbed a semiautomatic pistol and fired a single shot into Fox's chest. "He was apparently choking her when the girl went and got the gun," Meredith said."[53]

— Clearwater, Florida: At 1:05 A.M., a man started banging on a patio door, briefly left to beat on the family's truck, but returned and tore open the patio door. At that point, after numerous shouts not to break into the home, a 16-year-old boy fired a single rifle shot, wounding the attacker.[54]

Unfortunately the parents of children like these risk facing criminal charges and jail in states with safe storage laws.

D. Did Safe Storage Laws Change the Rate at Which People Locked Up Guns?

While there is an economically and statistically significant increase in crime after the passage of safe storage laws, it would be helpful to actually prove people lock up their guns just because the new law instructs them to do so. Without that information, the possibility exists that passage of the law did not alter the rate at which individuals either locked up or owned guns. Fortunately, several types of survey data are available. One survey sponsored by the Police Foundation in 1997 asked 2,568 people whether they owned a gun and how they stored it.

A total of 2,562 people answered "yes" or "no" to the question of whether a gun in the home was stored loaded and unlocked, but missing information for other questions reduced the sample size in the estimates to 2,394. The survey included a great deal of information that allowed us to measure behavioral differences along racial lines, how safe the individual feels at home alone, whether he has ever used a gun for self-defense, whether he has had training in how to use a gun, the person's age, place where he lives, employment status, marital status, education, political views, veteran status, number of children, number of children under age three, how frequently he attends religious services, religious preferences, family income, whether he has ever been arrested, the respondent's sex, state codes, and information on whether the surveyor thinks that the person being surveyed fabricated claims of defensive gun use. A set of so-called "dummy" variables, where the variable equals one when the respondent answers "yes" and zero when the answer is "no," was used to identify these different characteristics.[55] Table 7.13 shows the complete list of the characteristics that were accounted for in analyzing the differences in those that stored their guns unlocked and loaded and those who claimed that they didn't.

To explain whether the respondent keeps a gun unlocked and loaded, an account is included for whether a safe storage law was in effect at the time of the polling in 1994, as well as another variable for the number of years (including parts thereof) that the safe storage law has been in effect.[56] The results shown in Table 7.13 indicate that states with safe storage laws had higher rates at which households left guns loaded and unlocked but that the rate fell the longer that the law was in effect. Six years after adoption of the law, states with safe storage laws have a lower percentage of homes with loaded, locked guns than do states without those laws.

Table 7.13: Examining the Impact of Safe Storage Laws On the Rate at Which Guns Are Stored Unlocked and Loaded

Variable	Coefficient	Variable	Coefficient
Dummy for safe storage law	0.69***	**Place (continued)**	
Number of years safe storage law in effect	-0.12*	Medium city	-0.77***
		Suburb	-0.90***
Dummy for arrest record	0.05	Large city	-0.72***
		Undocumented	-0.55
Race			
Black	-0.50***	**Employed**	
Hispanic	-1.13***	Part-time	-0.25
Asian	0.31	Homemaker	-0.35
American Indian	-0.59	Student	-1.83***
Don't know	-0.80	Retired	0.11
Refused	-0.70	Unemployed	-0.62
		Other	-0.57
How Safe Do You Feel at Home Alone		Undocumented	-0.73
Somewhat safe	0.12		
Safe	-0.60	**Marital Status**	
Very safe	-0.13	Widow	-0.12
Don't know	0.33	Divorced	0.01
Refused	1.74	Separated	-0.16
		Never	0.15
Self-defense use of gun (no=1)	-0.20	Undocumented	0.39
Training in how to use a Gun	-1.38		
		Education	
Age	0.05	Some high school	18.06***
Age squared	-0.0002	High school graduate	17.77***
Age cubed	-4.72e-6	Some college	17.77***
		Bachelor's degree	17.56***
Place Where You Live		Some graduate	17.36***
Farm	.23	Graduate degree	17.65***
Small city	-0.31	Undocumented	18.68***

The other results are basically what one would expect. People who have used a gun in self-defense or who feel the least safe are more likely to have a gun that is loaded and unlocked. Men and those living on farms are also more likely to have a gun that is loaded and unlocked. Other characteristics of people in this category are interesting, though less explicable: They are often Asian, Catholic, or earning a total household income between $50,000 and $75,000.

The decline in the rate of loaded and unlocked guns in the previous estimate could be due either to people with a gun starting to store them differently or a general decline in gun ownership. Therefore, the previous estimates were redone so that they solely focus on those

Variable	Coefficient	Variable	Coefficient
Political Views		**Religious Preference (continued)**	
Liberal	0.42	None	-0.19
Slightly liberal	0.50	undoc code	-0.31
Moderate	0.58		
Slightly conservative	0.89*	**Family Income**	
Conservative	0.63	<$5,000	-0.04
Extremely conservative	0.51	<$10,000	-0.38
Don't know	0.04	<$15,000	0.43
Undocumented	0.70	<$20,000	0.49
		<$30,000	0.62
Veteran		<$50,000	0.59
Current member of military	-0.22	<$75,000	0.65
Never in military	0.42***	>$75,000	-0.42
		Don't know	-0.40
Children under	-0.04	Undocumented	-0.01
age 3			
		Survey person thinks that	
# of Times Going to Religious Services		**defensive gun use invented**	
Few times a month	0.05	No	0.92
Few times a year	-0.03	Not reported	1.03
Once a year	0.34		
Once in a while	-0.02	Female	-2.06***
Not attend	0.19		
Undocumented	-0.21	Intercept	-18.55

*** The two-tailed t-test is significant at the 1 percent level.
** The two-tailed t-test is significant at the 5 percent level.
* The two-tailed t-test is significant at the 10 percent level.

Variable	Coefficient
Religious Preference	
Catholic	0.12
Jewish	-0.93
Other	-0.32

individuals who reported that they owned guns. Doing so produces very similar, though more significant, results.[57]

Other survey data are also available from the General Social Survey conducted by the National Opinion Research Corporation. While this survey has the advantage of having been conducted over many different years, it can only be used to investigate what happens to the number of guns owned, and not whether guns are being stored loaded and unlocked. Beside the concerns raised in Chapter 2, there are also a couple of other problems with the survey: Not all states are surveyed and the survey misses quite a few years, as it was only conducted in 1977, 1980, 1982, 1984, 1985, 1987 to 1991, 1993, 1994, and 1996. Especially compared with the Police Foundation survey, there were relatively few people questioned in any given year—ranging between 907 and 1,970.[58] To explain the percentage of the population with guns, I used the trends for the years before and after the adoption of the safe storage and concealed handgun laws as well as all the measures of income, state population, unemployment, poverty, and demographics used in earlier analyses. The results imply that gun ownership rates fell by one percentage point per year faster after the safe storage law than they did before (though the change was only marginally statistically significant).[59] If true, this represents a substantial change in gun ownership. After five years, the level of gun ownership in these states would be expected to fall from 28 to 23 percent.

There are several possible reasons for this reported decline in ownership, though the price of gun locks themselves does not seem particularly important. The most likely factors would be either the new possible criminal penalties for owning a gun or the increased perception of the risk of having a gun in the home given the media attention surrounding the law's passage. When the debate over safe storage laws takes place, many news reports emphasize the risk of having guns in the home. The new criminal penalties seem a less likely explanation since differentiating safe-storage-law states on the basis of whether they make violations a felony or a misdemeanor does not appear to make a difference in explaining the drop in gun ownership.

A final concern is more difficult and involves the accuracy of the polls themselves. People may be more likely to tell pollsters that they are locking up their guns after the passage of safe storage laws simply to give the impression that they are obeying the law. While the laws do not necessarily punish storing unlocked guns per se but only unlocked guns that are used improperly by juveniles, people might still be more reluctant to admit that they are behaving in what has become a socially disapproved manner. Social stigma is likely to lead to more secretive behavior as well as more locking up of guns, but it is not clear how to disentangle the relative sizes of these two effects.

Two responses are possible. First, the polling data do not stand on their own. The changes in storage and ownership coincide with changes in crime rates and in particular residential crimes. Second, to the extent that the level of criminal penalties measure stigma, the drops in ownership and increases in locking unloaded guns should be most common in states that treat violations as felonies. The bottom line is that the survey data are at least consistent with the previous results.

E. Gun Ownership Rates, Gun Accidental Deaths, and Gun Suicides

One question remains unaddressed: How closely are gun ownership rates related to accidental gun deaths and gun suicides? It would appear that more guns would almost by definition increase both types of deaths, though it is possible that the risks vary with the type of household buying guns. As noted earlier, accidental gun deaths are primarily committed by people with long criminal backgrounds. Surveys of gun ownership rates are unlikely to ascertain the gun possession rate of criminals, but are rather more likely to provide information on law-abiding households, where the risk of accidental death is low.[60]

It was surprisingly difficult to obtain statistically significant results. Using the survey data available in this book and in my previous book, one finds no positive statistically significant relationships between gun ownership rates and either accidental gun deaths or suicides for all ages. Mixed results were obtained when the 1998 data were used to plot the relationship between gun ownership rates that year and accidental gun deaths or gun suicides.

Figures 7.6 to 7.11 show that while there are weak trends that can be discerned between either juvenile gun or non-gun accidental deaths and suicides and gun ownership rates, one must look very carefully to see any relationship. The correlations are rarely statistically significant. What is surprising is that it is non-gun deaths—not gun deaths—that are always positively correlated with higher gun ownership rates, and that half the time the positive relationship is stronger for non-gun accidental deaths or suicides than it is for similar gun deaths. The simple graphs make it hard to claim that there is an obvious negative impact of gun ownership on juvenile deaths.

Table 7.14 more systematically examines the relationship between types of juvenile gun deaths and household gun ownership rates from 1978 to 1998.[61] Accounting for the factors used earlier to explain accidental gun deaths or suicides shows there is, if anything, more evidence that increases in gun ownership are significantly related to

Table 7.14: Does Higher Gun Ownership Increase Accidental Gun Deaths or Suicides?: Using General Social Survey State-Level Data on Household Gun Ownership Rates

	Accidental Gun Deaths				Suicide Gun Deaths	
	Under 5 Years of Age	5 to 9 Years of Age	10 to 14 Years of Age	15 to 19 Years of Age	Under 15 Years of Age	15 to 19 Years of Age
A. Gun Deaths						
Only Accounting for Gun Ownership Rate and the Average Differences Across States and Years						
Percent increase in deaths from increasing household gun ownership rate by one percentage point	0.5%	-0.16%	0.04%	0.1%	-0.06%	0.1%
Accounting for All Control Variables						
Household gun ownership rate from General Social Survey	0.7%*	0.1%	0.03%	0.1%	-0.0001%	-0.1%
B. Non-gun Deaths						
Only Accounting for Gun Ownership Rate and the Average Differences Across States and Years						
Household gun ownership rate from General Social Survey	-0.01%	0.09%*	0.02%	-0.02%	0.5%**	-0.1%
Accounting for All Control Variables						
Household gun ownership rate from General Social Survey	-0.1%	0.13%**	0%	-0.0001%	0.45%**	0.1%

*** The two-tailed t-test is significant at the 1 percent level.
** The two-tailed t-test is significant at the 5 percent level.
* The two-tailed t-test is significant at the 10 percent level.

Figure 7.6: Comparing Accidental Gun and Non-gun Deaths for Children Under 5 with Gun Ownership Rates by State in 1998

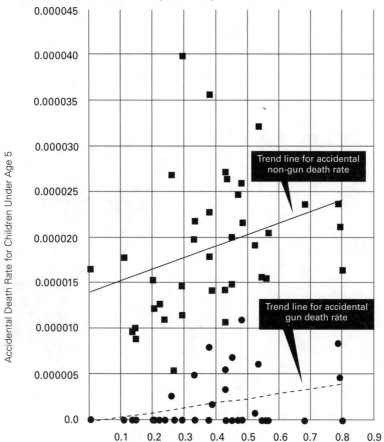

Percentage of the state's adult population owning a gun

Figure 7.7: Comparing Accidental Gun and Non-gun Deaths for Children
Between 5 and 9 with Gun Ownership Rates by State in 1998

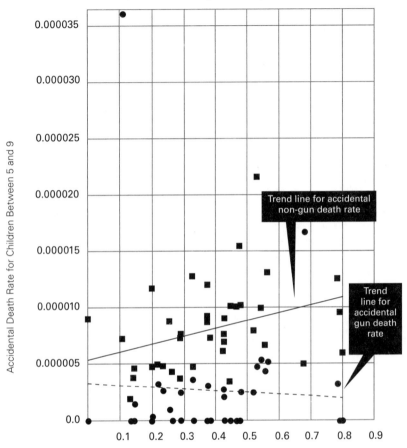

Percentage of the state's adult population owning a gun

Figure 7.8: Comparing Accidental Gun and Non-gun Deaths for Children Between 10 and 14 with Gun Ownership Rates by State in 1998

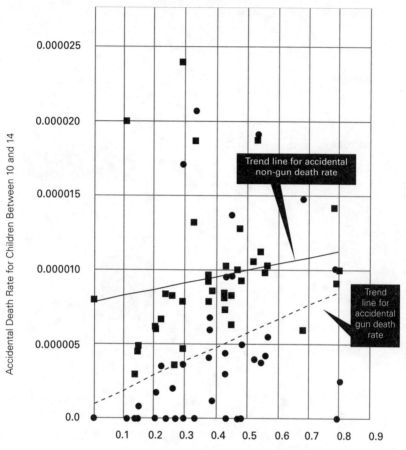

Percentage of the state's adult population owning a gun

Figure 7.9: Comparing Gun and Non-gun Deaths for Children Between 15 and 19 with Gun Ownership Rates by State in 1998

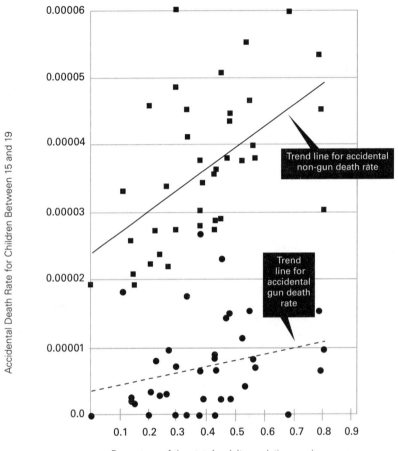

Percentage of the state's adult population owning a gun

Figure 7.10: Comparing Gun and Non-gun Suicides for Children Under 15 with Gun Ownership Rates by State in 1998

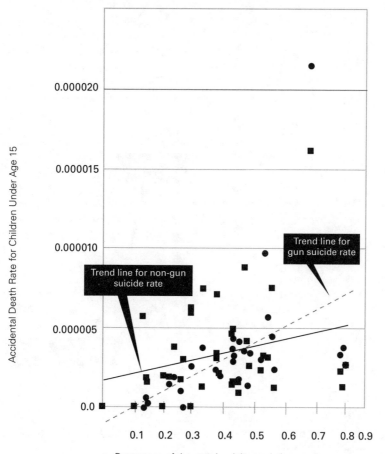

Percentage of the state's adult population owning a gun

Figure 7.11: Comparing Accidental Gun and Non-gun Suicides for Children
Between 15 and 19 with Gun Ownership Rates by State in 1998

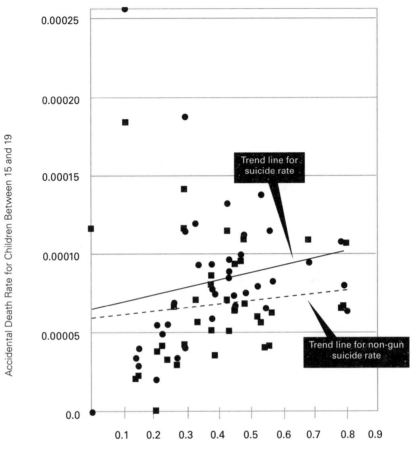

Percentage of the state's adult population owning a gun

non-gun accidental gun deaths or non-gun suicides. Four of the twelve results explaining non-gun deaths are statistically significant, while there is only one case of a statistically significant result for gun deaths. Yet, even in the few cases in which a statistically significant result occurs, the effect is relatively small. In nineteen of the twenty-four estimates, a one percentage point increase in gun ownership produces less than 0.2 of a percentage point change (either an increase or decrease) in gun deaths.

There was slightly more evidence of a relationship when state-level sales data from the Audit Bureau of Circulation for the largest five gun magazines (*American Rifleman, American Hunter, Handguns Magazine, Guns & Ammo,* and *North American Hunter*) were used. In 1996, these five magazines sold a total of 3,498,165 copies. By comparison, the five largest non-gun magazines (with the exception of the American Association of Retired Persons) sold 47,824,944 copies the same year. The setup is similar to that used earlier, with the exception that there is not a variable for accidental gun deaths or gun suicides by adults, because what I am trying to explain in this case is accidental gun deaths or gun suicides for the entire population.[62]

The sales of the largest five gun magazines were only positively and significantly related to accidental gun deaths when all the factors were accounted for, including the different gun control variables. The variable was consistently positively related to gun suicides, though in this case the coefficient was only statistically significant when all the control variables were not included except for the fixed year and state effects. To get an idea of how small these effects are, the only statistically significant result for accidental gun deaths indicates that increasing the average magazine sales in a state by 1,000 (or 1.1 percent) increases the number of accidental gun deaths in the state by 0.07 people (or 0.3%). The other results either imply a smaller increase or an actual drop in accidental gun deaths from more gun magazine sales. The percentage impact on suicides, while more consistent, was never as large as the impact on accidental gun deaths.

It is possible to break down these total sales into the individual gun magazines, but the pattern is not very obvious. Only *Guns & Ammo* magazine sales consistently imply significant and positive increases in accidental gun deaths and gun suicides.[63] But magazines devoted entirely to handguns (*Handguns Magazine*) or to hunting tend to have the opposite effects.

As a comparison, data from the five largest magazines (*TV Guide, Reader's Digest, National Geographic, Family Circle,* and *Better Homes & Gardens*) were examined. Surprisingly, these magazines were "better" predictors: They were always positively related to both accidental gun deaths and gun suicides, though the relationship was always statistically significant only for gun suicides. Increasing total sales by a thousand yielded a much smaller percentage increase in accidental gun deaths or suicides than the largest result implied for gun magazine sales. Often the effect was a tenth or less as large as for selling an additional gun magazine, though interestingly gun magazine sales are less than a tenth as large. So the same percentage change in non-gun magazines produces a consistently slightly larger percentage increase in gun suicides as the largest estimate implied for gun magazines. These results make it hard to believe that general gun ownership or gun accidents or suicide are related to gun magazine sales.

Generally, this section raises significant questions about the relationship between magazines and suicide rates as well as why there is so little relationship between measures of guns and accidental gun deaths. But there is little relationship between guns and either gun suicides or accidental gun deaths.

VI. CONCLUSION

Safe storage laws have no impact on accidental gun deaths or on total suicide rates. While there is some weak evidence that safe storage laws reduce juvenile gun suicides, those intent on committing suicide appear to easily substitute other methods, as the total number of juvenile suicides actually rises (however statistically insignificantly) after passage of safe storage laws. The patterns across ages and with regard to the different characteristics of the law also make it difficult to reconcile the theory that safe storage laws will reduce juvenile accidental gun deaths. The only consistent impact of safe storage laws is to raise rape, robbery, and burglary rates, and the effects are very large. My most conservative estimates show that safe storage laws resulted in 3,738 more rapes, 21,000 more robberies, and 49,733 more burglaries annually in the fifteen states with these laws. More realistic estimates indicate across-the-board increases in violent and property crimes. During the five full years after the passage of the safe storage laws, the fifteen states face an annual average increase of 309 more murders, 3,860 more rapes, 24,650 more robberies, and over 25,000 more aggravated assaults.

The impact of safe storage laws is consistent with existing research indicating that the guns most likely to be used in accidental shootings are owned by the least law-abiding citizens and thus are the guns least likely to be locked up after the passage of the law. The safe storage laws thus increase crime, yet fail to produce any significant change in accidental deaths or suicides. The plausible explanation for both phenomena is that the law-abiding households with low accidental-death risks are now the ones most likely to obey the law.

I have occasionally talked to members of the press about their coverage of accidental gun deaths and inquired why accidental gun deaths get the type of news coverage illustrated in Table 7.2. The explanation usually given is that such events are so rare—that "Man Bites Dog" stories are much more newsworthy than "Dog Bites Man" stories. While this is often what drives news coverage, something more appears to be going on here. First, there are many other rare ways that children die that get very little news coverage. Children accidentally kill themselves with everything from plastic water buckets to cigarette lighters. Unfortunately, children die in rare, gruesome ways, from combines on farms to decapitation. Yet, when was the last time that you saw a story about accidental deaths from other products? Secondly, even if the reason these stories are considered newsworthy is that they are so rare, that is surely not the impression those who hear these stories come away with. People don't hear these stories and think, "Boy, that sure is an unusual event." Instead, the effect is obviously that this is a problem about which something must be done. The results in this chapter indicate that this exaggerated impression created by the media and government officials who compile statistics takes a real cost on people's safety.

CHAPTER 8

DO GUN SHOWS AND ASSAULT WEAPONS INCREASE CRIME?

[Senator Joseph] Lieberman's beef with the gun lobby is that the distinct lack of background checks at gun shows provides terrorists (and anyone else for that matter) with a perfectly legal means for purchasing weapons, including assault rifles and hand grenades.

Peter Wendel, "After 9/11: Got Big Chutzpah?"
Campaigns & Elections, *February 2002*

...[S]tates that do not require criminal background checks at gun shows are flooding the nation with crime guns.

Jim Kessler, Policy and Research Director
at Americans for Gun Safety[1]

Why would a guy who doesn't want to be identified as a felon or a potential criminal show up at a gun show and buy a weapon in public when he could go buy it in—in some seedy hotel somewhere out of a suitcase? Why would he do that?

Chris Matthews, CNBC's Hardball, June 19, 2001[2]

I. INTRODUCTION

Labels are important. Labeling something a "loophole" in a gun law almost automatically generates a desire to "close" it, whatever it is. "Assault weapons" conjure up images of machine guns. As the Wendel quote indicates, to many people these issues are tied together. While many are concerned about gun shows or assault weapons and crime, since September 11 these fears have been further magnified as concerns rise that terrorists are acquiring weapons to use against Americans. Gun shows are frequently described as places where grenades and other bombs are sold and as an inappropriate "carnival atmosphere" associated with weapons.[3] Both their defenders and detractors view gun shows as opportunities for the pro-gun culture to solidify its base, in that gun shows provide a meeting place for people with similar interests and a way for them to learn about guns.

Polls suggest strong support both for closing the gun show "loophole" (that is, mandating background checks on the private transfer of guns at gun shows) and the assault weapons ban (a ban on certain semi-automatic weapons based either upon cosmetic features or merely their names). In early 2001, Opinion Research Corporation International found 82 percent of people support closing the loophole.[4] An NBC News poll indicated that over 70 percent of people wanted the assault weapons ban to remain in place.[5] In 2000, gun show regulation initiatives passed comfortably in Colorado and Oregon.

As discussed in Chapter 4, the notion of a gun show "loophole" is questionable simply because there are no different rules for buying a gun in a gun show than anywhere else.[6] Gun control groups, such as Americans for Gun Safety, identify eighteen states that have closed the "loophole," but interestingly, prior to 2000, only three of these had laws that even mentioned gun shows. What usually constitutes closing the loophole are laws that require background checks for private transfers of handguns. Since 1994, federal law has required background checks for all handguns purchased through dealers. The checks were extended to long guns in 1998. But regulating transfers by private individuals—such as those at gun shows—has been left to the states.

Chris Matthews's question gets to the bottom line for most Americans. Will stricter regulations of private transfers of guns at gun shows stop criminals? A related question is whether such regulations prevent law-abiding citizens from getting guns. Gun shows are an important place for relatively low-income people to obtain guns. To the extent that regulations put shows out of business, the regulations could make obtaining guns more costly for those people.

To help determine where criminals obtained their firearms, the Bureau of Justice Statistics conducted a survey of 18,000 state prison inmates in 1997, the largest survey of inmates ever conducted.[7] Less than one percent of inmates (0.7 percent) who had a gun indicated that they had obtained it at a gun show. When combined with guns obtained from flea markets, the total rises to 1.7 percent. These are tiny fractions compared with the estimated 40 percent of the criminals' guns that are obtained from friends or family, and the 39 percent that are obtained on the street or from illegal sources. The numbers had also changed little from a similar 1991 survey that indicated that 0.6 percent of inmates had gotten their guns from gun shows and 1.3 percent from flea markets.

Other surveys of criminals produce a similar range of estimates. A 1997 study of eight cities by the National Institute of Justice found that "less than 2 percent reported obtaining [handguns] from a gun show." An earlier study using data from the mid–1980s found that the percentage of guns from gun shows was so small that the researchers did not separately break out gun shows as a source.[8]

The only really contradictory claim arises from two very similar government studies by the Bureau of Alcohol, Tobacco, and Firearms based on tracing data. The 1999 study concludes that "Gun shows provide a large market where criminals can shop for firearms anonymously."[9] But the study provides no evidence that directly measures how important gun shows are to criminals obtaining guns. The report examines 314 selected investigations involving gun shows, including all gun show investigations from 1997 and 1998. "The remainder" come from 1994 to 1996, and there is one investigation each from 1991 and 1992. How this combination of years and cases was selected is never explained, and it leaves one concerned that the data were selectively chosen by the government to create a certain impression.

Yet, even if all the available tracing cases had been used, there is still the issue of which guns local police trace. Not all guns are traced, and those that are traced presumably are being traced because they are linked to the worst problems. So guns linked to criminal problems are overrepresented in the sample. To put it simply, as the Congressional Research Service noted, cases "selected for tracing do not constitute a random sample."[10]

In any event, of these 314 investigations, thirty-three were said to involve a felon purchasing a gun and twenty involved a straw purchaser. But no evidence is provided on the strength of these claims, or on the alleged wrongdoing. All the appendix notes is that "not all violations described will necessarily be charged as crimes or result in convictions." Yet, even if the fifty-plus cases of felons or straw purchasers over these seven years constitute real crimes, there is still the question of why such a small sample should drive policy considerations.

Despite all the emphasis on gun shows, there is no empirical research linking gun show regulations to crime rates. What evidence is usually utilized by the government does not deal directly either with gun shows or crime rates. Even ignoring those deficiencies, there are other problems with the evidence offered. By May 2002, Senator Joseph Lieberman notes, the Brady Act background checks had "stopped 700,000 criminals from buying a weapon."[11] But the 700,000 figure is actually the estimated number of initial denials. This is quite different from the number of criminals prevented from obtaining a gun. It includes people who were initially denied—incorrectly—because they had the same name as a criminal or because legal violations that should not have disqualified them under law, such as unpaid traffic tickets, slowed down their approval. The number is also not a "hard" number. Denials from a set of state reports are used to estimate the number of denials nationwide, but there have been serious questions about the accuracy of the numbers. The discrepancies between the number of reported initial denials submitted by the selected states and what the FBI has claimed that they were given has been as high as 1,300 percent.[12] Yet, the ultimate question is whether the Brady Act reduced violent crime, and I am not aware of any academic studies that have found any evidence of that.[13,14]

Surprisingly, only five states (California, Colorado, Maryland, Oregon, and Pennsylvania) have regulations that actually explicitly discuss gun shows, and two of those were not passed until November 2000. What is normally meant when gun control organizations claim that the gun show loophole is closed in a state is that private transfers require the same type of background check that is needed to buy a gun from a licensed gun dealer. (My assistant, Lydia Regopoulos, spent a great deal of time talking to Jim Kessler from Americans for Gun

Safety to make sure that the definition of gun show loopholes I use corresponded with their definition. Kessler's time was appreciated.)

One of these surveys provides some evidence on how many assault weapons are used by criminals. The Bureau of Justice Statistics' 1997 survey also indicates that about 1.5 percent of state and federal inmates who possessed a firearm used "military-style semi-automatic or automatic weapons" during the crime for which they were convicted, though virtually none of these is actually likely to involve a crime committed with a machine gun. The 1.5 percent includes both guns whose sales were stopped by federal or state assault weapons bans as well as ones that weren't affected. To be included as a military-style weapon in the survey, rifles or shotguns must have a pistol grip, folding stock, flash suppresser, or bayonet mount. Handguns are classified as military-style if the magazine or clip is visible. Just like other semi-automatic guns, these weapons fire just one bullet each time the trigger is pulled, and the bullets and speed of fire are the same.

There has been little study on the impact of the federal assault weapons ban that went into effect on September 13, 1994, and there have been no studies of the state assault weapons laws. The only study of the federal law that I know of was conducted by Jeffrey Roth and Christopher Koper of the Urban Institute. They found that while the ban clearly raised the price of assault weapons in anticipation of the fact that new guns could no longer be sold, "the ban's short-term impact on gun violence has been uncertain." However, their lack of results may have arisen simply because they studied the federal law for only the first year that it was in effect, 1995, and for only forty-two states. They were also unable to account for average differences across states in crime rates or for almost any of the controls that we have tried to account for in this book.[15]

The theory behind both gun show loopholes and assault weapon bans is fairly straightforward and very similar. To the extent that background checks on private transfers prevent criminals from getting guns, crime rates will be reduced. Similarly, if criminals use so-called assault weapons relatively more effectively to commit crime than those weapons are used to stop crime, banning them ought to reduce crime.

But background checks can prevent law-abiding citizens from getting guns—or at least prevent them from getting them quickly. Even though a friend is being threatened, people may be reluctant to loan out a gun for fear of violating the law. There is also simply the risk that so many additional laws make it likely that even the best-intentioned person will violate them. Recently even Sarah Brady, the chairman of the antigun Brady Campaign (formerly Handgun Control, Inc.) whose husband inspired the 1994 Brady Law requiring background checks for dealer sales, apparently violated Delaware law (and perhaps federal law as well) by purchasing a rifle in her own name which she intended to, and did, give to her son as a surprise present.[16] Referring to Sarah Brady's actions and state law, a spokeswoman for the Delaware Justice Department said, "You can't purchase a gun for someone else, that would be a 'straw purchase.' You've got a problem right there."

As Chris Matthews pointed out, there is also the issue of substitutes. Will law-abiding citizens bear the costs of following the increasingly complex legal process while criminals possibly move to other methods of obtaining a gun that are illegal but easy?

A similar substitution question exists for assault weapons. If other guns exist that are functionally equivalent to the banned weapons, why should the ban make any difference to criminals? To the extent that banning guns raises gun prices, the impact on crime depends upon whether ownership of guns by criminals is more or less sensitive to higher prices than is ownership by law-abiding citizens. Depending upon the answer, the effect on crime rates could go in either direction. If law-abiding citizens are more sensitive, higher prices could conceivably lead to more crime.

II. SOME BACKGROUND ON GUN SHOWS AND ASSAULT WEAPONS

Gun control organizations such as Americans for Gun Safety and the Brady Campaign classify a state as having closed a gun show loophole if background checks are required for the private transfer of handguns. Americans for Gun Safety explains this decision because "In truth, long guns are rarely used in crimes."[17]

By 1998, there were seventeen states that regulated the private transfer of handguns (Table 8.1).[18] Six of those seventeen states also

Table 8.1: Enactment Dates of Laws Requiring
Background Checks on the Private Transfer of Handguns

State	Date the law went into effect	Type of crime for not conducting check	Type of crime for providing false Information
California	1/1/91	Misdemeanor	Misdemeanor
Colorado	3/31/01	Class 1 misdemeanor	Class 1 misdemeanor
Connecticut	10/1/94	Class D felony	Fined not more than $500 and/or imprisoned for not more than 3 years
Hawaii	Pre-1977	Misdemeanor	Class C felony
Illinois	Pre-1977	Class A misdemeanor	Perjury
Indiana	Pre-1977	Class B misdemeanor	Class C felony
Iowa	7/1/91	Simple misdemeanor	Class D felony
Maryland	10/1/96	Misdemeanor	Misdemeanor
Massachusetts	Pre-1977	Felony	$500-1000 and/or 6 months, to 2 years imprisonment
Michigan	Pre-1977	Felony	Felony
Missouri	9/28/81	Class A misdemeanor	Class A misdemeanor
Nebraska	9/6/91	Class 1 misdemeanor	Class 4 felony
New Jersey	Pre-1977	Crime of the 4th degree	Crime of the 3rd degree
New York	Pre-1977	Class A misdemeanor	Class A misdemeanor
North Carolina	12/1/95	Class 2 misdemeanor	Class H felony
Oregon	12/7/00	Class A misdemeanor	Class A misdemeanor
Pennsylvania	10/11/95	Misdemeanor of the 2nd degree	Felony of the 3rd degree
Rhode Island	Pre-1977	Not more than $1000 and/or imprisonment of up to 5 years	Imprisonment of up to 5 years
Tennessee	Until 11/11/98	Class A misdemeanor	Class A misdemeanor

included background checks for long guns (California, Hawaii, Illinois, Massachusetts, New Jersey, and Rhode Island). Table 8.2 lists the regulations on transfers by dealers.

There is no national registry of gun shows, but the "Gun Show Calendar" provides a central source of advertisements for shows. According to the calendar, the number of gun shows rose steadily through the 1990s until reaching a peak of 2,907 in 1996, and then declined consistently through 2001 (Figure 8.1).[19] The peak in gun

Table 8.2
Enactment Dates of Laws Requiring Background Checks
on the Dealers Sales of Handguns

State	Date the law went into effect	Type of crime for not conducting check	Type of crime for providing false information
Alabama	2/28/94	$1000 max and/or 1 year max	Fine and/or 5 years max
Alaska	2/28/94	$1000 max and/or 1 year max	Fine and/or 5 years max
Arizona	2/28/94	$1000 max and/or 1 year max	Fine and/or 5 years max
Arkansas	2/28/94	$1000 max and/or 1 year max	Fine and/or 5 years max
California	Pre-1977	Misdemeanor	Misdemeanor
Colorado	2/28/94	Class 1 misdemeanor	Class 1 misdemeanor
Connecticut	2/28/94	Class D felony	Fine not more than $500 and/or imprisoned not more than 3 years
Delaware	1/20/91	Class A misdemeanor	Class G felony
Florida	10/1/90	Felony of the 3rd degree	Felony of the 3rd degree
Georgia	2/28/94	$1000 max and/or 1 year max	Fine and/or 5 years max
	1/1/96	Misdemeanor	Misdemeanor
Hawaii	Pre-1977	Misdemeanor	Class C felony
Idaho[1]	2/28/94	Misdemeanor	Misdemeanor
Illinois	Pre-1977	Class A misdemeanor	Perjury
	1991	Class A misdemeanor	Class 2 felony
	1995	Class A misdemeanor to aquire without FOID card, Class 3 felony if eligible for FOID; to transfer to someone without a FOID is a class 4 felony	Class 2 felony
Indiana	Pre-1977	Class B misdemeanor	Class C felony
	12/1/95	Class A misdemeanor	Class D felony
Iowa	7/1/91	Simple misdemeanor	Class D felony
	7/1/94	Aggravated misdemeanor	Class D felony
Kansas	2/28/94	$1000 max and/or 1 year max	Fine and/or 5 years max
Kentucky	2/28/94	$1000 max and/or 1 year max	Fine and/or 5 years max
Louisiana	2/28/94	$1000 max and/or 1 year max	Fine and/or 5 years max
Maine	2/28/94	$1000 max and/or 1 year max	Fine and/or 5 years max
Maryland	Pre-1977	Misdemeanor	Misdemeanor
Massachusetts	Pre-1977	Felony	$500—1,000 and/or 6 months, to 2 years imprisonment
Michigan	Pre-1977	Felony	Felony
Minnesota	Pre-1977	Gross misdemeanor	Gross misdemeanor

State	Date the law went into effect	Type of crime for not conducting check	Type of crime for providing false information
Mississippi	2/28/94	$1000 max and/or 1 year max	Fine and/or 5 years max
Missouri	9/28/81	Class A misdemeanor	Class A misdemeanor
Montana	2/28/94	$1000 max and/or 1 year max	Fine and/or 5 years max
Nebraska	9/6/91	Class 1 misdemeanor	Class 4 felony
Nevada	2/28/94	$1000 max and/or 1 year max	Fine and/or 5 years max
N. Hampshire	2/28/94	$1000 max and/or 1 year max	Fine and/or 5 years max
	1/1/95[2]	Misdemeanor	Misdemeanor
New Jersey	Pre-1977	Crime of the 4th degree	Crime of the 3rd degree
New Mexico	2/28/94	$1000 max and/or 1 year max	Fine and/or 5 years max
New York	Pre-1977	Class A misdemeanor	Class A misdemeanor
North Carolina	2/28/94	Misdemeanor	Class H felony
	12/1/95	Class 2 misdemeanor (reclassified but same sentence as previously)	Class F felony
North Dakota	2/28/94	$1000 max and/or 1 year max	Fine and/or 5 years max
Ohio	2/28/94	$1000 max and/or 1 year max	Fine and/or 5 years max
Oklahoma	2/28/94	$1000 max and/or 1 year max	Fine and/or 5 years max
Oregon	1/1/90	Class C felony	Class C felony
	7/1/96	Class A misdemeanor	Class A misdemeanor
Pennsylvania	2/28/94	Misdemeanor of the 1st degree	Misdemeanor of the 1st degree
	3/22/95	Misdemeanor of the 2nd degree	Felony of the 3rd degree
Rhode Island	Pre-1977	Not more than $1000 and/or imprisonment of up to 5 years	Imprisonment of up to 5 years
South Carolina	2/28/94	$1000 max and/or 1 year max	Fine and/or 5 years max
South Dakota	2/28/94	$1000 max and/or 1 year max	Fine and/or 5 years max
Tennessee	Pre-1977	Class B misdemeanor	Class B misdemeanor
	11/11/89	Class A misdemeanor	Class A misdemeanor
Texas	2/28/94	$1000 max and/or 1 year max	Fine and/or 5 years max
Utah	2/28/94	Felony of the 3rd degree	Felony of the 3rd degree
Vermont	2/28/94	$1000 max and/or 1 year max	Fine and/or 5 years max
Virginia	11/1/89	Class 1 misdemeanor	Class 5 felony
	3/23/93	Class 6 felony	Class 5 felony
Washington	7/24/83	Misdemeanor	Gross misdemeanor
West Virginia	2/28/94	$1000 max and/or 1 year max	Fine and/or 5 years max
Wisconsin	12/1/91	Fined $500–10,000 and/or imprisoned for up to 9 months	Fined $500–10,000 and/or imprisoned for up to 9 months
Wyoming	2/28/94	$1000 max and/or 1 year max	Fine and/or 5 years max

[1]Brady for 5 months
[2]State provision added that changed the penalty

Figure 8.1: The Number of Gun Shows Since 1989

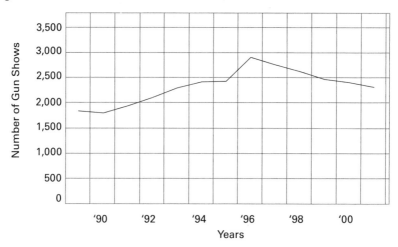

shows occurred a couple of years after the 1993–94 peak in the domestic production of guns. Given the time lag in setting up shows, it is
possible that what generated the increased demand for sales also generated increases in the number of shows. If national laws such as the
Brady Act or the federal assault weapons ban discourage gun shows,
Figure 8.1 does not indicate an obvious effect. Both laws went into
effect in 1994. Yet, there was a large increase in the number of gun
shows in 1996, and it was not until 2000 that the number of gun
shows returned back to their 1994 levels.

While there are a few surprises, the distribution of cases across
states is also generally what one would expect (Table 8.3). The per
capita number of shows in 1998 is greatest in the west, particularly
in states such as Wyoming, Montana, and South Dakota where the
rate of gun shows was 2.1 to 4.3 times the national average. By contrast, states like New York, California, Massachusetts, New Jersey,
and Hawaii have very few gun shows, with rates that are one-third or
less of the national average. There are a couple of surprises, particularly Utah and Alaska, which have high gun ownership rates and relatively few gun shows. But a very simple regression linking the per
capita number of gun shows with the General Social Survey's gun
ownership rate indicates that higher gun ownership states have sig-

Table 8.3: The Number of Gun Shows by State in 1998
(Collected from the Gun Show Calender)

State	Gun Shows per 100,000 people	No. of Shows	State	Gun Shows per 100,000 people	No. of Shows
Wyoming	5.62	27	North Carolina	1.03	78
Montana	4.89	43	Louisiana	1.03	45
South Dakota	2.74	20	Michigan	0.98	96
Oregon	2.59	85	Virginia	0.93	63
West Virginia	2.48	45	Kentucky	0.92	36
Nevada	2.41	42	Illinois	0.85	103
Iowa	2.34	67	Delaware	0.81	6
Wisconsin	1.88	98	Maine	0.80	10
Nebraska	1.87	31	Alabama	0.78	34
Colorado	1.64	65	New Hampshire	0.76	9
Idaho	1.62	20	Ohio	0.75	84
North Dakota	1.57	10	Washington	0.74	42
Minnesota	1.50	71	South Carolina	0.73	28
New Mexico	1.50	26	Maryland	0.70	36
Oklahoma	1.44	48	Rhode Island	0.61	6
Arkansas	1.42	36	Vermont	0.51	3
Kansas	1.40	37	Utah	0.43	9
Indiana	1.37	81	New York	0.39	71
Tennessee	1.36	74	California	0.37	122
Missouri	1.29	70	Connecticut	0.37	12
Mississippi	1.27	35	Alaska	0.33	2
Arizona	1.20	56	Massachusetts	0.28	17
Florida	1.19	178	New Jersey	0.14	11
Georgia	1.17	89	Hawaii	0	0
Pennsylvania	1.15	138	**Average**	**1.30**	**53.63**
Texas	1.08	213			

nificantly more shows, with a one percent increase in gun ownership rates increasing the gun show rate by 0.6 percent.[20]

Some have used this type of cross-sectional data from 1998 to make several points about requiring background checks on private transfers. Americans for Gun Safety claims that background checks on private transfers do not interfere with gun shows: "Of the five states that host the most gun shows, three states—Pennsylvania, Illinois, and California—have already closed the gun show loophole."[21] Yet, this seems to be what one would expect simply because these are all large states. For example, Wyoming has less than 1.5 percent of the population of California and it is difficult to see why one would expect the smaller states to have more total shows than the larger ones. Just as Wyoming or Montana have fewer Wal-Marts than California because of their smaller populations, it is not surprising that they would also have fewer total gun shows. On a per capita basis Pennsylvania, Illinois, and California ranked, respectively, only 25th, 32nd, and 45th.[22] In 1998, seventeen states that required background checks on private transfers averaged 0.89 gun shows per 100,000 people, while thirty-three states without these regulations had over a 70 percent higher gun show rate (1.52 shows per 100,000 people).

Another issue involves whether the checks make it more difficult for criminals to get guns. While no previous evidence has been presented on how gun show regulations affect crime rates, Americans for Gun Safety points out that the criminals in states that do not require gun show background checks are more likely to obtain their guns from within their states and thus are relatively less likely to get them from other states.[23] On average they claim that criminals are 36 percent more likely to get their guns from the state that they are living in when the gun show loophole is "open" than in "closed" states. But there is also the question of how plentiful guns were from other sources in those states. For example, open states also have much higher gun ownership rates; indeed, the gun ownership rate in open states is 39 percent higher. To the extent that criminals obtain guns through theft, those criminals living in closed loophole, low gun ownership states are going to be much less successful on average in obtaining guns through theft.

While many gun laws are accounted for in this research, the other gun control law that we will focus on in this chapter is the assault weapons ban, enacted nationally in September 1994. There are also five states that had this law in effect for at least some period of time prior to the end of 1998 (see Table 8.4). Most gun laws, once they go on the books, are rarely repealed. California is unusual with respect to the assault weapons ban in that the ban the state enacted in 1990 was declared unconstitutional by an intermediate appellate court in early 1998.[24] An injunction kept this appellate court decision from having an effect, but it appears to have prevented prosecutions. A new law was not enacted until the beginning of 2000, thus providing an interesting experiment for whether there was a drop in crime when

Table 8.4: Assault Weapons Ban

State	Date law went into effect	Penalty for Violation
California	1/1/90 3/4/98—state appellate court ruled that the ban was unconstitutional* 1/1/00—a new assault weapons bill took effect**	Felony: 4-8 years in prison
Hawaii	7/1/92	Class C felony: 5 years in prison
Maryland	6/1/94	fine of $1,000-10,000 and/or 1-10 years imprisonment
Massachusetts	10/21/98	Felony: not more that 3 yrs. or $5,000 or both
New Jersey	5/30/90	Crime of the 3rd degree, knowingly violating provisions is a crime of the 4th degree

* State appellate court ruled that the Roberti-Roos bill was unconstitutional because the law violated the equal protection provisions of the constitution because in many cases guns banned under the law are no different than guns allowed to be sold legally.
** The new law specifically defined the banned by characteristic instead of listing individual models to be prohibited.
6/29/00-California Supreme Court reversed decision of court of appeals stating that Roberti-Roos did not violate due process protections, nor did it violate either the equal protection or separation of powers doctrines.

the law was enacted and a corresponding increase when it was ruled unconstitutional.

III. Explaining Why the Number of Gun Shows Changes Over Time

Obviously other things explain gun show rates, and as we have discussed in Chapter 5, purely cross-sectional data are problematic. In addition to the percent of the population owning guns, different gun laws could affect the number of gun shows. Background checks, because of delays and breakdowns in the computer checks or other inconveniences, could discourage people from going to gun shows. From September 1999 to December 2000 the system was available on average about 94 percent of the time, or down about one hour for every 16.7 hours of operation.[25] When the system does go down, it tends to go down for a few large blocks of time as opposed to many

short periods of time.[26] An additional difficulty, though, is that neither customers nor sellers are informed as to how long any particular
outage is expected to last.

The system shutdowns affect all transactions, but the delays were
also significant even when the system was in operation. While 71 percent of the checks during 2000 and 72 percent during 1999 were conducted within an average of thirty seconds, 23 percent took up to two
hours and the remaining 5 percent took an unspecified but longer
amount of time.[27]

Finally, there are issues over whether some transactions are
stopped that shouldn't be stopped. The National Instant Check System reports that "many records lack not only final dispositions, but
post-judgment relief data as well."[28] Some problems arise because of
the similarity of people's names. All these factors could impose a significant cost on transactions and discourage sales, though no estimates have been made of lost sales. A loss of 10 or 15 percent of sales
could force many gun sellers out of business.

On the other hand, it is possible that any drop could be due to criminals no longer finding gun shows an attractive source of weapons. If
this last explanation was important, the background check should be
associated with a drop in crime or, if close substitutes are available, at
least no increase in crime.

Much of the debate over recent federal gun show background check
legislation has centered over whether to allow three days for background checks to be conducted. The NRA has claimed that a three-
day waiting period could "very well close down firearms shows and
we oppose that."[29] Other laws that ban the sales of assault weapons
or inexpensive guns (e.g., Saturday night specials) restrict what can be
sold and thus could reduce the demand for gun shows. Similarly, one-
gun-a-month rules could reduce demand for guns and thus reduce the
number of shows, while right-to-carry concealed handgun laws could
also increase the number of shows by increasing demand for handguns. But survey data indicate that the large majority of permit holders already owned a gun.

In addition to various gun control laws, I also control for state population, different measures of income, unemployment rate, poverty
rate, and demographics, as well as the average differences across states

Table 8.5: Explaining the Number of Gun Shows in States

Percent Impact on Number of Gun Shows from the Following:	(1)	(2)	(3)
Background Checks for "Gun Shows"	-14%**	-24%***	-11%**
Background Checks by Dealers	-8%	-4%	-4%
Assault Weapons Ban	-27%***	-28%***	-23%***
Saturday Night Special Ban	0.7%	-23%	0.8%
Waiting Period (Impact on Number of Gun Shows for each additional day that waiting period is lengthened)	-1.4%***	-1.4%***	-0.5%*
Right-to-Carry Law	.02%	0.3%	-4.3%
One-gun-a-month Rule	7%	2%	2%
Percent of Population Owning a Gun (Survey Data from General Social Survey)	0.2%**	0.25%***	
Violent Crime Rate		0.06%***	
Number of Observations	263	259	495

Note: These estimates account for not only the average differences across states and years in the number of gun shows but the state population, unemployment rate, poverty rate, per capita income, per capita welfare payment, per capita unemployment insurance, average income support payments to those over 65 years of age, and the thirty-six different demographic categories by age, sex, and race that we have used throughout the book.

*** The two-tailed t-test is significant at the 1 percent level.
** The two-tailed t-test is significant at the 5 percent level.
* The two-tailed t-test is significant at the 10 percent level.

and years that have been used throughout the rest of the book. The different measures of income and demographics are used to help explain some of the changing demand for gun shows.

The results in Table 8.5 provide consistent evidence that closing the gun show loophole, enacting the assault weapons ban, and instituting waiting periods significantly reduce the number of gun shows. Both types of background checks reduce the number of gun shows, but only the effect of background checks on private transfers is statistically significant and quite large, with estimates implying between an 11 to 24 percent drop in gun shows. An assault weapons ban produces an even more consistently massive and statistically significant effect, reducing the number of shows by between 23 to 28 percent.

Waiting periods also decrease the number of shows, but the effect is much smaller than for assault weapons or the gun show loophole. A waiting period of one day reduces the number of gun shows by 0.5 to

Figure 8.2: Impact of Gun Show Regulations
on the Number of Gun Shows

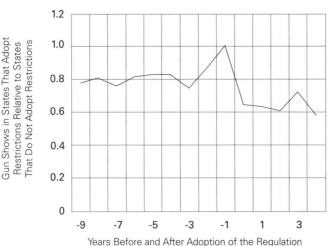

Years Before and After Adoption of the Regulation

1.4 percent. A three business day waiting period, as was put forth in the federal legislation sponsored by Senators John McCain and Joseph Lieberman, reduces the number of shows by 1.5 to 4.2 percent.[30]

The other gun laws (Saturday night special ban, right-to-carry laws, one-gun-a-month rules) have no statistically significant effect on the number of gun shows. An increase in the percentage of a population that owns a gun and a higher violent crime rate both work to increase the number of shows. Increasing the number of violent crimes by one per 1,000 people increases the number of gun shows by 6 percent. Including all these additional factors also reduces the importance of gun ownership rates in explaining the number of gun shows. Increasing the percentage of the population owning a gun by one percentage point increases the number of gun shows by 0.25 percent.

Figure 8.2 shows the year-by-year changes in the number of gun shows before and after the adoption of the gun show regulations. The graph compares the rate at which shows occur in states that will adopt the regulations relative to the states that are not changing their rules. The states adopting the regulations tended to have relatively few gun shows even before they instituted the rules, but they fell even farther behind after they were implemented. In only the year immediately preceding the passage of the gun show law did the rate of gun shows reach parity between the states that would have regulations and those that never adopted the regulations. During the rest of the pre-law period, states that would eventually adopt the regulations were at a fairly consistent 80 percent, but in four of the six years with the regulations in effect the rate of gun shows fell to around 60 percent.

IV. The Impact of Gun Show and Assault Weapons Bans on Crime

The Raw Data

The simplest approach to start with is to examine how crime rates changed in states with and without a particular gun law. There are nine states that had the gun show loophole closed for at least a full four years by the end of 1998, and the average state had adopted the regulations by 1990.

Figure 8.3 graphs the change in different violent crime rates before and after the "closing" of the loophole for these nine states relative to the change in these crime rate categories for the thirty-three states that never adopted the law. While violent crime rates are falling relatively faster in states with the law after adoption, that pattern was also true before the law was enacted and certainly well before the first full year that the law was in effect (Year 1). Murder and robbery rates, the crimes that one would expect to be most reduced by the law if it is preventing criminals from obtaining weapons, actually begin declining after Year -3, four years before the first full year that the law was in effect.

The assault weapons ban's benefits are even less obvious in Figure 8.4. Four of the five states with assault weapons bans had them in effect for at least four full years prior to the end of 1998, and the average state adopted the ban in 1991. The comparison group here is the forty-five states that did not adopt a ban. For both murder and robbery rates, the states adopting assault weapons bans were experiencing a relatively faster drop in violent crimes prior to the ban and a relatively faster increase in violent crimes after it. For rapes and aggravated assaults, the trends before and after the law seem essentially unchanged.

Figure 8.3: Ratio of Violent Crime in States
With and Without Gun Show Check

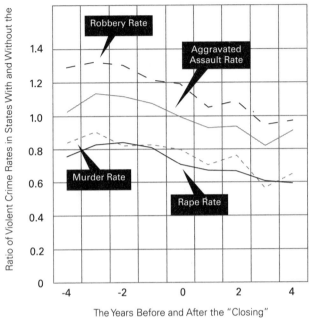

The Years Before and After the "Closing"
of the Gun Show Loophole

Figure 8.4: Ratio of Violent Crime in States
With and Without an Assault Weapons Ban

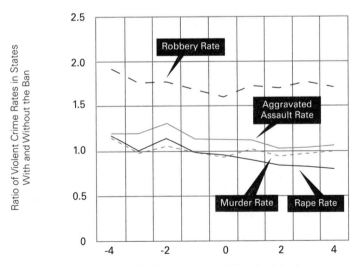

The Years Before and After the Adoption
of an Assault Weapons Ban

Figure 8.5: California's Rape and Murder Rates

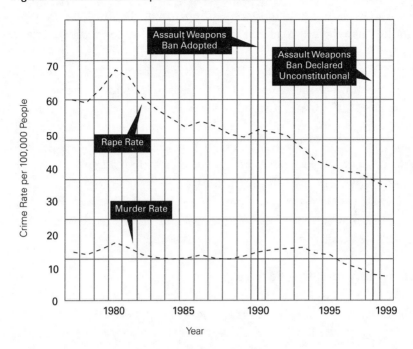

Figure 8.6: California's Robbery and Aggravated Assault Rates

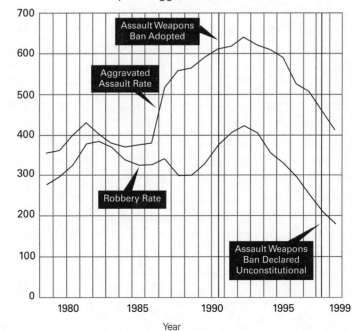

As mentioned earlier, California provides a relatively unique example in that it both enacted an assault weapons ban in January 1990 and then had the law declared unconstitutional in early 1998. Figures 8.5 and 8.6 indicate that there is little impact on the state's violent crime rates from the law. For murder, robbery, and aggravated assaults, those crime rates were rising before the law and continued rising after it. Similarly, when the law was declared unconstitutional, those same crime rates continued their trend, as they were falling prior to the court decision and continued falling in 1998 and 1999. With respect to rape, while there was a tiny upward spike in 1990, rape rates were largely falling uninterruptedly since 1980.

These four graphs make it pretty hard to argue that either closing the gun show loophole or banning assault weapons produced any noticeable benefit in terms of lower crime rates.

Accounting for Other Factors

Many factors can affect crime rates. Table 8.6 examines the average impact of the gun show background checks and the assault weapons ban on crime rates. All the factors that were accounted for in the previous chapters, as well as all the gun control laws that we have discussed, are again used here. An initial look at the simplest results imply that both of these laws increase murder and robbery rates. The impacts also appear to be quite large with respect to closing the gun show loophole: it raised murder and robbery rates by 9 and 14 percent, respectively. Under the assault weapons ban, murder and robbery rates rose by 12 and 10 percent.

An initial warning flag is raised by the large increases in larceny rates which are unlikely to involve guns, though it is possible that creating more of a criminal environment in which robbery flourishes may also encourage other types of crime. This might arise if only because of the "broken window" phenomenon discussed by James Q. Wilson and George Kelling. As robbery and murder rates rise in an area, people might avoid the area and thus make it easier for criminals to commit other property crimes, since there are less likely to be witnesses.

Unlike our earlier discussions of concealed handguns, it is not obvious that either closing the gun show loophole or banning assault

Table 8.6: The Impact of Closing the Gun Show "Loophole"
and Assault Weapons Ban

These estimates account for different gun control laws (safe storage, right-to-carry, one-gun-a-month rules, waiting period, penalties for using guns in the commission of crimes), the average differences across states and years (so-called year and state fixed effects), the state population, unemployment rate, poverty rate, per capita income, per capita welfare payment, per capita unemployment insurance, average income support payments to those over sixty-five years of age, and the thirty-six different demographic categories by age, sex, and race that we have used throughout the book.

| Variable | Average Crime Rate Before and After Adoption of the Law | |
	Gun Show Background Check	Assault Weapons Ban
Violent Crime	5.4%	1.5%
Murder	9.2%**	11.9%***
Rape	-4.3%	3.2%
Robbery	14.3%***	9.9%**
Aggravated Assault	3.1%	-4.8%
Property Crime	3.8%*	6.7%***
Auto Theft	15.9%***	-12.4%**
Burglary	4.8%	6.3%**
Larceny	4.3%*	5.4%**

*** The two-tailed t-test is significant at the 1 percent level.
** The two-tailed t-test is significant at the 5 percent level.
* The two-tailed t-test is significant at the 10 percent level.
†† F-test significant at the 1 percent level.
† F-test significant at the 10 percent level.

weapons should have an increasing impact on crime rates over a long period of time. Much was made by the Clinton administration in recent years about the short time period between when guns are purchased and when they are used in crime. If that is true, whatever beneficial effects these laws produced should have been quickly observable.

Yet, looking at the changes in crime by each year before and after the adoption of the background checks makes it hard to accept that this law has made much of a difference. Figure 8.7 shows that the murder and robbery rates were rising relatively faster in the states adopting the law prior to the law being adopted. It is possible that the growth rate increases slightly for robbery, but the effect is not very large. The diagram shows why the average crime rates are higher in the postadoption period, but the increase is not due to some sudden

Figure 8.7: Impact of Closing Gun Show "Loophole" on Crime Rates

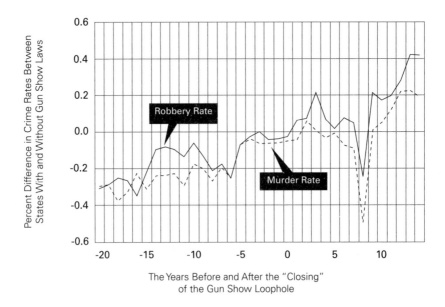

The Years Before and After the "Closing"
of the Gun Show Loophole

Figure 8.8: Impact of Closing Gun Show "Loophole" on Crime Rates

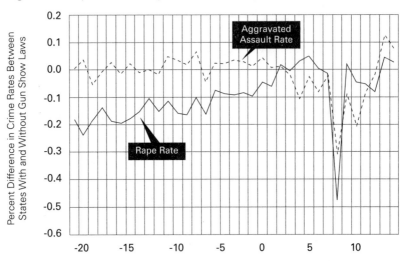

The Years Before and After the "Closing"
of the Gun Show Loophole

Figure 8.9: Impact of the Assault Weapons Ban on Crime Rates

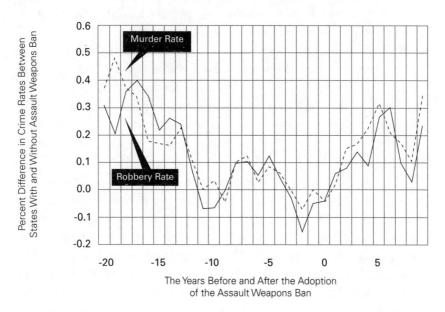

Percent Difference in Crime Rates Between States With and Without Assault Weapons Ban

The Years Before and After the Adoption
of the Assault Weapons Ban

Figure 8.10: Impact of the Assault Weapons Ban on Crime Rates

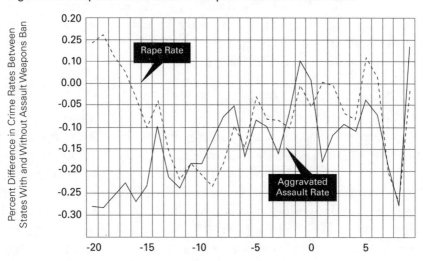

Percent Difference in Crime Rates Between States With and Without Assault Weapons Ban

The Years Before and After the Adoption
of the Assault Weapons Ban

increase in crime after adoption of the gun show provision. Whatever upward trend exists after adoption is merely a continuation of an upward trend that was occurring over the entire period.

While rape rates eventually rise back up above their rates prior to the implementation of the gun show background check (see Figure 8.8), the rape rate was actually lower for most of the period after the law was adopted. Just as was the case for murder and robbery rates, aggravated assaults appear to be rising over the whole period and it is difficult to see any unusual change in growth that occurred after adoption.

Presumably if assault weapons are to be used in any particular crimes, they will be used for murder and robbery, but the data appears more supportive of an adverse effect of an assault weapons ban on murder and robbery rates (Figure 8.9), with both crime rates rising after the passage of the bans. The figure shows something of a "U" shape, with the drop in crime rates leveling off before the ban is adopted. Murder and robbery rates started off relatively high in the states that eventually adopted a ban, but the gap disappears by the time the ban is adopted. Only after instituting the ban do crime rates head back up. There is a very statistically significant change in murder and rape rate trends before and after the adoption of the ban.

As can readily be seen from Figure 8.10, it is very difficult to observe any systematic impact of the ban on rape and aggravated assault rates.

Differences in Effects Across States and by Level of Enforcement

A couple of further tests help confirm doubts about the lack of systematic impact of gun show checks or assault weapons bans on crime. Table 8.7 examines the impact of the laws across states on average. Take the tests for the gun show checks: While some changes in crime are statistically significant, it is very difficult to see any systematic pattern across states for any particular crime or even across crimes for any particular state. There is not enough data to determine an effect for all states, but nine states had higher average violent crime rates after gun show checks were imposed, and six states experienced a decline. For murder, eight states experienced an increase, while five experienced a decline.

The trend estimates reported in Table 8.8 provide slightly stronger evidence that violent crime rates were rising more after the law, with six states showing an increase and two a decline. But just as indicated in Figure 8.7, the states showing an increase after the law were experiencing an increase before the law. The large differences across states seem to imply that the results are due more to randomness than to any systematic effect of gun show checks on crime rates.

While the assault weapons ban tends to produce higher crime rates, Tables 8.7 and 8.8 show that even this effect varies by state. The results show a more consistent increase in murder and robbery rates.

Given the differences across states, I also tried to see whether the penalties imposed for violating the various laws could explain the differences, but the results only further confirm that the laws are randomly related to crime rates. In some cases, misdemeanor penalties for improperly transferring a gun reduce violent crime, but felony penalties increase it. But then the reverse impact of penalties is observed for murder. Or treating false background check information as a misdemeanor significantly increases violent crime, but treating it as a felony produces only a small, insignificant increase.

V. OTHER RECENT PROPOSALS

After the 2002 sniper attacks in the Washington, D.C., area, government officials and the media hastily declared ballistic fingerprinting to be the new, magic crime-solving tool. By the fall elections, politicians such as California's attorney general and numerous gubernatorial candidates were calling for law enforcement to record the markings made on bullets for all new guns.[31]

Unfortunately, there was a lot of confusion about what ballistic fingerprinting can and cannot do. Using ballistic fingerprinting to identify a recently fired gun is not the same thing as setting up a computerized database by test-firing all new guns before they are sold. The question provides a typical example of where it is necessary to look at both the costs and benefits of new gun laws. Before taking resources from traditional police activities that work and moving to other enforcement efforts, it would be nice to know which activity has the greater ability to reduce crime.

Table 8.7: The Impact of Closing the Gun Show "Loophole" and Assault Weapons Ban Across the States That Have Enacted These Rules: Changes in Average Crime Rates Before and After the Laws

Variable	Violent Crime	Murder	Rape
The Impact in Different States from Closing the Gun Show Loophole			
California	0.4%	12.3%	-5.2%
Connecticut	16.3%	77.8%***	56.2%***
Hawaii	-38.7%		
Illinois	2.2%		27.8%
Indiana	-72%***	-31.5%	11.8%
Iowa	2.8%	25.4%**	-14.6%
Maryland	-12.4%	-7.6%	-11.1%
Massachusetts	-12.1%		39.5%
Michigan		34.4%	71.7%***
Missouri	-14%**	-4.2%	-26.6%***
Nebraska	24.9%**	2.5%	-18.4%
New Jersey		-7.6%	
New York	83.1%**		67%**
North Carolina	7.2%	16.3%	5.2%
Pennsylvania	24.6%***	31.8%***	18%**
Rhode Island	-52.5%	-43.4%	14.1%
Tennessee	14.1%	16.3%	27%**
The Impact in Different States from the Assault Weapons Ban			
California	10.1%**	19.7%***	7.8%
Hawaii	54.8%**	45%	37.1%
Maryland	-14.1	11.7%	25.1%**
Massachusetts			
New Jersey	-5.9%	-1.6%	-8.3%

These estimates account for different gun control laws (safe storage, right-to-carry, one-gun-a-month rules, waiting period, penalties for using guns in the commission of crimes), the average differences across states and years (so-called year and state fixed effects), the state population, unemployment rate, poverty rate, per capita income, per capita welfare payment, per capita unemployment insurance, average income support payments to those over 65 years of age, and the thirty-six different demographic categories by age, sex, and race that we have used throughout the book.

Despite frequent comparisons, ballistic fingerprints are not like human fingerprints or DNA. Recording a child's fingerprints or DNA allows for identification much later in life. But friction in gun barrels causes wear and changes the markings over time.

A better analogy is the tread on car tires. It is possible to take the tire tracks left at the crime scene and match them with the criminal's car. But tires wear over time. If six months go by and the car is dri-

Robbery	Aggravated Assault	Property Crime	Auto Theft	Burglary	Larceny
13.4%	-7.4%	7.9%	12.4%	13.2%**	6.4%
77.4%***	9.8%	29.5%**	-1.9%	42.3%**	37.5%***
	266%		104%***	68.3%***	48.3%***
61.2%**	-12.2%		15.6%		26.6%
-12.1%	-125%***	-25.5%	-102%***	-79.5%***	-16.6%
-12.4%	9.7%	-18.2%***	-2.9%	-10%	-23%
-20.8%	-3.2%	-5.3%	-34.2%	-11.1%	1.1%
107%**		35.3%	-5.6%	12.6%	23%
34.7%		11.1%		-25.5%	9.1%
-11.8%	-8.8%	-.12%	1%	-10%	5.3%
17.9%	38.2%***	7.7%	21.9%	9.6%	4.3%
130%***		49.2%***		25.7%	48.6%***
	22.5%		115%**		69.4%***
42.3%***	-7.5%	16%***	36.4%***	21.5%***	16.6%***
41.1%***	13.1%	6.9%	33.6%***	5%	8.7%
60.3%			5.3%	13.8%	53%**
14.6%	-3.8%	5.1%	-35.1%	14.2%	6.4%
17.3%***	7.5%	7.8%**	.8%	5.5%	6.7%**
95.4%***	-6.7%	59.1%***	62.8%	46.5%	49.4%***
-7.5%	-27.2%**	-2.3%	-56.3%***	-16.2%	-2.4%
5.2%	-9.87%	2.8%	-23.6%***	8.4%	-2.5%

*** The two-tailed t-test is significant at the 1 percent level.
** The two-tailed t-test is significant at the 5 percent level.
* The two-tailed t-test is significant at the 10 percent level.

ven, the original print marks on the tires may not be of much use in solving the crime.

Nor does it make much sense to create a registry of tire treads on new tires on the off chance that a tire mark will be left at a crime scene. New tires are essentially identical, leaving investigators with limited information on only the brand and model.

The very friction that creates markings on bullets also creates wear. Except for the cheapest guns, the same models of new guns produce

Table 8.8: The Impact of Closing the Gun Show "Loophole" and Assault
Weapons Ban Across the States that have Enacted these Rules: Crime Rate
Trends After the Law

Variable	Violent Crime (1)	Murder (2)	Rape (3)
The Impact in Different States from Closing the Gun Show Loophole			
California	-3.9%***	-3.9%**	-3.4%***
Connecticut	4.5%	15.8%**	9%*
Iowa	3.3%*	.8%	.6%
Maryland	6%	-7.9%	-18%
Missouri	-1.3%	-2.3%**	-2%***
Nebraska	6.4%***	.7%	-4.1%**
North Carolina	3.1%	9%**	1.7%
Pennsylvania	7.6%**	11.3%***	7.5%**
The Impact in Different States from the Assault Weapons Ban			
California	1.6%**	3.2%***	.3%
Hawaii	14.7%	-2.1%	-4.2%
Maryland	-9.2%	7.2%	12%*
New Jersey	-1.5%	1.1%	-3.2%***

These estimates account for different gun control laws (safe storage, right-to-carry, one-gun-a-
month rules, waiting period, penalties for using guns in the commission of crimes), the average differences across states and years (so-called year and state fixed effects), the state
population, unemployment rate, poverty rate, per capita income, per capita welfare payment,
per capita unemployment insurance, average income support payments to those over 65 years
of age, and the thirty-six different demographic categories by age, sex, and race that we have
used throughout the book.

the same markings on bullets. And markings change slightly each
time a gun is fired. For inexpensive guns with softer metal barrels,
after fifty or one hundred rounds are fired, it can be very difficult to
match bullets.[32]

Ballistic fingerprinting faces other difficulties. The process is easily defeated by replacing the gun's barrel or scratching part of the
inside of a barrel with a nail file to cover up a crime. Putting tooth-
paste (a mild abrasive) on a bullet before firing it would also alter the
markings created by future bullets on the barrel.

Even if a gun were not used much between when the ballistic fingerprint was originally recorded and the occurrence of the crime, and
so therefore the gun was traceable to its place of purchase, police
must still trace the gun to the criminal. Yet only 12.1 percent of guns
used in crimes are obtained by the criminals through retail stores or
pawn shops.[33]

Robbery (4)	Aggravated Assault (5)	Property Crime (6)	Auto Theft (7	Burglary 8)	Larceny (9)
-.3%	-5.9%***	-.6%	-1%	1.4%	-.2%
15.2%**	6.8%	3.1%	1.2%	2.9%	6%
1.6%	4.5%**	-1.3%	3.7%	1.4%	2.4%**
-8.4%	15.3%	2.3%	28.3%	9.2%	3.6%
-1.7%	-1.2%	-1.25%**	-1.7%	-1.4%*	-.8%
4%	9.2%***	1%	5.5%*	1.2%	.15%
17.5%***	-2.5%	6.5%***	16%***	8.7%***	6.8%***
16.9%***	3.2%	1.7%	11.8%**	1.5%	2.5%
2.5%**	1.2%	1.3%***	.47%	1.4%**	.99%**
30.9%**	-15.4%	8.9%	6.2%	8%	6.5%
-2.6%	-14%	-3.7%	-37.2%***	-12.3%	-2.3%
1.6%	-1.3%	.09%	-4.7%***	1.5%	.48%

*** The two-tailed t-test is significant at the 1 percent level.
** The two-tailed t-test is significant at the 5 percent level.
* The two-tailed t-test is significant at the 10 percent level.

Because of collinearity the impacts on all states from the law could not be estimated. Those states where no estimates were found are not reported.

The sniper attacks in Washington are a good example of how the system works. The bullets were matched fairly quickly to the weapon. In the sniper case, the attacker was proud and wanted police to know the same person was committing the crimes. But doing that is not the same thing as setting up a database on new sales and making matches after guns have been used often.

Two states, Maryland and New York, have started recording the ballistic fingerprints of all new handguns sold in early 2001. Maryland's program cost $1.1 million to start and another $750,000 a year to run.[34] New York's startup costs were $4.5 million, with no estimates of yearly costs.[35] Dealers, gun makers, and prospective gun owners face far greater costs.

Yet, not one violent crime has been solved in New York or Maryland. The databases have been used only once: identifying two handguns stolen from a gun shop in Maryland.[36]

Gun control advocates cite a May 2002 Treasury Department study showing ballistic fingerprinting works.[37] But they confuse using the process to match guns soon after they are used with a database on all new guns. The advocates ignore the report's warning in its preface that the two approaches are "significantly different."

The Fraternal Order of Police also released a report in October 2002 that emphasized the difference between the approaches.[38] It noted that "[ballistic fingerprinting] has proved to be very effective to investigators, enabling them to link multiple shootings in which the same firearm was used (such as the recent murders in the Washington area) and to definitively connect recovered firearms to a particular shooting and/or crime."

But the police point out that: "In all cases, it is necessary that investigators recover a bullet or shell casing from the crime scene which is intact enough to allow forensic analysis to be able to identify the ballistic markings. The firearm must then be recovered in order for the gun and the bullet or shell casing to be conclusively linked.... Ballistics imaging and comparison technology [using a computer database] is very limited in accomplishing the latter."

A recent study done by the California Department of Justice confirms the Fraternal Order of Police's concerns about using a computer database with ballistic fingerprinting.[39] The report tested 790 pistols firing a total of 2,000 rounds, an average of just 2.5 shots per pistol. With cartridges from the same manufacturer, computer matching failed 38 percent of the time. When cartridges from different manufacturers were compared, the failure rate rose to 62 percent. The study does not even begin addressing difficulties involving wear.

The evidence is overwhelming that "fingerprinting" all new guns would divert police resources from normal police work and make it costlier for law-abiding citizens to own guns.

VI. Conclusion

Despite all the furor over gun shows and assault weapons, when one looks at the data, it is hard to see any benefits from the laws restricting them. Indeed, if there is any effect, the assault weapons ban appears to increase murder and robbery rates. Like most gun laws, closing gun show loopholes and assault weapon bans can have both benefits and costs.

Once one takes a step back from the political debate, the finding that background checks at gun shows have no impact on crime is probably not particularly surprising. The tiny percent of crime that arises from weapons purchased at gun shows indicates that there are probably a great number of substitute methods of obtaining guns for crime. Claims that background checks will mean the end of gun shows also appear excessive. While the background checks have a statistically significant impact on the number of shows, the total drop in the number of shows is between 11 and 24 percent. That is a sizeable reduction, but it is not correct to say that these rules eliminate shows. Other rules, such as the assault weapons ban or long waiting periods, have a much bigger depressant impact on the number of shows. A three-day waiting period combined with closing the gun show loophole, the type of proposed federal legislation that has generated so much controversy, implies a total reduction in gun shows by someplace between 12.5 and 28 percent.

What is possibly more surprising is the impact of the assault weapons ban on murder and robbery rates. My results find an *increase* in the average murder rate after a state enacts a ban on assault weapons. An examination of trends finds an even larger change. It is difficult to say why banning certain guns that are functionally identical to other still legal weapons should have such a large impact. The law does greatly reduce the number of gun shows (and, for similar reasons, possibly also reduces the number of gun dealers), and that could discourage law-abiding citizens from owning guns. Yet, the fact that this effect is neither uniform across states nor consistent with respect to the penalties for violations gives significant reason to pause. The bottom line, however, is this: No evidence exists that a ban reduces crime, whereas there is some weak evidence that the opposite is true.

Many gun control organizations frequently say that they favor "sensible" gun regulations, not the abolition of private gun ownership. Americans for Gun Safety portrays itself as one of the more moderate gun control organizations and says that it supports the "rights of law-abiding gun owners."[40] During 2002, I appeared with

Jim Kessler, the group's research director, on a local cable broadcast discussing a ballistic fingerprint database for new guns and other gun regulations. After the debate, Jim and I discussed gun show regulations. Jim believes those regulations will produce large reductions in crime rates and he expressed frustration about how difficult it was to get them passed. On the other hand, the NRA is concerned (correctly, according to the results presented here) that the regulations will eliminate many gun shows. In response, I made a simple suggestion, which I thought would make everyone happy. Since Kessler believes that benefits from reduced crime would greatly exceed the costs of gun shows performing the checks, why not offer to cover the costs to the gun shows to do the checks? It would take away the NRA's objection to the program and, if he is correct about the benefits, still make society better off.[41] In any case, it is not clear why only gun owners should pay for something that is going to benefit everyone. Needless to say, the idea went nowhere.

CHAPTER 9

CONCLUSION

The debate on gun control would be very different if even a few defensive gun use cases were covered better in the news. Too often, the debate over guns is a philosophical one, pitting the freedom of gun owners against the safety of everyone else.[1] Freedom is extremely important to Americans, but so is safety. Many people will understandably trade some freedom for more safety if that's the choice. But at least in the case of guns, that is often a false choice.

By disarming law-abiding citizens, gun control has frequently put Americans in danger.

Laws with seemingly obvious benefits—such as safe storage restrictions—result in higher crime rates and appear to do nothing to reduce juvenile accidental gun deaths and suicides. Likewise, so-called "gun-free safe zones" turn out to be neither "gun free" nor "safe" zones. And instituting background checks on the private transfers of handguns (closing the so-called "gun show loophole") or banning assault weapons is more apt to increase than decrease violent crime.

This book started by noting the obvious: Guns make it easier for bad things to happen. No one in the United States, or actually any place else in the world, could be unaware of this. Worldwide news coverage focuses on the bad things that happen with guns, such as the public school shootings or the 2002 sniper attack in the Washington, D.C., area. The puzzle is why dramatic cases in which people use guns to save lives are virtually never covered. Some of the difference in treatment is understandable. Dead bodies are more newsworthy than mere brandishings that cause criminals to run away. Dead bodies of innocent victims are probably also more newsworthy than dead bodies of criminals, but it is suspicious when the media are already covering a story and leaves out how the crimes were stopped.

The government has made the problem worse by measuring only the bad consequences of guns. While the government releases an annual report on the top ten crime guns, there is no corresponding list of top ten guns used defensively. The gun control debate raises the question of whether guns used in crime should be banned, but fails to ask whether the same characteristics make those guns even more useful in defensive situations. Each year the government releases reports on the number of crimes committed with guns, but the government surveys don't directly ask people the other side of the issue, whether they have used a gun to stop crime. Government public service ads also grossly exaggerate the risks of guns, without any mention of the benefits.

If we care about saving lives, we need to consider not only the bad newsworthy events, but also the events that never became newsworthy because people defended themselves. Yet, it seems undeniable that what is covered by the media drives the political debate. When gun crimes occur, I am sometimes asked to appear on television or radio shows to debate the need for more gun control. I have never been asked to debate whether we should remove gun control laws after such laws have prevented a victim from defending himself.

Terrorism has surely focused more attention on guns. For example, during June 2002 many Brooklyn Jews were alarmed by a CBS *60 Minutes* report that the terrorists who targeted the World Trade Center in 1993 originally planned to blow up Brooklyn Jewish neighborhoods. The terrorists apparently switched their target to the Trade Center only because they believed most of its occupants were Jewish. A terrorist interviewed by CBS gave the impression that Brooklyn Jews were still a prime target.

As a result of this scare, Rabbi Yakove Lloyd, founder of the Jewish Defense Group, tried organizing armed patrols in some heavily Jewish areas of Brooklyn, saying they "will be a very effective deterrent against terrorism directed at American Jews and other targets."[2] Even though Lloyd and some local politicians asked police for more protection, no additional protection was offered. But other New York City Jews, concerned about people running around with guns—even off-duty police officers or those with permits—opposed the Brooklyn patrols.[3] Even more seriously, New York City police commissioner Ray Kelly announced that the police would not tolerate it, and that "anyone attempting to patrol the streets armed with a weapon will be arrested."[4] Mayor Bloomberg declared, "We will not tolerate people going around with guns in this city, acting unto themselves."[5]

But the risks of attacks on heavily Jewish areas in New York City aside, there are simply too many vulnerable targets for the police to protect all of them. In addition, we hamstring the police. We trust police with guns when they are on the job, but some jurisdictions no longer trust officers to carry a gun off-duty. Even when police are allowed to carry their guns off-duty, they can't carry them when they travel across state lines.

What could possibly be the goal of increased regulations if gun control doesn't reduce crime and frequently increases it? Certainly one effect is reduced gun ownership. Indeed while handgun sales were increasing nationally after September 11, there were a few states where sales plummeted. In 2001 California saw a reduction of almost 23 percent, down by 46,000; Massachusetts by over 85 percent, or about 35,000; and Maryland saw no handguns sold during the first half of the year.[6] Gun control organizations applauded the drop and claimed that the drop in California was simply because "there's been a dramatic change in people's attitudes toward handguns."[7] More likely, the drop was due to new regulations. California banned the sale of relatively inexpensive handguns and required "safety" tests so that guns would withstand several sixty-foot drops onto concrete and still fire 600 rounds without jamming.[8] In Massachusetts, there were new permit regulations and restrictions on what types of guns could be sold.[9] No handguns were sold in Maryland during the first six months because of new regulations that gun makers pick up the costs of setting up a ballistic "fingerprinting" program.

Over time, I have come to believe that the ultimate objective of most gun control advocates is to gradually eliminate the private ownership of guns.[10] Pete Shields, the founder of Handgun Control, Inc., is well known for his statement that: "The first problem is to slow down the number of handguns being produced and sold in this country. The second problem is to get handguns registered. The final problem is to make possession of all handguns and all handgun ammunition— except for the military, police, licensed security guards, licensed sporting clubs, and licensed gun collectors—totally illegal."[11]

The Brady Campaign, Handgun Control's successor organization, has funded many suits against gun makers when guns were used improperly. Their lawyer in a suit against a Florida gun distributor in 2002 explained the motivation behind their actions: "This case is simply about a product that should never have been on the market. This gun has no business—it's not collectible, it's not used for hunting, it's not used for target practice. It's only used for what you heard about in that courtroom, and that is to hurt people."[12] The very notion of guns for self-defense, to deter criminals, is thus not recognized as a legitimate motivation for owning a gun.

The natural inclination when crimes are committed with guns is to get rid of the guns. While an understandable reaction, looking at only the costs of guns does not make good policy. But considering the very unbalanced media coverage and government reports about guns, it is no wonder that most people are unaware of the extensive benefits of gun defense. Unfortunately, this bias against guns costs lives.

SOME RECENT EVIDENCE ON GUNS AND CRIME

A. THE NUMBERS

After my book *More Guns, Less Crime* first appeared in 1998 (with the second edition appearing in 2000), a host of new empirical research was undertaken. With the exception of one study that looks at the Brady Act, virtually the entire focus of the new research by others has been on the impact on just one part of my previous work—the impact concealed handguns have on crime rates. Even though the data sets that I gave out to other researchers contained the work that I did on other gun control laws, such as state waiting periods and background checks, one-gun-a-month rules, and penalties for using guns in the commission of a crime, none of these other laws was included in subsequent analysis. That may have happened simply because my results on concealed handguns received the most media attention, but in the current policy debates, these other issues receive at least as much attention.

My previous book reviewed a large number of papers that had studied concealed handgun laws and crime.[1] The results ranged from little or no reduction to large reductions in violent crime. The most recent research continues that pattern, with seven new papers finding reductions in violent crime from concealed handgun laws, although the magnitude of the benefits varies: One new piece claims that the benefits are small or nonexistent, and one new working paper claims the first evidence that concealed handguns may increase crime.[2]

For example, of the seven recent papers published in the *Journal of Law and Economics* that found a benefit from right-to-carry laws, here are some of the comments: Florenz Plassmann and Nicolaus Tideman conclude that "right-to-carry laws do help on average to reduce the number of these crimes." Carl Moody states that his findings "confirm and reinforce the basic findings of the original Lott and Mustard study." While calling for more research, David Olson and Michael Maltz found "a decrease in total homicides," though the different data set they use indicates that the decline was driven entirely by a drop in gun homicides. My work with John Whitley concludes that "the longer a right-to-carry law is in effect the greater the drop in crime." The different research approaches the problem from a variety of perspectives: using new statistical techniques, different data sets, additional control variables, or examining a variety of specifications.

Plassmann and Tideman break down the impact of concealed handgun laws not only across states but also by each year before and after the law for the years 1977 to 1992. Their big innovation involves solving what is called the "truncation problem." No matter how effective a law is, it can't lower the crime rate below zero. The problem is that a lot of counties actually have zero crime rates. This problem is particularly important for murder and rape. For murder, 80 percent of the counties in the country have zero in any given year. Including these counties in estimating the impact of right-to-carry laws (or any gun laws for that matter) biases the results towards finding that the law increases the crime rate.

Appendix Figure 1.1 here reproduces the results that they obtained for murder, and the results are striking. For the ten states that adopted concealed handgun laws during the period that they studied, murder rates were rising or constant in all the states and falling after the law was passed. Indeed, with one exception, all the coefficients for murder, rape, and robbery for all ten states enacting the law from 1977 through 1992 imply that crime rates fell during the first full year that the laws were in effect. Even in that one exception (Oregon for robbery), the robbery rates still were much lower in the first three full years after enactment than in any of the five years before the law. Robbery rates (again with the exception of the single year for Oregon) indicate a bigger drop in robbery rates for each additional year that the law is in effect.

David Olson and Michael Maltz use county-level data from the Supplemental Homicide Report (SHR). This report unfortunately only provided data at the state level when I did my research. The advantage of the Supplemental Homicide Report is the richness of its data: It includes much more detailed characteristics of the victims and murderers than is provided by the FBI's Uniform Crime Reports (UCR). Further, its county level data are preferable to state level data. When you examine changes in crime rates solely at the state level you miss a lot of what may be happening within a state.[3] There is no reason to expect that changes in law enforcement or other factors are going to have the same impact on crime rates in all counties in a state. Maltz has another new paper where he discusses some problems with the way that the FBI determines the crime rate at the county level, and he indicates that.[4]

The overall drop in homicides that Olson and Maltz find is roughly similar to what I originally reported using county level UCR data, but the county-level SHR data do produce different results in terms of how murders are committed and who benefits from gun ownership. Their results show that the criminals who continue to murder after passage of concealed handgun laws rely much less frequently upon guns to commit murders. The results are striking: Murders with guns fall by 21 percent while non-gun murders actually rise by 10 percent, though this latter result is not statistically significant.

Using data from 1984 to 1996, David Mustard finds that while waiting periods rarely have a significant effect one way or the other on police deaths, concealed handgun laws are consistently and significantly related to fewer killings of police.

The only study that tried to replicate my results for the Brady Act was by Jens Ludwig and Philip Cook, and they also found that the law had no statistical impact on murder rates or overall accidental gun deaths or suicides. Their study did not examine the one crime category for which I found an increase in crime: rapes.[5] Even though they concede that the Brady Act had no effect on total suicides, they claim that it reduced suicides for those over age fifty-five. According to Ludwig and Cook, this is what we should expect, since making it more

Appendix Figure 1.1: Examining the Before-and-After Trends for Murder Using Plassmann and Tideman's Results

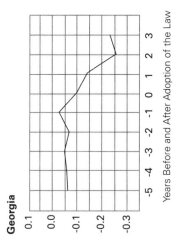

Percentage Difference in Murder Rate Between the State Being Examined and States Without Right-to-Carry Laws

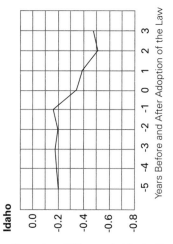

Percentage Difference in Murder Rate Between the State Being Examined and States Without Right-to-Carry Laws

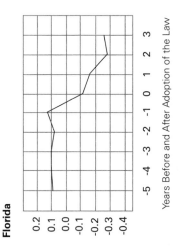

Percentage Difference in Murder Rate Between the State Being Examined and States Without Right-to-Carry Laws

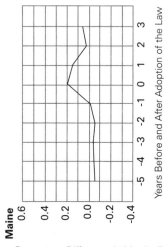

Percentage Difference in Murder Rate Between the State Being Examined and States Without Right-to-Carry Laws

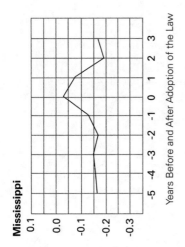

Mississippi

Percentage Difference in Murder Rate
Between the State Being Examined and
States Without Right-to-Carry Laws

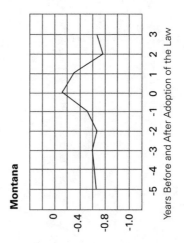

Montana

Percentage Difference in Murder Rate
Between the State Being Examined and
States Without Right-to-Carry Laws

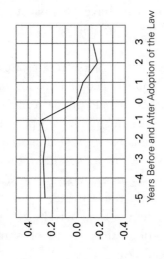

Oregon

Percentage Difference in Murder Rate
Between the State Being Examined and
States Without Right-to-Carry Laws

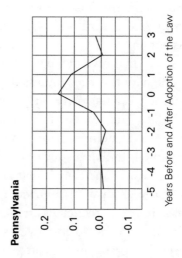

Pennsylvania

Percentage Difference in Murder Rate
Between the State Being Examined and
States Without Right-to-Carry Laws

Appendix Figure 1.1 (continued)

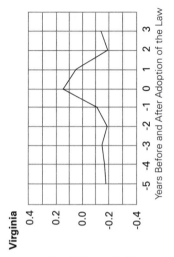

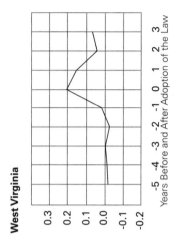

Percentage Difference in Murder Rate
Between the State Being Examined and
States Without Right-to-Carry Laws

Percentage Difference in Murder Rate
Between the State Being Examined and
States Without Right-to-Carry Laws

difficult to obtain guns will impact those who have the lowest gun
ownership rate and the highest suicide rate, which they say is true for
this age group.

Yet, even their own poll data show that gun ownership rates are at
least as high for this age group as it is for younger people.[6] In addition,
a closer look at a narrower age grouping contradicts the pattern that
they predict. The reduced incidence of firearm suicides for persons
over 54 is overwhelmingly driven by the change for just those from
ages 55 to 64, but this subcategory has the lowest suicide rate for
those over age 54 and they have the highest gun ownership rate. The
different age groups experienced apparently random increases and
decreases in firearm suicides after enactment of the law: The groups
aged 35 to 44 years, 45 to 54 years, and older than age 85 all show
increases in firearm suicides after the Brady Act.[7]

As mentioned earlier, a recent study by Mark Duggan disagrees
with my finding that increased gun ownership is associated with
reduced crime rates. In place of using survey data on gun ownership,

Duggan relies on sales of the fourth largest gun magazine, *Guns & Ammo*, and finds that changes in its sales precede by one and two years changes in murder rates. Unfortunately, though, as will be shown in Appendix 2, this seems to be the only gun magazine whose sales exhibit such a relationship. Duggan claims that he focused on this one magazine because he was particularly interested in the impact of handguns on crime and about 53 percent of the magazine's gun product reviews were on handguns.[8] But there are two exclusively handgun-oriented magazines whose sales figures are available, and neither of them is significantly related to murder rates. Only one of the three largest gun magazines shows a statistically significant result, and that implies that increases in magazine sales are associated with fewer murders.[9]

There are other problems with using magazines as a proxy for gun ownership. For example, for *Guns & Ammo*, anywhere from 5 to 20 percent of its national sales in a particular year were purchases by the magazine itself in order to meet its guaranteed sales to advertisers.[10] The copies were then given away for free to dentists' and doctors' offices. Because the purchases were meant to offset any unexpected declines in sales, self-purchases systematically smooth out any national changes. While a precise breakdown of how these free samples are counted towards the sales in different counties is not available, they were very selective and these significant national swings would have produced very large swings in these selected regions. More importantly, these self-purchases were apparently related to factors that helped explain why people might purchase guns, and these factors included changing crime rates. In the final analysis, the claim that this fourth largest gun magazine accurately measures changes in gun ownership is especially questionable since survey data continue to imply that murder rates decline when gun ownership rates rise.[11]

Duggan claims in his Table 12 that my statistically significant results on concealed handguns disappear for several of the violent crime categories when one correctly calculates the statistical significance, but Duggan has simply misreported his own results. To obtain the level of statistical significance for his Column 2, one must divide the coefficients by the reported standard errors. When that is done, four of the five violent crime rates indeed show a statistically significant

AppendixTable 1.1: Reporting the Results on Violent Crime Rates from Critical Studies of My Work (Using the National Coefficients from the Most Critical Studies Listed in Footnote 17 of the Report)

Study	Tables in the Study	Positive Effect	Zero Effect	Negative Effect***
Black and Nagin	Tables 1 & 2			
	(National Effects)	1	8	12
Duggan	Table 12	1	15*	14*
Ludwig	Tables 4 and 5	0	19	0
Ayres and Donohue	Table 1	0	13 (16)**	30 (27)**
Totals		**2**	**55 (58)**	**56 (53)**

*Duggan's study has typos mislabeling the statistical significance of two of his results. See column 2 in table 12 (p. 1110) and the results for rape and aggravated assault. For rape a coefficient of -0.052 and a standard error of 0.0232 produce a t-statistic of 2.24. For aggravated assault a coefficient of -.0699 and a standard error of 0.0277 produce a t-statistic of 2.52. (Mark Duggan, "More Guns, More Crime." *Journal of Political Ecomony*, October, 2001, pp. 1086–1114.

**Because of downward rounding to 1.6, it is not possible to tell whether the t-statistics reported in Ayres and Donahue are statistically significant at the 10 percent level. The values in parentheses assume that a t-statistic of 1.6 is not significant at that level while the first values assume that a t-statistic rounded up to 1.6 is significant at that level. (See Ian Ayres and John Donohue, "Nondiscretionary concealed weapons laws: a case study of statistics, standards of proof, and public policy," *American Law Economics Review* 1999 1: 436–470.

***Some of these negative significant coefficients are a result of the authors replicating my earlier work. If these were removed, the numbers for negative significant coefficients would be as follows: Black and Nagin, 8; Duggan, 9; Ayres and Donohue, 25 (22) andTotals, 42 (39). (Dan Black and Dan Nagin, "Do Right-to-Carry Laws Deter Violent Crime?" *Journal of Legal Studies*, January 1998, pp. 209–220 and Jens Ludwig, "Concealed-Gun-Carrying Laws and Violent Crime," *International Review of Law and Economics*, September 1998, pp. 239–254.)

reduction in crime from the passage of the right-to-carry law, with the t-statistics exceeding at least 2.3 in those four cases.

Two other points need to be made. First, Duggan provides no evidence that the adjustments that he makes are appropriate (indeed, my original paper with Mustard discussed these adjustments). Second, examining the before-and-after trends produces extremely statistically significant results. Duggan chose only to report the results for the before-and-after averages.

To date, four critical papers have been published using national data that follow the change in crime rates as right-to-carry laws are adopted. Besides the paper by Duggan, other pieces have been written by Black and Nagin, Ludwig, and Ayres and Donohue. Appendix Table 1.1 shows the results for the four papers listed in the footnote that I would cite as truly critical (the papers by Black and Nagin, Ayres and Donohue, Duggan, and Ludwig). Out of 113 coefficients reported by these critics, only 2 coefficients imply a statistically sig-

Appendix Figure 1.2: Ayres and Donohue's Examination of Right-to-Carry Concealed Handgun Laws Over the Years from 1977 to 1997

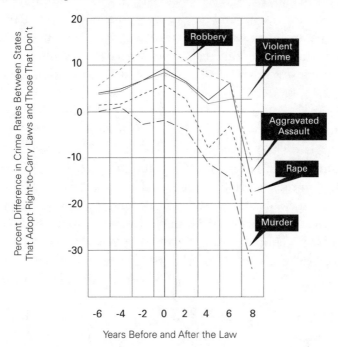

nificant increase in crime after the passage of the law, 55 imply no statistically significant change, and 56 a statistically significant decline in crime. In other words, half the time my results are confirmed, and in only 2 percent of cases are the results reversed—and these are fairly dubious regressions.[12]

It is also possible to provide a listing for Black and Nagin's state-by-state breakdown. At the 10 percent level, three coefficients imply a statistically significant increase, twenty-two no significant change, and fifteen a statistically significant decline.[13] Of course, as mentioned in the introduction to the second section of this book, examining only simple before-and-after averages can be quite misleading, and all these critical estimates report only these estimates.

Finally, there is new research by John Donohue (and an almost identical paper by Ian Ayres and John Donohue) that claims that crime rates actually rise with the passage of right-to-carry laws. They provide results for a variety of specifications using data from 1977 to 1997, but their most general results report the relative crime rates by year, before and after the adoption of the law, showing significant declines in all violent crime categories with patterns which are very similar to those shown for Plassmann and Tideman (see Appendix Figure 1.2).

Donohue doesn't use simple dummies for each year. Instead they aggregate years into two-year groupings (Year Zero and Year One, Year Two and Year Three, Year Four and Year Five, Year Six and Year Seven, and Years Eight or More). A similar aggregation is used for years prior to the adoption of the law. This is an unusual approach, but they do it to obscure in their results the large drop that occurs between the year of passage and the first full year that the law is in effect for their sample period. Combining Year Zero and Year One together produces an average of the crime rate in those two years and obscures the peak in crime rates that occurred immediately before the law went into effect.

Donohue argues that these results provide no evidence that right-to-carry laws reduce violent crime because the coefficients for crimes like robbery are positive for up to six to seven years after the enact-ment of the law.[14] Yet, this is not how these coefficients should be interpreted. A positive coefficient implies that the crime rates in right-to-carry states are higher than non-right-to-carry states, but if the coefficient becomes smaller after the law, it means that the crime rates in right-to-carry states are falling relative to the crime rates in non-right-to-carry states. The crime rate in right-to-carry states is still higher, but not by as much as had previously been the case. Appendix Figure 1.2 provides fairly dramatic evidence that even Ayres and Donohue's own results show that violent crime rates fall after right-to-carry laws are adopted.

Appendix Figures 1.3 to 1.8 show the same breakdown for the 1977 to 2000 data that Ayres and Donohue reported, and the figures show a large drop in violent crime rates when right-to-carry laws are adopted. While the year-by-year breakdown is by far the most reliable, the figures also show the changes in crime rates predicted by three other types of empirical tests (whether the law is in effect or not, a

Appendix Figure 1.3: Violent Crime: Weighted Least Squares Estimates Using County-Level Data from 1977 to 2000

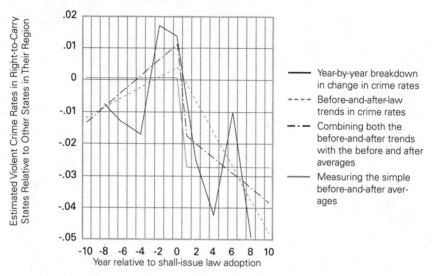

Appendix Figure 1.4: Murder: Weighted Least Squares Estimates Using County-Level Data from 1977 to 2000

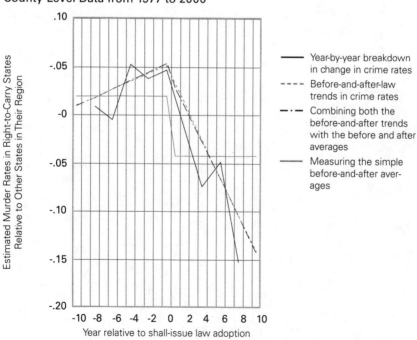

Appendix Figure 1.5: Rape: Weighted Least Squares Estimates Using County-Level Data from 1977 to 2000

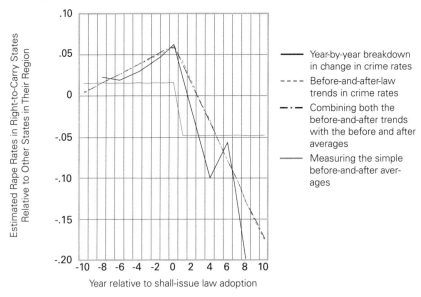

Appendix Figure 1.6: Robbery: Weighted Least Squares Estimates Using County-Level Data from 1977 to 2000

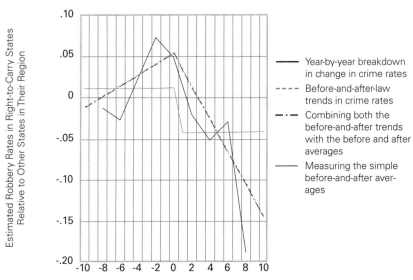

Appendix Figure 1.7: Aggravated Assault: Weighted Least Squares
Estimates Using County-Level Data from 1977 to 2000

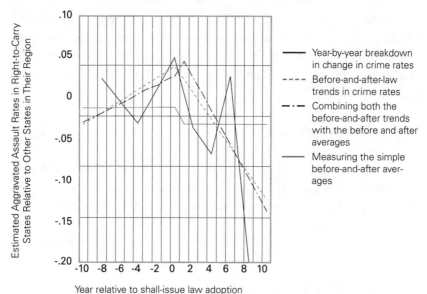

Year relative to shall-issue law adoption

Appendix Figure 1.8: Property Crimes: Weighted Least Squares Estimates
Using County-Level Data from 1977 to 2000

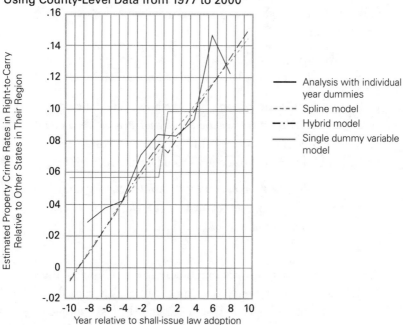

Year relative to shall-issue law adoption

comparison of before-and-after law trends in crime, and a "hybrid" model that combines those three specifications).

Despite all the work that has been done on the topic of concealed handguns, it is remarkable that no academic study has found a bad effect from these laws. It is even more remarkable that no one has challenged the results that I have gotten for all the other different gun control laws.

B. The Political Debate

> I know that a lot of his [Lott's] studies have been paid for by the gun lobby. ....I think that he is trying to sell guns here, and I think that he is trying to increase the gun lobby's ability to carry out their work.
>
> [Lott] talks about the National Association of Chiefs of Police, which is funded by the gun lobby.

Statements by John Shanks of the Brady Campaign during a debate on KMOX radio (St. Louis) on May 14, 2002

> Gun control advocates say the gun industry funded [John Lott's] research.

Regina Brett, "Having a gun, does it end fear?" Plain Dealer (Cleveland, Ohio), May 23, 2002

> He's argued after the tragedy at Jonesboro, Ark., the school shooting there, that if the teachers had been armed, they could have prevented the shooting. This is extremist, someone who believes that everyone in society should be armed at all times.

Matt Bennett, Spokesman for Americans for Gun Safety Foundation, appearance on Fox News Channel's Special Report with Brit Hume, July 5, 2002

> The current debate is based upon a fellow in Chicago, John Lott, who told us if everybody on the street was armed, we would have an appropriate response. And there's a couple of

problems I have with that. The first one is that Mr. Lott has done a couple of different studies. He found that if we take law enforcement [agents] and they happen to be minorities or women, and we put them on the street, rather than crime going down, it actually goes up. And my feeling is that African-Americans and women are part of the citizenry, so he is inconsistent with that.

> *Charlie Blek Jr., director of the Bell Campaign from*
> *www.apbnews.com, Friday, September 24, 1999*[15]

Gun control advocates all too frequently use these types of arguments in debates.[16] These are old attacks, and I have addressed them more in depth before. However, given that gun control organizations, such as the Brady Campaign and the Bell Campaign, continue to make these statements, I should briefly respond here.[17] Unfortunately, no matter how many times I deny or address these charges, they are still made.

The claim that the gun industry funded my research was originally made while I was at the University of Chicago Law School and was based upon the fact that the conservative Olin Foundation had given money to the University of Chicago Law School for law and economics. Stephen Chapman, a columnist in the *Chicago Tribune*, studied these claims back in 1996 and wrote:[18]

> Another problem is that the [Olin] foundation didn't 1) choose Lott as a fellow, 2) give him money or 3) approve his topic. It made a grant to the law school's law and economics program (one of many grants it makes to top universities around the country). A committee at the law school then awarded the fellowship to Lott, one of many applicants in a highly competitive process.
>
> Even the committee had nothing to do with his choice of topics. The fellowship was to allow Lott—a prolific scholar who has published some 75 academic articles—to do research on whatever subject he chose....
>
> To accept their conspiracy theory, you have to believe the following: A company that derives a small share of its earnings

> from sporting ammunition somehow prevailed on an indepen-
> dent family foundation to funnel money to a scholar who was
> willing to risk his academic reputation (and, since he does not
> yet have tenure, his future employment) by fudging data to
> serve the interests of the firearms lobby—and one of the pre-
> mier research universities in the world cooperated in the fraud.

Before the gun control organizations started making these charges, I
had no knowledge of any details about the Olin Foundation. As Chapman notes, I had not myself raised any money from the organization
nor had I any contact with it. The money was given to the university
and not to me.

Even after I left the University of Chicago, Handgun Control, Inc.
continued to try and show that some link existed between the Olin
Foundation and me. Doug Weil, then research director at Handgun
Control, went so far as contacting the Yale Law School to find if my
new position was in anyway funded by the Olin Foundation.

Americans for Gun Safety may view me as an "extremist," but just
because I am concerned about the unintended consequences of gun-
free zones does not imply that I believe that "everyone in society
should be armed at all times." As Chapter 6 noted, even if only a fraction of people carry guns (say 5 or 10 percent), in large enough groups
the probability that someone will be available to defend others is
close to 100 percent. One doesn't need one hundred armed people to
stop someone intent on causing harm. Even a few people unknown to
the attacker can make all the difference. My research has also found
that certain people benefit more than others from owning or carrying
guns. Among those benefiting the most are poor blacks living in high
crime urban areas and people who are relatively weaker physically,
such as women.

The Brady Campaign (their predecessor, Handgun Control, Inc.),
the Million Mom March, and the Violence Policy Center have frequently claimed that I supposedly "found that if we take law enforcement [agents] and they happen to be minorities or women, and we put
them on the street, rather than crime going down, it actually goes
up." A Violence Policy Center representative made these claims again
as recently as October 24, 2002, on the CNN*fn* cable news network.

My research analyzed the impact of consent decrees, decrees which had been imposed on cities by the federal government, and which reduced reliance on cognitive skill tests and physical strength tests in hiring police officers. First, the questions posed in my research were not about whether hiring African-Americans or women increased crime. Instead, my research examined how crime rates compared in cities that hired minority officers with and without consent decrees being imposed. The change in crime rates was thus a question about *under what rules* they were hired, not the hiring of these groups per se. Indeed, I tried to point out that the relationship I found was largely driven by the reduced quality of *all* new officers, including whites and Asians. In the abstract I noted that "this apparently arises because lower hiring standards involved in recruiting more minority officers reduces the quality of both new minority and new non-minority offi-cers."[19] Secondly, I found little evidence that hiring women had any "consistent evidence that crime rates rise" when physical strength standards were set so that there were equal pass rates for men and women.[20]

My research was concerned with evaluating how best to increase the share of different groups in police departments. The discussion was over whether it is best to create different standards for different groups or whether one should alter the content of tests to create equal pass rates, and found that altering the tests so as to create equal pass rates generated increased crime that primarily harmed minority residents in high-crime cities.

OTHER MEASURES
OF GUN OWNERSHIP

A. MAGAZINE SALES

Academics have used many proxies for gun ownership rates. They have ranged from the number of accidental gun deaths or gun suicides to the sales of gun magazines to survey data. Each measure has some problem. For example, accidental gun deaths seem to be more likely to tell you the level of gun ownership among criminals than the general population. Gun owners may be reluctant to tell pollsters that they own a gun. This might stem from either a concern that someone will try to take away their guns, or that it is not socially acceptable to own one. The changing social acceptability might help explain the growing gap between married men and women and their reported rates of gun ownership. Underreporting is also likely to be greater among those who own guns illegally.

For a couple of decades, magazine sales have been used to proxy gun ownership. Even a registration system produces a very imprecise measure of gun ownership, and the guns that are registered are unlikely to be the guns which are producing criminal problems. In Canada, around 2 million people registered their guns when surveys had indicated between 5 and 7 million owned guns prior to the registration process. After registration began, surveys indicated only about 2.4 million people admitting to owning a gun, though it is surprising that more people would admit to a surveyor that they illegally own an unregistered weapon.[1]

A recent study by Mark Duggan revisits the issue of using magazine sales and relies on one magazine: *Guns & Ammo*, the fourth largest gun magazine by sales. He provides two reasons for using this particular magazine: 1) "[S]ales data for this magazine are available annually at both the state and the county levels" and 2) "More important, *Guns & Ammo* is focused relatively more on handguns than [*American Rifleman, American Hunter,* and *North American Hunters*]."[2] It is indeed true that 42 percent of *American Rifleman's* product reviews from 1981 to 1998 focused on handguns, 11 percent less than the product reviews done by *Guns & Ammo*.[3] Handgun reviews in the *American Hunter* and *North American Hunters* are very infrequent. But if the 11 percent higher rate of handgun reviews is important enough to single out this publication, it is possible to examine gun magazines whose product reviews are 100 percent devoted to handguns. The two biggest exclusively handgun-oriented magazines are *Handguns* (published by the same company that publishes *Guns & Ammo*) and *American Handgunner*.[4] *Handguns* magazine's sales are also available at the county level.[5] Florenz Plassmann and I have used this data elsewhere, and we could not find any relationship between magazine sales and murder or other crime rates.[6] Duggan doesn't seem to attach a lot of significance to whether the data is available at the county level in part because he says that the results are very similar for both state and county data.

Duggan's claim is that the presence of guns doesn't make violent crime more or less likely, but only makes it more violent and more likely to produce a fatality. Increased sales of *Guns & Ammo* is shown to precede by one or two years the number of gun homicides, but it is not significantly related to any other crime category.

A little background on the subscribers to *Guns & Ammo* might be helpful. Generally, these subscribers hardly fit the normal description of a typical criminal. They have relatively high family incomes and are well educated, with 63 percent having a college education, 46 percent holding professional/managerial jobs, and over 10 percent working for the police or military.[7] The types of guns owned by subscribers is also reflective of the close to 50-50 split between handgun and long-gun reviews: 93 percent own handguns, 89 percent rifles, 81 percent shotguns, 52 percent pellet guns. A full 98.8 percent of subscribers

AppendixTable 2.1: The Sizes of Different Gun Magazines

Name	Average Annual Sales 1990–1999	Average Annual National Sales 1990–1999
American Handgunner	152,541	147,110
American Hunter	1,212,882	1,027,854
American Rifleman	1,478,541	1,328,805
Guns & Ammo	560,276	569,109
Handguns	143,055	148,308
North American Hunter	584,052	766,326

already own a gun. The average subscriber owns 15.4 guns (excluding pellet guns). Even if they inclined to commit a crime, it hardly seems like their ability to do so is dependent upon obtaining another gun.

Duggan has declined to provide anyone with his data. So I purchased state level sales data for the four largest gun magazines: *Guns & Ammo, American Rifleman, American Hunter,* and *North American Hunter.*[8] I also obtained data for the two handguns magazines that sales data are available for: *Handguns* and *American Handgunner.*

Appendix Table 2.1 shows the relative sizes of these different magazines over the last decade. The two largest dwarf *Guns & Ammo* with two to three times more sales. *North American Hunter* actually started out the decade less than half the size of *Guns & Ammo,* but by 1999 *North American Hunter* had a 35 percent higher circulation. The exclusively handgun-oriented magazines averaged only around 150,000 sales during the decade, and they have remained fairly constant in terms of size.

An important first question is: How closely do the different magazine sales numbers track gun ownership surveys? Gun-magazine sales to consumers may well track changes in future purchases, but they may be by people who already own guns. And more importantly, what is listed as sales by the Audit Bureau of Circulation is not always sales to customers. In order to keep circulation promises to advertisers, a nontrivial portion of sales (something between 5 and 20 percent for *Guns & Ammo*) is actually to the magazine itself.[9] The self-purchased copies are then distributed free to doctors' offices and other venues in a few dozen counties. The counties selected to receive these free copies are picked based upon factors that could stimulate future sales. Among those factors were high hunting rates or increased crime, and thus the possibility of increased demand for guns for self-defense. This is not a problem with magazines that are sold by the NRA to its members, since their sales are not dependent on newsstands and are more predictable.

With 99 percent of *Guns & Ammo* subscribers already owning a gun, changes in subscriptions seem much more likely to tell us that existing gun owners are purchasing an additional gun than it is to tell us that non-gun owners are buying a gun. It is difficult to see how more *Guns & Ammo* magazine sales could possibly proxy for more people getting access to guns.

There is also the issue of what determines magazine sales. With the Internet and other sources of information, drops in magazine sales might not necessarily signal a drop in gun sales. Likewise, higher paper or postage costs might produce a substitution away from magazines towards other sources of information. Thus it is not surprising that the changes in gun-magazine circulation over time and across states track very closely the changes in non-gun magazine circulation. What is surprising is that the total sales of the largest five non-gun magazines explain as much or more of the variation in the sales of the *American Rifleman, American Hunter,* and *North American Hunter* than does *Guns & Ammo.*[10]

Appendix Table 2.2 examines whether changes in gun-magazine sales are related to changes in gun ownership rates. Changes in sales of the six gun magazines are related to the gun ownership rate in a state.[11] Information on gun ownership rates is from the National Opinion Research Corporation's General Social Survey. Survey data was readily available from 1977 to 1998, though it is not available for every year and the sample size is relatively small.[12] While I have used the larger CBS News General Election Exit Poll or the Voter News Survey in the past,[13] I will use the General Social Survey here because Duggan references it.[14] Two different measures of gun ownership were derived from General Social Survey: a simple rate at which people own guns and the rate at which households owned guns.[15]

The regressions in Appendix Table 2.2 attempted to account for the average differences in gun ownership across states and any national changes in gun ownership rates across years. What the table shows is that the gun magazines that most closely proxy the survey data are the two NRA publications, *American Hunter* and *American Rifle-*

Appendix Table 2.2: Are Changes in Gun Magazine Sales Related to Changes in Gun Ownership Rates as Measured by Poll Data?

Name	Percent Change in Individual Gun Ownership Rates from Increasing Magazine Sales One Year Earlier by 1 Percent	Percent Change in the Rate That Guns are Owned in Households from Increasing Magazine Sales One Year Earlier by 1 Percent
Guns & Ammo	0.12%	0.28%
American Handgunner	0.11%	0.19%
Handguns	0.47%*	0.50%*
American Hunter	0.34%*	0.58%***
American Rifleman	0.52%**	0.79%***
North American Hunter	0.02%	0.10%

*** The result is significant at the 1 percent level for a two-tailed t-test.
** The result is significant at the 5 percent level for a two-tailed t-test.
* The result is significant at the 10 percent level for a two-tailed t-test.

man, and *Handguns* magazine. For these three types of magazines, increasing magazine sales by 1 percent is associated with an increased gun ownership rate of anywhere from 0.34 to 0.52 percent.

Guns & Ammo is positively related to the survey data, but the relationship is not statistically significant and is only about a third to a half as large as for the three most closely related magazines. Duggan provides a similar analysis using only *Guns & Ammo* and claims to provide a significant positive relationship between survey data and magazine sales, but while he uses the data at the state level, he weights the polling data by regional, and not state level, demographic characteristics. Of the six magazines, *Guns & Ammo* ranked fourth in its ability to explain changes in the survey data, and its effect was never statistically different than zero.

So, do increases in either gun magazine sales or survey data precede changes in murder? To answer this I added in the sales of the different gun magazines into the crime regressions reported earlier in this book and in *More Guns, Less Crime*. This allows us to account for the impact that other factors have on murder rates. These include: the arrest rate for murder, the death penalty execution rate, population density, unemployment rate, poverty rate, per capita income, per capita welfare payments, and detailed demographic information with the share of the population by age, sex, and race.[16]

AppendixTable 2.3: Do Sales of Gun Magazines Precede Changes in Murder Rate?

Name	Percent Change in Murder Rate from Increasing Magazine Sales One Year Earlier by 1 Percent	Percent Change in Murder Rate from Increasing Magazine Sales Two Years Earlier by 1 Percent
Guns & Ammo	0.25% ***	0.17% **
American Handgunner	0.04%	0.03%
Handguns	0.10%	0.002%
American Hunter	0.19%	-0.31% *
American Rifleman	0.32%	-0.12%
North American Hunter	-0.11%	-0.08%

*** The result is significant at the 1 percent level for a two-tailed t-test.
** The result is significant at the 5 percent level for a two-tailed t-test.
* The result is significant at the 10 percent level for a two-tailed t-test.

The results are reported in Appendix Table 2.3. If more sales of a gun magazine lead in a year or two to higher murder rates, it appears to only occur for the fourth largest magazine, *Guns & Ammo*, where a 1 percent increase in magazine sales increases murder rates by 0.24 percent the following year and by 0.17 percent two years later. What is puzzling with these results is that handguns are used to commit most murders (indeed that is the reason that Duggan claims to focus on *Guns & Ammo*). Yet, the relationship between the two purely handgun magazines and murder rates is essentially zero, with coefficients that are less than 18 percent of the size of the *Guns & Ammo* coefficients in three of the four cases. Almost the same results are obtained when homicide or firearm homicide data are used. *Guns & Ammo* magazine is the only magazine that ever implies a statistically significant relationship for both previous years of sales.

The same process is repeated by replacing the magazine sales with the General Social Survey polling data on gun ownership (see Appendix Table 2.4). Both the individual ownership rate and the household ownership rate data imply that increased gun ownership reduces murder, though only the measure of household gun ownership is statistically significant at the 5 percent level. Again, looking at homicide rates or homicides with firearms produces similar results.

Appendix Table 2.4: How is Gun Ownership Survey Data Related
to Murder Rates?

	Percent Change in the Murder Rate from Increasing the Percent of the Population Owning Guns by 1 Percent
GSS polling data weighted by population demographics in each state	-0.05%
GSS polling data on whether you live in a household that owns a gun,† weighted by demographics in each state	-0.12%**

*** The result is significant at the 1 percent level for a two-tailed t-test.
** The result is significant at the 5 percent level for a two-tailed t-test.
* The result is significant at the 10 percent level for a two-tailed t-test.
† Same as the first row except that married women are assumed to own guns at the same rate as married men

There is another result of Duggan's that does not stand up to close scrutiny. He argues that the presence of guns makes existing crimes more likely to result in a fatality and that guns should have only "a much weaker relationship" to "other crime rates."[17] While the other gun sales measures are pretty much unrelated to any of the crime categories, both the single and two year lags of *Guns & Ammo* sales seem pretty much statistically related to virtually all the different crime categories (Appendix Table 2.5). In the case of auto theft and robbery, the single year lag in magazine sales predicts an increase in future crime as large or larger than the *Guns & Ammo* magazine sales had for murder. Auto theft is particularly puzzling since by definition this crime category does not involve direct contact between the victims and criminals and rarely involves the use of a gun.

I also re-estimated these relationships for the other gun magazines. Generally, the other gun magazines rarely imply that past gun sales precede any type of change in crime rates.[18] The partial exception to that rule involves property crimes. Of the forty possible lagged sales coefficients for the other five magazines for the four crime categories, eight are positive and three are negative and significant. One can also contrast these results with those using the General Social Survey. The survey measure of gun ownership in the home implies that a higher

AppendixTable 2.5: Do the sales of Guns & Ammo Magazine Precede
Changes in Other Violent Crime Rates and Different Property Crime Rates?

Name	Percent Change in the Specific Crime Rate from Increasing Guns & Ammo Magazine Sales One Year Earlier by by 1 Percent	Percent Change in the Specific Crime Rate from Increasing Guns & Ammo Magazine Sales Two Years Earlier by by 1 Percent
Different Crime Rates	0.14%**	0.10%
Violent Crime	0.15%***	0.12%**
Rape	0.25%***	0.21%***
Aggravated Assault	0.04%	0.13%*
Property Crime	0.12%***	0.13%***
Auto Theft	0.32%***	0.14%*
Burglary	0.08%	0.14%***
Larceny	0.11%***	0.13%***

*** The result is significant at the 1 percent level for a two-tailed t-test.
** The result is significant at the 5 percent level for a two-tailed t-test.
* The result is significant at the 10 percent level for a two-tailed t-test.

gun ownership rate is associated with fewer violent and property crimes. Only murder and rape were statistically significant at better than the 10 percent level. Each 1 percent increase in gun ownership is associated with a 0.04 percent reduction in both murder and rape rates.

Appendix Table 2.5 raises another possibility. If *Guns & Ammo* magazine sales are so closely related to all the different crime rates, people who bought the magazine may have done so simply because they anticipated crime rates to rise.

The results suggest few options. Even if one accepts that the positive impact that *Guns & Ammo* magazine sales have on murder is because it is the only true proxy for handgun sales (even though two other magazines focus exclusively on handguns), there is still the problem of explaining why *Guns & Ammo* magazine sales produce an even bigger impact on auto theft than murder, and why its sales precede such strong and significant increases in all the property crime rates. There is also the evidence that other gun magazines are even more significantly related to survey data on gun ownership.

Yet the real puzzle is to think of a theory for why a study would only look at the fourth largest gun magazine to predict handgun sales. One is tempted to think that this single magazine (*Guns & Ammo*) was just accidentally related to future crime rates.

B. Gun Homicides and Suicides

Other proxies for gun ownership have included firearm homicide or suicide rates, and sometimes the two measures are combined. While these are plausible measures, there are also significant problems with them. For example, two jurisdictions may have the same firearms ownership rates simply because they have different levels of drug gang violence. If I were to compare a city and rural area with the same gun ownership rate, it would not be particularly surprising that firearm homicides would differ. Similar problems exist for firearm suicides. For example, we know that women and men as well as African-Americans and whites commit suicides with guns at different rates. Different age groups commit suicides with guns at different rates. At least for suicides, controlling for extensive demographic information can help account for these differences, though detailed demographics are never accounted for in this work.

One recent paper receiving significant attention using these measures of gun ownership was published in the *Journal of Trauma*.[19] Britain's *Economist* magazine announced the study proved that "More guns kill more children."[20] The study, which received no critical comments in the press, examined accidental gun deaths, gun suicides, and gun homicides of five to fourteen year olds from 1988 to 1997. While the *Journal of Trauma* study did account for the percent of state population living in poverty, the percent of the adult population with at least a high school education, and the percent of state populations living in urban areas, it did not account for the average differences across states or years that we argued in Chapter 5 were necessary, nor many other variables such as any demographics or income. Given that they only have three control variables, it is particularly important that they try to account for these average differences across states that might be attributable to factors other than the adult homicide or suicide rates.

In fact, their results are entirely determined by one factor: their failure to account for these average differences across states. Appendix Table 2.6 replicates the *Journal of Trauma* for the measures of gun ownership based upon the sum of gun homicides and suicides or gun suicides with their limited set of control variables. In place of household

Appendix Table 2.6: Examining the *Journal of Trauma's* Measures of Gun Ownership Using the Control Variables Without Accounting for Average Differences Across States and Years, Also Using State-Level Survey Data on Gun Ownership

These estimates account for only the percent of the state's population living in poverty, the percent of the adult population with at least a high school education, and population density per square mile.

	MEASURES OF GUN OWNERSHIP				
	Homicides and suicides with guns by those over age 20	Suicides with guns by those over age 20	Accidental gun deaths involving those over age 20	Family or household gun ownership rates in states using NORC data	Individual gun ownership rates by state using the NORC data
Accidental gun deaths for 5- to 9-year-olds	0.09%***	0.17%***	1.1%***	-0.12%	-0.08%**
Accidental gun deaths for 10- to 14-year-olds	0.08%***	0.13%***	0.92%***	0.08%	0.39%**
Gun suicides for those 15 years old	0.05%***	0.14%***	0.4%***	0.0095%	0.23%
Gun homicides for 5- to 9-year-olds	0.033%***	0.07%***	0.5%***	0.11%	0.23%
Gun homicides for 10- to 14-year-olds	0.06%***	0.07%***	0.4%***	-0.21%*	0.19%

*** The result is significant at the 1 percent level for a two-tailed t-test.
** The result is significant at the 5 percent level for a two-tailed t-test.
* The result is significant at the 10 percent level for a two-tailed t-test.

Appendix Table 2.7: Examining the *Journal of Trauma's* Measures of Gun Ownership Using the Control Variables Used Throughout This Book.

These estimates account for not only the average differences across states and years in the number of gun shows but the state population, unemployment rate, poverty rate, per capita income, per capita welfare payment, per capita unemployment insurance, average income support payments to those over 65 years of age, and the thirty-six different demographic categories by age, sex, and race that we have used throughout this book.

MEASURES OF GUN OWNERSHIP

	Homicides and suicides with guns by those over age 20	Suicides with guns by those Over age 20	Accidental gun deaths involving those over age 20	Family or household gun ownership rates in states using NORC data	Individual gun ownership rates by state using the NORC data
Accidental gun deaths for 5- to 9-year-olds	0.004%	-0.1%	0.19%	0.16%	0.05%
Accidental gun deaths for 10- to 14-year-olds	0.02%	0.04%	0.16%	0.04%	0.21%
Gun suicides for those 15 years old	0.03%*	0.05%	0.25%	-0.04%	0.04%
Gun homicides for 5- to 9-year-olds	0.014%	-0.004%	0.3%	-0.16%	-0.3%
Gun homicides for 10- to 14-year-olds	0.05%*	-0.002%	0.08%	-0.26%	-0.1%

*** The result is significant at the 1 percent level for a two-tailed t-test.
** The result is significant at the 5 percent level for a two-tailed t-test.
* The result is significant at the 10 percent level for a two-tailed t-test.

survey data for a "nonrandom" selection of states or their use of regional, instead of state, level National Opinion Research Center survey data, I used National Opinion Research Center state level survey data at the family and individual level for all available states. I also included the number of adult accidental gun deaths as a similar measure to the gun homicides and suicides.

Using the *Journal of Trauma* methods, the first three measures (gun homicides and suicides, gun suicides, and accidental gun deaths for adults) are all statistically significantly related to juvenile accidental gun deaths, gun suicides, and gun homicides. Yet, when survey data is used for all states, even their limited control variables show little relationship between gun survey data and the harm from guns. While family gun ownership rates are significantly negatively related to gun homicides for 10- to 14-year-olds and individual gun ownership rates are significantly positively relatively to accidental gun deaths for 10- to 14-year-olds, none of the other types of gun deaths are related to the survey data.

Yet, Appendix Table 2.7 shows how sensitive their results are to controlling for the controls used in this book. While including factors such as demographics reduces the statistical significance and size of the effects, trying to account for the average differences across states by itself essentially eliminates any statistical significance. The results are not statistically significant, but all the survey data indicate a negative relationship between family or individual gun ownership and gun homicides.

C. Conclusion

It is difficult to measure gun ownership, but one has to wonder why anyone would take seriously the idea of using only one gun magazine's sales to proxy for ownership. There are also serious concerns about using gun homicide or suicide data for adults to predict gun homicides, accidents, or suicides among juveniles and then interpret a higher rate of gun deaths among juveniles as due to higher gun ownership rates. However, even putting the interpretations aside, the relationships using gun homicides or suicides disappear when even the most basic controls that we discussed in Chapter 5 are accounted for.

Survey data, which would appear to be the most obvious measure of gun ownership, consistently show a negative relationship between gun ownership and homicides or murders, though only higher family gun ownership rates imply a statistically significantly reduction in murder rates.

D. Survey on Defensive Gun Use

Below is the survey that was used to identify defensive gun use.

Hello, my name is _____, and I am a student at _____ working on a very brief survey on crime. The survey should take about one minute. Could I please ask you a few questions?

1) During the last year, were you ever threatened with physical violence or harmed by another person or were you present when someone else faced such a situation?

(Threats do not have to be spoken threats. Include physically menacing attacks such as an assault, robbery or rape.)

    a) Yes
    b) No
    c) Uncertain
    d) Declined to answer

(Just ask people "YES" or "NO." If they answer "NO" or "Decline to answer," go directly to demographic questions. If people are "Uncertain" or say "YES," proceed with Question 2.)

2) How many times did these threats of violence or crimes occur? _____

3) Which of the following best describe how you responded to the threat(s) or crime(s)? Pick one from the following list that best described your behavior or the person who you were with for each case faced.

    a) behaved passively
    b) used your fists
    c) ran away

    d) screamed or called for help
    e) used a gun
    f) used a knife
    g) used mace
    h) used a baseball bat or club
    i) other

(Rotate these answers (a) through (h), place a number for 0 to whatever for each option. Stop going through list if they volunteer answer(s) that account for the number of threats that they faced.)

4) This is only done if the respondent answers "e" (a gun) to Question 3.

If a gun was used, did you or the other person you were with:
    a) brandish it
    b) fire a warning shot
    c) fire at the attacker
    d) injure the attacker
    e) kill the attacker

(Again, place a number for 0 to whatever number is appropriate for each option. Rotate answers.)

5) Were you or the person you were with harmed by the attack(s)?
    a) Yes
    b) No
    c) Refused to answer

(We obviously have the area code for location, write down sex from the voice if possible, otherwise ask.)

Two demographic questions asked of all participants:
    What is your race? black, white, Hispanic, Asian, Other.
    What is your age by decade? 20s, 30s, 40s, so on.

Question for surveyor: Is there any reason for you to believe that the person was not being honest with you?

a) Didn't believe respondent at all

b) Had some concerns

c) Had no serious concerns

The survey was conducted over eight evenings (Mondays through Thursdays) during November and December 2002. When a surveyor received no answer, a busy signal, or an answering machine, they called that telephone number two more times on different days in order to try to reach the party.

In all defensive gun uses, the surveyors were debriefed that night or the following morning about the call. All the respondents in these cases had volunteered extensive details of what happened with the defensive gun use. None of the defensive gun uses recorded involved defensive uses by police. A number of calls (from the surveyor's end) were randomly monitored as they were made. Two of our surveyors had previous experience conducting telephone surveys and they went through the survey with the surveyors before everyone started. As a result of callbacks, over 50 percent of telephone numbers produced completed interviews. Finally, at least two respondents for each surveyor who had indicated that they had felt threatened over the last year were called back by me to double check their answers. In almost all cases it was possible to reach the respondent and in all cases the answers matched what had been given to the surveyor.

I assume that there were 206.99 million adults over age nineteen in December 2002 (the census estimated that there were 288.68 million Americans at that time, and the 2000 Census indicated that 71.7 percent are over nineteen years of age). 1,015 people were surveyed, and the estimates were weighted by race (black, white, other) and gender. The telephone numbers were collectd from a program called Select Phone Pro Version 2.4 made by infoUSA. The telephone numbers were randomly selected by area code so that the same precentage of each area code was sampled. Defensive gun uses by law enforcement were excluded. The confidence interval for these surveys islarge for brandishing, but combining the 41 defensive-gun uses reduces it. Kleck and Kates discuss other surveys.

Overall the survey results here are similar to one I conducted primarily during January 1997 which identified 2.1 million defensive

gun uses, and that in 98 percent of them, the gun was simply brandished. The time of James Knowles, Jill Mitchell, Carl Westine, Susan
Follett, Matt Trager, Arnaud Bonraisin, Andrei Zlate, and Sandra Long
in conducting this survey was greatly appreciated.

SUPPLEMENTAL TABLES FOR CHAPTERS 6, 7, and 8

Appendix 6.1: Examining the Means for States That Did Not Change Their Concealed Handgun Laws During the 1977 to 1997 Period Using State Averages to Compute Rates

Year	Murders in Multiple Victim Public Shootings Per 100,000 People	Injuries in Multiple Victim Public Shootings Per 100,000 People	Murders and Injuries in Multiple Victim Public Shootings Per 100,000 People
(1)	(2)	(3)	(4)
1977	0.0131	0.0840	0.0970
1978	0.0252	0.0543	0.0794
1979	0.0031	0.0294	0.0325
1980	0.0020	0.0060	0.0080
1981	0.0282	0.0215	0.0496
1982	0.0145	0.0504	0.0649
1983	0.0036	0.0059	0.0095
1984	0.0120	0.0250	0.0370
1985	0.0095	0.0126	0.0221
1986	0.0052	0.0090	0.0143
1987	0.0149	0.0213	0.0362
1988	0.0238	0.0250	0.0487
1989	0.0168	0.0232	0.0400
1990	0.0038	0.0103	0.0141
1991	0.0153	0.0113	0.0266
1992	0.0105	0.0139	0.0244
1993	0.0212	0.0156	0.0368
1994	0.0150	0.0092	0.0242
1995	0.0070	0.0034	0.0104
1996	0.1061	0.3432	0.4494
1997	0.0627	0.1142	0.1768

Number of Shootings Per 100,000 People	Number of Murders in Public Shootings	Number of Injuries in Public Shootings	Number of Murders and Injuries in Public Shootings	Number of Shootings
(5)	(6)	(7)	(8)	(9)
0.0059	19	35	54	5
0.0148	14	10	24	7
0.0069	10	19	29	7
0.0015	5	11	16	3
0.0195	21	29	50	18
0.0097	12	72	84	8
0.0048	5	11	16	8
0.0081	31	52	83	12
0.0067	15	16	31	9
0.0052	11	24	35	11
0.0115	18	26	44	15
0.0122	32	42	74	18
0.0140	21	58	79	15
0.0047	16	38	54	16
0.0043	29	30	59	8
0.0053	27	43	70	14
0.0072	73	61	134	25
0.0087	13	19	32	9
0.0033	13	7	20	7
0.1421	72	194	266	89
0.0446	55	94	149	41

Appendix 6.2: More Detailed Set of Regression Coefficients from the
Simple Estimate Reported in Table 6.5 (Number of observations = 1045)

Exogenous Variables	Column 3 Explaining Total Deaths and Injuries		Column 4 Explaining the Number of Shootings	
	Incidence Rate Ratio	Absolute z-statistic	Incidence Rate Ratio	Absolute z-statistic
Shall Issue Law Dummy	0.2151	9.609	0.3280486	3.82
Arrest Rate for Murder	0.9960666	2.942	0.9952213	1.818
Execution Rate	0.9715	1.209	0.9931	0.505
Waiting Period Dummy	0.8975358	0.71	4.198896	1.515
Waiting Period in Days	0.9939132	0.584	0.6725213	1.425
Waiting Period in Days Squared	1.014414	0.09	1.016592	0.982
One-gun-a-month Law	1.109443	0.191	0.8748271	0.144
Safe Storage Gun Law	1.073774	0.459	0.8250622	0.628
Penalty for using a gun in a commission of crime	2.91E+13	3.078	0.6718624	1.166
State Population	0.9999999	0.712	1	0.92
State Population Squared	1	1.573	1	0.243
Real Per Capita Personal Income	1.000023	0.239	1.000258	1.355
Real Per Capita Income Maintenance	1.005806	3.131	1.002375	0.666
Real Per Capita Unemployment Insurance Payment	1.001974	1.136	0.9986415	0.364
Real Retirement Payments Per Person Over 65	0.9998008	0.612	0.9997663	0.378
State Unemployment Rate	1.343001	6.553	1.24501	2.424
State Poverty Rate	0.9480791	2.37	1.026594	0.617
Percent of the Population That Is:				
Black Males 10-19 Yrs. old	0.0309393	0.992	0.2262022	0.21
Black Females 10-19 Yrs. old	5341.427	2.433	137.6209	0.704
White Males 10-19 Yrs. old	23.66847	1.9	25.9636	0.941
White Females 10-19 Yrs. old	1.27E+01	1.2	0.0341304	0.939
Other Males 10-19 Yrs. old	8.28E+08	4.998	1891463	1.775
Other Females 10-19 Yrs. old	1.70E+13	6.707	3.23E+08	1.996
Black Males 20-29 Yrs. old	0.8167172	0.108	0.1138905	0.58
Black Females 20-29 Yrs. old	20.24739	1.549	69.20485	1.09
White Males 20-29 Yrs. old	0.1132487	3.417	0.2358618	1.12
White Females 20-29 Yrs. old	14.88749	3.919	2.971733	0.773
Other Males 20-29 Yrs. old	265.2411	1.65	0.975273	0.004
Other Females 20-29 Yrs. old	9.35E+01	0.02	0.0163516	0.63
Black Males 30-39 Yrs. old	1.56E+06	5.426	0.0017685	1.248
Black Females 30-39 Yrs. old	6622.304	4.514	16.02969	0.706
White Males 30-39 Yrs. old	2931.809	5.823	5.983502	0.703
White Females 30-39 Yrs. old	8.18E+04	5.521	0.1100072	0.909
Other Males 30-39 Yrs. old	0.0000256	2.906	0.0125477	0.587
Other Females 30-39 Yrs. old	15353.86	2.78	55.37337	0.572

Exogenous Variables	Column 3 Explaining Total Deaths and Injuries		Column 4 Explaining the Number of Shootings	
	Incidence Rate Ratio	Absolute z-statistic	Incidence Rate Ratio	Absolute z-statistic
Black Males 40-49 Yrs. old	0.0897098	0.868	0.0864408	0.45
Black Females 40-49 Yrs. old	4475.959	3.33	1263.454	1.435
White Males 40-49 Yrs. old	2.284444	0.736	1.268709	0.103
White Females 40-49 Yrs. old	5.264373	1.394	1.866689	0.252
Other Males 40-49 Yrs. old	2050366	2.98	105.0116	0.491
Other Females 40-49 Yrs. old	1.71E+06	3.288	0.0061294	0.661
Black Males 50-64 Yrs. old	0.0007524	2.163	0.0019288	0.967
Black Females 50-64 Yrs. old	0.5939145	0.184	0.2258918	0.266
White Males 50-64 Yrs. old	2092.919	6.121	2.955171	0.439
White Females 50-64 Yrs. old	0.0012159	6.487	0.1355853	0.953
Other Males 50-64 Yrs. old	5.89E+08	4.036	10895.66	0.968
Other Females 50-64 Yrs. old	5921817	3.279	35.11413	0.378
Black Males Over 64 Yrs. old	6.30E+07	4.656	2.94E+06	2.012
Black Females Over 64 Yrs. old	21782.44	4.657	17103.05	2.201
White Males Over 64 Yrs. old	16.42544	2.886	0.5631965	0.298
White Females Over 64 Yrs. old	4.65E+01	1.153	1.23927	0.161
Other Males Over 64 Yrs. old	9.49E+02	1.134	1.87E+08	1.637
Other Females Over 64 Yrs. old	1.97E+12	5.233	6.26E+10	2.161
Year Fixed Effects				
1978	0.6144086	1.867	1.55637	0.774
1979	2.419846	3.374	2.874282	1.671
1980	1.345762	0.854	2.543089	1.205
1981	1.40725	0.792	6.546625	2.087
1982	0.7702999	0.511	2.975671	1.035
1983	0.2209044	2.601	2.13218	0.65
1984	0.8123332	0.327	3.5013	0.98
1985	0.4271977	1.21	2.893901	0.759
1986	0.383171	1.235	2.158159	0.5
1987	0.2857228	1.512	2.550774	0.575
1988	0.2195504	1.69	1.829284	0.344
1989	0.1474414	1.975	1.44242	0.195
1990	0.0431717	2.975	0.7075152	0.17
1991	0.0214102	3.356	0.3822376	0.437
1992	0.0058973	4.132	0.211221	0.653
1993	0.0074061	3.645	0.2843393	0.491
1994	0.0011508	4.742	0.0693321	0.986
1995	0.0017162	4.008	0.1080188	0.735
1996	0.0094291	2.905	1.262951	0.077
1997	0.006131	3.195	0.7214349	0.108
State Fixed Effects				
Alaska	9.28E+07	2.873	2273.677	0.872
Arizona	315.1895	2.014	1601230	2.571

Appendix 6.2: (continued)

Exogenous Variables	Column 3 Explaining Total Deaths and Injuries		Column 4 Explaining the Number of Shootings	
	Incidence Rate Ratio	Absolute z-statistic	Incidence Rate Ratio	Absolute z-statistic
Arkansas	4.365399	1.162	186.3471	2.072
California	2.440504	0.346	166.7339	0.976
Colorado	21.46203	1.059	48874.94	1.956
Connecticut	58.64235	1.669	15476.08	2.031
Delaware	1.02E+06	0.046	7.05E+07	0.065
D.C.	0.0421282	0.616	2.05E+06	1.281
Florida	4.83E+02	2.938	4327.855	1.915
Georgia	0.345945	1.496	0.1434456	1.332
Hawaii	6.39E+33	5.461	1.98E+07	0.615
Idaho	3.145178	0.355	173727.4	1.933
Illinois	2.457148	0.566	33.78523	1.06
Indiana	735.1607	3.191	28185.45	2.505
Iowa	11.55945	0.829	81700.39	1.957
Kansas	231.4512	2.136	296075.2	2.521
Kentucky	275.7836	2.507	12924.33	2.147
Louisiana	0.3802884	1.299	0.1998901	1.169
Maine	8.050525	0.643	106969.7	1.862
Maryland	1.465251	0.32	26.21247	1.439
Massachusetts	1153.813	2.694	74088.35	2.16
Michigan	19.02617	1.887	210.9348	1.716
Minnesota	16.10909	0.947	92580.94	2.005
Mississippi	0.0282325	2.601	0.0018076	2.31
Missouri	62.75716	2.238	3059.725	2.198
Montana	0.1028048	0.645	425725.4	1.934
Nebraska	64.66929	1.491	93351.13	2.086
Nevada	4.73E+11	0.078	0.0208509	0.012

Exogenous Variables	Column 3 Explaining Total Deaths and Injuries		Column 4 Explaining the Number of Shootings	
	Incidence Rate Ratio	Absolute z-statistic	Incidence Rate Ratio	Absolute z-statistic
New Hampshire	4.496229	0.449	108751.2	1.837
New Jersey	20990.25	1.702	6.433943	0.216
New Mexico	340.1913	1.806	1967074	2.282
New York	26342.01	1.705	0.1482885	0.211
North Carolina	59.80803	4.83	74.89252	2.578
North Dakota	1.712374	0.158	2069468	2.197
Ohio	106.9125	2.57	645.0559	1.727
Oklahoma	109.1635	1.849	54169.02	2.186
Oregon	5.277829	0.539	288417.7	2.135
Pennsylvania	515.5245	3.071	2975.216	1.897
Rhode Island	238.1297	1.915	118140.2	2.07
South Carolina	0.8126614	0.232	0.4070634	0.553
South Dakota	0.0000363	0.033	22.12971	0.009
Tennessee	1.188541	0.119	27.37615	1.283
Texas	683.977	3.75	317.7401	1.526
Utah	756.0805	2.12	276217.5	2.012
Vermont	49.71928	1.195	226144.5	1.949
Virginia	146.215	3.742	1348.581	2.842
Washington	2.719711	0.333	184117.6	2.123
West Virginia	58.00059	1.497	109994.8	2.197
Wisconsin	5.079271	0.626	38522.63	2.088
Wyoming	0.019079	1.082	26236.05	1.473
Model ChiSquare	5260.4		1210.6	
Log Likelihood	2080.7		679.7	

Appendix 6.3: Simultaneous Poisson-Logit Estimates for Multiple Victim Public Shootings

(The regressions control for sex, race, age; population, population squared, state unemployment rate, state poverty rate, real per capita personal income, unemployment payments, income maintenance payments, retirement payments, arrest rate for murder, and state and year fixed effects. The first stage estimates do not report the various demographic and fixed effects that were in the regression. Incidence rate ratios are reported for the second stage estimates. Absolute z or t-statistics are shown in parentheses.)

Second Stage Estimates

Endogenous Variables

Exogenous Variables	Murders in Multiple Victim Public Shootings	Injuries in Multiple Victim Public Shootings	Murders and Injuries in Multiple Victim Public Shootings
Right-to-Carry Law Dummy Variable	0.534 (2.223)	0.3116 (4.672)	0.3842 (5.249)
Model Chi-Square	4287.95	7893.02	11379.8
Log Likelihood	-1591.7	-1997.8	-2862.02
Number of Observations	984	984	984

First Stage Estimates

Exogenous Variables

Endogenous Variable	Right-to-Carry Law Dummy Variable
Chi-Square	823.6
Log likelihood	-216.88
% Rep. Pres. in State Vote * Year Dummy 1995-98	0.3142 (5.116)
% Rep. Pres. in State Vote * Year Dummy 1991-94	0.2942 (3.192)
% Rep. Pres. in State Vote * Year Dummy 1987-90	0.2401 (3.141)
% Rep. Pres. in State Vote * Year Dummy 1983-86	0.1751 (2.632)
% Rep. Pres. in State Vote * Year Dummy 1979-82	0.022 (0.396)
% Rep. Pres. in State Vote * Year Dummy 1977-78	0.045 (0.397)
Change in Property Crime Rate	0.00007 (.118)
Change in Violent Crime Rate	0.0075 (2.346)
Lagged Property Crime Rate	-0.00009 (0.305)
Lagged Violent Crime Rate	-0.0089 (4.869)

Appendix 6.4: Means and Standard Deviation of Variables

	Obs.	Mean	Std. Dev.
Shall Issue Law Dummy	1071	0.2586368	0.4380902
Arrest Rate for Murder	1045	88.17906	52.77598
Murders in Multiple Victim Public Shootings Per 100,000 Persons	1071	0.0188385	0.0782509
Injuries in Multiple Victim Public Shootings Per 100,000 Persons	1071	0.0307867	0.1806079
Murders and Injuries in Multiple Victim Public Shootings Per 100,000 Persons	1071	0.0496252	0.2380429
Murders in Multiple Victim Public Shootings	1071	0.8618114	2.622253
Injuries in Multiple Victim Public Shootings	1071	1.420168	4.614375
Murders and Injuries in Multiple Victim Public Shootings	1071	2.281979	6.678102
Attempted or Actual Bombings Per 100,000 Persons	1071	0.5768352	0.4942879
Attempted or Actual Incendiary Bombings Per 100,000 Persons	1071	0.1543275	0.2231764
Attempted or Actual Other Bombing Incidents Per 100,000 Persons	1071	0.7380498	0.6925256
Attempted or Actual Bombings	1071	27.13259	43.94869
Attempted or Actual Incendiary Bombings	1071	8.420168	19.3333
Attempted or Actual Other Bombing Incidents	1071	30.53035	45.27652
Deaths per shooting	293	1.616356	1.44935
Injuries per Shooting	293	2.655577	4.085048
Deaths or Injuries per Shooting	293	4.271933	4.426812
Number of Shootings	1071	.5620915	1.533922
Number of Shootings per 100,000 Persons	1071	.0128497	.0656067
Murders per 100,000 Persons	1068	7.532612	7.571831
Death Penalty Execution Rate	1068	0.0012488	0.0057638
Waiting Period Dummy	1071	0.3582726	0.4759902
NRA Members Per 100,000 Persons	1071	4766908	5181944
State Population	1071	4.96E+14	1.24E+14
State Population Squared	1071	13082.76	2377.003
Real Per Capita Personal Income	1071	170.1907	67.42687
Real Per Capita Income Maintenance	1071	70.53992	43.68931
Real Per Capita Unemployment Insurance Payment	1071	394.2354	610.888
Real Retirement Payments Per Person Over 65	1071	355.6367	1382.601
Unemployment Rate	1071	6.41378	2.087943
Poverty Rate	1071	13.49024	4.193104

Percent of the Population That is:

Black Males 10-19 Yrs. old	1071	1.000924	1.073925
Black Females 10-19 Yrs. old	1071	0.9861901	1.08779
White Males 10-19 Yrs. old	1071	6.522034	1.554608
White Females 10-19 Yrs. old	1071	6.212554	1.518811
Other Males 10-19 Yrs. old	1071	0.3739574	0.7276978
Other Females 10-19 Yrs. old	1071	0.3619659	0.7037917

Appendix 6.4: (continued)

	Obs.	Mean	Std. Dev.
Black Males 20-29 Yrs. old	1071	0.9357873	1.002613
Black Females 20-29 Yrs. old	1071	1.010992	1.181078
White Males 20-29 Yrs. old	1071	7.05599	1.303731
White Females 20-29 Yrs. old	1071	6.904337	1.339297
Other Males 20-29 Yrs. old	1071	0.362629	0.6881269
Other Females 20-29 Yrs. old	1071	0.3671231	0.6964837
Black Males 30-39 Yrs. old	1071	0.7481225	0.8423609
Black Females 30-39 Yrs. old	1071	0.8550366	1.002243
White Males 30-39 Yrs. old	1071	6.746516	1.202193
White Females 30-39 Yrs. old	1071	6.692243	1.196271
Other Males 30-39 Yrs. old	1071	0.3210689	0.67081
Other Females 30-39 Yrs. old	1071	0.3520146	0.7068117
Black Males 40-49 Yrs. old	1071	0.5086571	0.5992915
Black Females 40-49 Yrs. old	1071	0.5975951	0.7313905
White Males 40-49 Yrs. old	1071	5.158535	1.146857
White Females 40-49 Yrs. old	1071	5.170353	1.114372
Other Males 40-49 Yrs. old	1071	0.2235525	0.5198493
Other Females 40-49 Yrs. old	1071	0.2504653	0.5625374
Black Males 50-64 Yrs. old	1071	0.5150453	0.6695444
Black Females 50-64 Yrs. old	1071	0.6479795	0.8692419
White Males 50-64 Yrs. old	1071	5.740179	1.032121
White Females 50-64 Yrs. old	1071	6.146133	1.212804
Other Males 50-64 Yrs. old	1071	0.207363	0.6047414
Other Females 50-64 Yrs. old	1071	0.2421665	0.6969355
Black Males Over 64 Yrs. old	1071	0.3613871	0.4908613
Black Females Over 64 Yrs. old	1071	0.5593317	0.8077022
White Males Over 64 Yrs. old	1071	4.374812	1.160827
White Females Over 64 Yrs. old	1071	6.357397	1.686213
Other Males Over 64 Yrs. old	1071	0.1328229	0.4933583
Other Females Over 64 Yrs. old	1071	0.1559203	0.5368273
Violent Crime Rate Per 100,000 Persons	1061	487.6289	339.2621
Murder Rate Per 100,000 Persons	1068	7.532612	7.571831
Rape Rate Per 100,000 Persons	1061	34.05506	15.72533
Aggravated Assault Rate Per 100,000 Persons	1068	287.2832	179.6146
Robbery Rate Per 100,000 Persons	1068	161.1047	174.7755

Appendix Table 7.1: Does Higher Gun Ownership Increase Accidental Gun Deaths or Suicides?: Using Information on Gun Magazine Subscriptions as a Proxy for Gun Ownership Rates (Coefficients are incident rate ratios, where a value of one implies that there is no change in the endogenous variable. The control variables are listed below and described in more detail in Section IV in the paper.)

	Accidental Gun Deaths for the Entire Population				Gun Suicides for the Entire Population			
	Only fixed effects		All other control variables used, except gun control laws	All other control variables used, including gun control laws	Only fixed effects		All other control variables used, except gun control laws	All other control variables used, including gun control laws
	(1)	(2)	(3)	(4)	(5)	(6)	(7)	(8)
State-level sales of the five largest gun magazines	0.9999 (1.359)	0.9999 (1.334)	1 (0.271)	1.000003 (1.844)*	1.000001 (2.488)**	1.000001 (2.039)**	1 (1.234)	1 (0.215)
Number of non-gun accidental deaths (columns 1-4) or number of non-gun suicides (columns 5-8)		0.9994 (0.932)	0.9999 (0.083)	0.9988 (1.531)		1.000198 (2.066)**	1.000046 (0.405)	0.99997 (0.178)
Chi Square	8712.3	8713.2	8804.9	570.86	103975.4	103979.6	104147.8	9587.75
	(9)	(10)	(11)	(12)	(13)	(14)	(15)	(16)
State level sales of the five largest magazines	1.0000005 (1.051)	1 (0.112)	1.0000006 (1.398)	1.000009 (1.956)*	1.0000001 (12.258)*	1.0000001 (9.860)***	1 (3.654)***	1 (3.415)***
Number of non-gun accidental deaths (columns 1-4) or number of non-gun suicides (columns 5-8)		1.0003 (1.430)	1.0019 (0.677)	1.0019 (0.520)		1.00031 (8.479)***	1.000239 (4.931)***	1.000279 (5.293)***
Chi Square	25601.4	25603.43	25874.95	24722.5	261128	261200	261569.5	248050

Note: All regressions are Poisson regressions and use state and year fixed effects. Coefficients are incident rate ratios. A value greater than one means that accidents or suicides are increasing, whereas a value less than one implies a decline. The coefficients show the percent increase or decrease from a one unit change in the independent variable. Not reported for the other specifications are the 36 demographic variables, state population and population squared, unemployment, poverty rate, income variables, or the fixed effects that are discussed in Section IV. The gun control variables are: right-to-carry laws, one-gun-a-month purchase rules, states that border one-gun-a-month states, waiting periods, and mandatory prison penalties for using guns in the commission of a crime. (Number of observations = 918)

*** The two-tailed t-test is significant at the 1 percent level; ** The two-tailed t-test is significant at the 5 percent level; * The two-tailed t-test is significant at the 10 percent level.

Appendix 7.2: The Descriptive Statistics for Endogenous Variables

Variable	Obs	Mean	Std. Dev.	Min	Max
Accidental Gun Death Rate for Ages					
Under 5	918	2.62e-06	5.01e-06	0	.0000455
5 to 9	918	4.21e-06	7.31e-06	0	.0000604
10 to 14	918	.000011	.0000123	0	.0000875
15 to 19	918	.0000182	.0000211	0	.000208
Non-gun Accidental Death Rate for Ages					
Under 5	918	.0001995	.0000788	-1.10e-12	.0005212
5 to 9	918	.0001164	.0000483	0	.0003763
10 to 14	918	.0001229	.0000484	0	.0003382
15 to 19	918	.0004679	.0001598	.0000347	.0012447
Suicide Rates for Those Under Age 15					
by gun	918	3.38e-06	3.47e-06	0	.0000285
by other method	918	2.48e-06	2.83e-06	0	.0000242
total	918	5.86e-06	4.75e-06	0	.0000449
Suicide Rates for Those Between 15 and 19					
by gun	918	.0000763	.0000426	0	.0003402
by other method	918	.00004	.0000232	0	.0001844
total	918	.0001162	.0000527	0	.000431
Natural Log of Crime Rates					
Violent	1010	5.9692	.7013274	2.68	7.979955
Murder	1017	1.749346	.7675413	-2.3	4.39
Rape	1010	3.412765	.4988437	0	4.9
Robbery	1017	4.658273	.9991612	1.17	7.4
Aggravated Assault	1017	5.450054	.6910092	2	7.350902
Property	1017	8.346207	.3342765	6.4	10.02
Burglary	1017	6.961164	.4242595	4.65	9.8
Larceny	1017	7.922934	.3196749	6.08	8.81
Auto Theft	1017	5.846315	.6062313	3.28	7.517467

Appendix 8.1: The Number of Gun Shows by State by Year (Collected from the Gun Show Calendar)

State	'89	'90	'91	'92	'93	'94	'95	'96	'97	'98	'99	'00	'01
Alabama	38	33	28	22	27	30	26	26	39	34	42	28	35
Alaska	0	0	0	1	0	1	1	1	5	2	1	2	3
Arizona	34	39	56	56	56	59	44	49	59	56	43	39	44
Arkansas	23	25	21	28	26	28	32	47	40	36	35	33	33
California	139	66	79	94	140	119	150	164	131	122	108	106	104
Colorado	45	51	45	55	58	55	42	65	63	65	62	61	60
Connecticut	12	18	15	15	13	14	17	11	15	12	5	11	9
Delaware	11	7	7	8	8	9	8	7	9	6	6	4	4
Florida	113	129	132	134	163	170	202	233	187	178	164	135	133
Georgia	36	51	61	65	81	74	105	101	114	89	91	78	89
Hawaii	0	0	0	0	0	0	0				2	2	2
Idaho	10	12	12	13	17	20	22	28	23	20	16	16	16
Illinois	84	98	97	95	78	91	74	99	95	103	83	78	83
Indiana	72	81	61	63	58	75	74	88	90	81	77	70	78
Iowa	32	50	52	58	39	60	39	73	75	67	69	65	54
Kansas	24	29	25	18	25	24	31	42	36	37	37	35	31
Kentucky	42	41	33	29	35	28	27	32	35	36	38	40	33
Louisiana	34	30	39	34	34	38	42	47	46	45	51	58	49
Maine	4	7	6	7	6	6	4	7	10	10	8	7	6
Maryland	40	36	44	49	52	52	50	49	38	36	30	28	22
Msschstts	5	5	8	10	13	16	15	22	16	17	10	9	9
Michigan	78	78	74	98	78	59	63	96	113	96	80	91	84
Minnesota	29	30	31	39	46	51	53	71	75	71	73	58	58
Mississippi	15	14	7	7	16	25	32	35	40	35	28	29	32
Missouri	33	42	51	50	61	68	52	68	68	70	75	69	59
Montana	15	20	22	27	32	24	31	43	36	43	36	37	39
Nebraska	14	12	10	13	9	18	15	27	35	31	33	21	25
Nevada	14	19	34	40	33	40	49	42	48	42	40	34	29
N. Hmpshr	2	4	9	10	14	5	10	16	9	9	9	14	8
New Jrsy	9	11	9	12	7	18	3	4	6	11	12	9	2
New Mxco	5	11	10	10	6	5	19	24	21	26	20	13	16
New York	57	57	57	58	74	72	77	91	89	71	73	59	52
N. Crlna	44	40	48	60	54	65	59	78	82	78	72	65	68
N. Dakota	3	3	6	6	5	8	4	14	17	10	11	15	14
Ohio	94	61	81	80	132	132	120	126	110	84	83	96	94
Oklahoma	47	53	61	46	46	50	47	74	59	48	45	62	45
Oregon	58	49	62	60	63	75	77	91	72	85	74	78	65
Pnnsylvna	97	111	110	117	123	144	132	138	144	138	129	122	128
Rhd Islnd	4	1	1	0	0	0	5	5	4	6	4	1	1
S. Carolina	0	6	18	14	24	36	26	24	28	28	19	23	18
S. Dakota	15	11	19	14	12	17	16	20	20	20	15	14	16
Tennessee	44	33	38	40	49	53	56	63	64	74	74	68	76
Texas	133	149	157	179	230	244	248	227	217	213	190	208	198
Utah	9	6	6	15	8	10	4	10	11	9	15	12	10
Vermont	4	1	0	3	2	2	3	4	6	3	4	2	2
Virginia	49	47	39	61	58	54	72	91	72	63	65	63	59
Washington	77	30	48	57	49	48	46	65	39	42	41	57	58
W. Virginia	9	8	10	16	22	32	24	43	41	45	47	50	44
Wisconsin	57	60	74	84	88	82	80	102	90	98	107	105	98
Wyoming	26	25	17	26	25	9	9	24	29	27	25	23	29
Total	**1839**	**1800**	**1930**	**2096**	**2295**	**2415**	**2437**	**2907**	**2771**	**2628**	**2477**	**2403**	**2324**

Notes

*Data referenced in this book can be examined
online at www.johnlott.org.

Introduction: Why Almost Everything You've Ever Heard About Gun Control Contains Bias

1. The Zogby poll is discussed in: "Bush Best Man For Crisis; Airline Anti-Terrorism Measures Rate Well With Americans; Second Amendment Freedoms Important," Associated Television News, Washington, D.C. (Internet Wire), 15 October 2001 (http://biz.yahoo.com/iw/011015/02033037_1.html).
2. John R. Lott, Jr. "Armed Citizens Can Diffuse Terrorist Threat," *USA Today*, 17 June 2002, 13A, for the final numbers on the increase in the number of purchasers. For an earlier number on the number of purchasers and the concealed handgun permits see Geraldine Sealey, "Gunfight Packs New Heat," ABC-News.com, 19 March 2002. (http://abcnews.go.com/sections/us/DailyNews/concealedguns020319.html). Al Baker, "Steep Rise in Gun Sales Reflects Post-Attack Fears," *New York Times*, 16 December 2001, A1.
3. Editorial, "Targeting Illegal Gun Sales," *Chicago Tribune*, 20 August 1999, 26.
4. Based upon a discussion with James Valentino, the lawyer representing the store in the case.
5. Debra J. Saunders, "Taxing Ways," *San Francisco Chronicle*, 2 April 2002, A17.
6. Most murder, especially involving the young, primarily involves criminals killing criminals. Major urban trauma care centers report that knife and bullet wounds are "a chronic recurrent disease peculiar to unemployed, uninsured law breakers." See R. Stephen Smith, et. al. "Recidivism in an Urban Trauma Center," *Archives of Surgery* (1992): 668, 670.
7. Lois Romano, "At Tulsa Gun Show, Searching for Safety," *Washington Post*, 22 October 2001, A3.
8. Quote by Luis Tolley in Geraldine Sealey, "Gunfight Packs New Heat," ABC-News.com, 19 March 2002 (http://abcnews.go.com/sections/us/DailyNews/concealedguns020319.html). Luis Tolley was the Western Regional Director of Handgun Control, Inc.

9. Editorial, "Gun Crazy: An Armed Citizenry Will Not Win the War on Terror," *Telegram & Gazette*, 24 December 2001, A6.

10. Nicholas D. Kristof, "Chicks with Guns," *New York Times*, 8 March 2002, A21.

11. The caveat on this is that ownership levels are usually based upon surveys.

12. Lyda Longa, "Accidental gun victim, 6, mourned," *Atlanta Journal and Constitution*, 7 June 1999, B1.

13. Gwen O'Brien, "11-year-old shoots, kills assailant threatening his grandmother," *South Bend Tribune*, 6 February 2002. http://www.southbendtribune.com/breakingnews/posts/293.html.

14. ABC News carried such concerns from Sarah Brady, the chairwoman of the Brady Center to Prevent Gun Violence (formerly Handgun Control): "If you must keep a gun in the home, we urge you to keep it locked up and stored out of the reach of children," and noted that "[Sarah Brady] cited a new report about a 3-year-old Virginia boy who accidentally shot and killed himself with a handgun his father purchased for protection after the terrorist attacks." (http://abcnews.go.com/sections/us/DailyNews/WTC_terrorismgun-run_011001.html)

15. While we will deal later with whether such differential rules actually exist and the possible impact that they have on crime rates, the debate itself is interesting. On one side, the NRA wants to "enforce the existing federal gun laws on the books against the violent felons" and raises concerns about "freedom." However, this response leaves many unsatisfied, particularly those in the middle of the debate who might value "freedom," but to whom the bottom line is what impact a law will have on crime rates. Many who hear the NRA position, including those in the gun control movement, simply say, "Great, let's enforce the existing laws, but let us also have new ones where necessary." Gun control organizations raise the issue of stopping criminals from getting guns and now claim that the regulations are necessary to stop terrorists. They point to the number of people with disqualifying backgrounds who have been stopped from buying a gun. But as Chris Matthews, the host of *Hardball* on MSNBC, recently asked in response to these claims: "How do you know those people that were stopped were actually going to commit crimes?" Unfortunately, Matthews's question was never answered. (Chris Matthews, anchor, "Wayne LaPierre, NRA, and Dennis Henigan, Brady Campaign, Discuss Senator McCain and the Issue of Gun Control," *Hardball with Chris Matthews*, 19 June 2001.)

16. Reuters, "Police: Jerusalem bomber was a young woman," Reuters, 12 April 2002. (http://story.news.yahoo.com/news?tmpl=story&u=/nm/20020412/ts_nm/mideast_bomber_woman_dc_1&printer=1)

17. David Germain, "Jewish Center Shooting May Be Call to Arms, but for Whom?" Associated Press, 16 August 1999.

18. Tom Hundley, "A Killer and a Cause," *Chicago Tribune*, 7 November 1995, 12.

19. Even toy guns are sometimes successfully used to stop crime. In England, a "homeowner, armed with a toy gun, managed to detain two burglars who had

broken into his house, while he called the police." (Joyce Lee Malcolm, "Trigger Unhappy," *Financial Times*, 21 June 2002.)

20. "Montgomery County Crime Watch," *Washington Post*, 18 October 2001, T21.
21. "Anne Arundel Crime Watch," *Washington Post*, 19 July 2001, T10.
22. See for example the discussion in my book, *More Guns, Less Crime*.
23. See Wright and Rossi (1986): 150.
24. Ibid., 146.
25. Richard T. Wright and Scott H. Decker, *Burglars on the Job: Streetlife and Residential Break-ins*, (Boston: Northeastern University Press, 1994), 112.
26. Ibid., 112–113.

CHAPTER 1: THE GOOD AND THE BAD

1. Don Grigas, "Program emphasizes gun danger message," *Chicago Suburban Newspapers*, 19 May 2002 (http://reporter-met.chicagosuburbannews.com/display/inn_news/BOLINGBROOK/C9203.TXT).
2. http://www.bradycampaign.org/facts/story.asp?url=http%3A%2F%2Fwww%2Eadn%2Ecom%2Falaska%2Fstory%2F925097p%2D1025618c%2Ehtml&headline=Man + accused + of + helping + his + wife + commit + suicide
3. http://www.bradycampaign.org/facts/story.asp?url=http%3A%2F%2Fwww%2Emcall%2Ecom %2Fnews%2Flocal%2Fall%2Db1%2D3murderapr12%2Estory%3Fcoll%3Dall%252Dnewslocal%252Dhed& headline=Monroe + woman + is + slain + in + home
4. http://www.bradycampaign.org/facts/story.asp?url=http%3A%2F%2Fwww%2Enews%2Drecord%2Ecom%2Fnews%2Flocal%2Fgso%2Fmccain12%2Ehtm&headline=Man + enters + guilty + plea + in + death + of + taxi + driver
5. http://www.bradycampaign.org/facts/story.asp?url=http%3A%2F%2Fwww%2Enewsok%2Ecom%2Fcgi%2Dbin%2Fshow%5Farticle%3FID%3D847115%26pic%3Dnone%26TP%3Dgetarticle&headline= Guns + found + in + toilet + tank + believed + murder + weapons
6. http://www.thedesertsun.com/news/stories/local/1018747484.shtml
7. http://seattlepi.nwsource.com/local/66435_shooting13.shtml
8. http://www.kdfw.com/dynamic/story.asp?category=2
9. Ronald D. Stephens, "School-Associated Violent Deaths," *National School Safety Center's Report*, 16 May 2001. A gang shooting of high school students at an elementary school took place at Pomona, California.
10. About 60 percent of these cases came from KeepandBeararms.com and the NRA *Armed Citizen*. Robert Waters also helped in collecting cases.
11. "Alleged Intruder Shot, in Critical Condition," *Gainesville Sun*, 11 March 2001. (http://www.sunone.com/articles/2001-03-10j.shtml)
12. WIS Television (http://www.wistv.com/Global/story.asp?S=265529&nav=0RaM).

13. "Shooting hurts man, cancels kids' recess," *Arkansas Democrat-Gazette*, 13 March 2001.

14. David G. Grant, "Gunman found dead after police standoff," *Detroit News*, 13 March 2001. (http://www.detnews.com/2001/metro/0103/13/d10-198791.htm)

15. Chris Barker, "After two attacks, man shoots assailant," *Palm Beach Post*, 14 March 2001, 5B.

16. Ellen Miller, "Man faces suspects accused of attacking him after getting ride," *Rocky Mountain News*, March 14, 2001.

17. "Victim Turns Tide on Assailant, Holds Him at Bay with Gun," *Hungry Horse News*, 15 March 2001. (http://www.hungryhorsenews.com/archives/ index.inn?loc=detail&doc=/store/2001/March/15-509-news01.txt)

18. "Pawn Shop Shootout," *Salt Lake Tribune*, 14 March 2001. (:http:// www.sltrib.com/2001/mar/03142001/utah/79517.htmChanged:3:18). See also Brady Snyder, "Shop owner credits guns with saving lives in attack," *Deseret News*, 15 March 2001.

19. Melissa Moore, "Homeowner Kills Intruder, Police Say," *Advocate*, 15 March 2001. (http://www.theadvocate.com/news/story.asp?StoryID=19987)

20. Greg Rickagaugh, "Woman kills former boyfriend," *Augusta Chronicle*, 26 July 2001. (http://augustachronicle.com/stories/072601/met_174-5876.001.html).

21. "Man who shot intruder faces no charges," *Herald-Journal* (Spartanburg, S.C.), 25 July 2001. (www.keepandbeararms.com/information/ XcIBPrintItem.asp?ID=2275)

22. Sheila Burke, "CCW permit holder shoots armed robber," *Tennessean*, 27 July 2001. (www.keepandbeararms.com/information/XcIBPrintItem.asp?ID=2288).

23. Cathi Carr and Kathy Ciotola, "Newspaper carrier shoots, injures man," *Gainesville Sun* (Florida), 22 July 2001 (http://www.sunone.com/articles/2001-07-22c.shtml).

24. Lilla Margza, "Woman fatally shoots intruder," *WKRN News 2*, 25 July 2001. (http://www.wkrn.com/Global/story.asp?S=412650&nav=1ugB).

25. Brenna R. Kelly, "Pizzeria manager shoots 2 robbers," *Tampa Tribune*, 25 July 2001.

26. Tyrone Walker, "Lost motorist shoots attacker," *Post and Courier* (Charleston, S.C.), 22 July 2001, B1.

27. See the end of Appendix 2 for details of the survey. The numbers, if accurate, are dramatic. Compare the 274,119 gun crimes that were reported in the Uniform Crime Reports to the estimate here of 2.3 million defensive gun uses in 2002.

CHAPTER 2: THE MEDIA ON GUNS

1. Peter Bronson, "Packin' Heat, Queen City of the Wild West," *Cincinnati Enquirer*, 17 April 2002. (http://enquirer.com/editions/2002/04/17/loc_bronson_packin_heat.html).

2. Ibid., 126.

3. This problem of misimpressions created by the media occurs in similar ways in other areas. For example, *Time* magazine wrote about how women are overly optimistic about being able to have children when they are in their late thirties and their forties.

> [The researchers] say they are just trying to correct the record in the face of widespread false optimism. Her survey found that nearly 9 out of 10 young women were confident of their ability to get pregnant into their forties. Last fall the A.I.A. conducted a fertility-awareness survey on the women's website iVillage.com. Out of the 12,524 respondents, only one answered all fifteen questions correctly. Asked when fertility begins to decline, only 13 percent got it right (age 27); 39 percent thought it began to drop at forty. Asked how long couples should try to conceive on their own before seeking help, fully 42 percent answered thirty months. That is a dangerous combination: a couple that imagines fertility is no problem until age forty and tries to get pregnant for thirty months before seeing a doctor is facing very long odds of ever becoming parents. . . . [The question] is simply how information is shared. Childlessness is a private sorrow; the miracle baby is an inevitable headline. "When you see these media stories hyping women in their late 40s having babies, it's with donor eggs," insists Stanford's Adamson, "but that is conveniently left out of the stories." (Nancy Gibbs, "Making Time for a Baby," *Time*, 15 April 2002.)

4. Don B. Kates, "The Value of Civilian Arms Possession as Deterrent to Crime or Defense Against Crime," *American Journal of Criminal Law* (1991).

5. The quotes below are from two articles: Rex Bowman, "I was sick, I need help," *Richmond Times-Dispatch*, 18 January 2002, A1; and Diane Suchetka, "Ex-Charlottean: I Helped Nab Suspect," *Charlotte Observer*, 18 January 2002, A2.

6. The two Nexis hits that mentioned that the students retrieved guns from their cars but did not use them were from the *New York Times* and NBC's *Today*. One newspaper op-ed that I wrote on this topic incorrectly implied that the *New York Times* had completely ignored that the students who stopped the attack had a gun. The number 208 was also transposed so that it was listed incorrectly as 280.

7. Not everyone agrees with this formulation of the facts. Kent Markus, a professor at Capital University Law School in Columbus, Ohio, and a close friend of L. Anthony Sutin, the former dean of the Appalachian Law School and one of the victims of the shooting, said that, "The gun lobby, without much sensitivity or attention, has distorted what actually happened for their own political benefits. I think it is a shameful exploitation of a tragedy" (Jim Oliphant, "A Tragedy Compounded: A Triple Murder Draws Unlikely Attention from Pro-gun Activists and Nigerian Immigrants," *Legal Times*, 17 June 2002, 1). However, when I called up Markus to find out exactly which facts he was referring to, he was unwilling to provide me any details.

8. Maria Glod and Fredrick Kunkle, "Va. Town, Law School Linked in Mourning," *Washington Post*, 18 January 2002, B1.

9. Alfonso A. Castillo, "Dean Was Man of Compassion," *Newsday*, 18 January 2002, A6.

10. Adam W. Lasker, "Faculty here remember law prof slain in Va.," *Chicago Daily Law Bulletin*, 18 January 2002, 1; Stephanie Simon, "Expelled Law Student Kills 3 on Campus," *Orlando Sentinel*, 17 January 2002, A3; Global News Wire, "Three Killed in Shooting," *Financial Times Information*, 17 January 2002; and Chris Kahn, "School massacre accused 'sick'," *Daily Telegraph* (Sydney), 19 January 2002, 24.

11. Francis X. Clines, "Coal Town's Hopes Clouded by Killings of 3 at Law School," *New York Times*, 18 January 2002, A1.

12. Jeffrey Gettleman, "In Appalachia, an Unlikely Setting for a Triple Murder," *Los Angeles Times*, 18 January 2002, 24. Others have made the last point made in the text (see The Week, *National Review*, 25 February 2002).

13. The interview took place on 28 January 2002.

14. Another surprise also surfaced from that radio interview in which I participated with Tracy Bridges which I had not seen mentioned in any newspaper stories that I had read. Tracy stated that he had been told by the police that when he, Mikael, and Ted stopped Peter, Peter was almost out of ammunition and was on his way to his car to get more. We can only wonder how many lives were saved by these men's quick actions.

15. Maria Glod also emphasized to me how busy she had been that day, with the memorial service, the interviews, and a 6 P.M. deadline.

16. Rick Montgomery, "NRA charges news media ignore popularity of guns," *Kansas City Star*, 4 March 2002.

17. This quote is based upon a conversation that I had with Mr. Getler. It should be noted that a later piece in the *Washington Post* somewhat corrected the false impression created earlier. Fredrick Kunkle, one of the reporters on the earlier story whom I had talked to wrote ("After the Tragedy, Resilience," 11 May 2002, A1): "Odighizuwa emerged from the school and put the handgun down. It is unclear whether he did so because he had exhausted his ammunition or because two students with law enforcement backgrounds confronted him with guns. Students subdued him."

18. Jeffrey Gettleman and Stephanie Simon, "Dean, Professor and Student Killed at Law School in Va; Crime Students Tackle the Gunman Minutes After the Shooting," *Los Angeles Times*, 17 January 2002, A14.

19. Laurence A. Elder, "The media that couldn't shoot straight," Townhall.com, 13 February 2002 http://www.townhall.com/columnists/larryelder/welcome.shtml.

20. Gary Kleck and Don B. Kates, *Armed: New Perspectives on Gun Control*, (Amherst, N.Y.: Prometheus Books, 2001), 288–289.

21. The restriction on nonpolitical murders appears to have been used to exclude the Oklahoma City bombing. Many of the killings in their list were committed with methods other than guns. Ford Fessenden, "They Threaten, Seethe and Unhinge, Then Kill in Quantity," *New York Times*, 9 April 2000, 1, Section 1; Ford Fessenden, "How Youngest Killers Differ: Peer Support," *New*

York Times, 9 April 2000, Section 1, 1; Laurie Goodstein and William Glaberson, "The Well-Marked Roads to Homicidal Rage," *New York Times*, 10 April 2000, A1; Fox Butterfield, "Hole in Gun Control Law Lets Mentally Ill Through," *New York Times*, 11 April 2000, A1; William Glaberson, "Man and His Son's Slayer Unite to Ask Why," *New York Times*, 12 April 2000, A1; Editorial, "A Closer Look at Rampage Killings," *New York Times*, 13 April 2000, A30.

22. Editorial, "A Closer Look at Rampage Killings," *New York Times*, 13 April 2000, A30.

23. Dean Baquet, "Response to John Lott," APBNews.com, May 2000.

24. Editorial, "Rampage Killings," *Virginian-Pilot* (Norfolk, Va.), 13 April 2000, B10 and Derek Rose, "Rivier professor backs study of video games, violence," *Union Leader* (Manchester, N.H.), 20 April 2000, B1.

25. Editorial, "A Closer Look at Rampage Killings," *New York Times*, 13 April 2000, A30.

26. Again, this denial was despite the fact that his article briefly noted that it "does not include every attack."

27. While the *New York Times* did not publish any of my letters to the editor detailing my concerns regarding their series, APBNews.com did publish a piece by me and asked the *New York Times* to respond. Dean Baquet, the *New York Times*'s national editor, wrote the following response:

"In the weeks since publication of The *Times*'s series, most experts have praised it as an aggressive and objective look at a complex, emotion-laden problem. Professor Lott, obviously, disagrees with the other experts, though I wonder whether his point of view is influenced by the fact that he has a strongly-held belief regarding the nation's gun laws, specifically that more guns means less crime. Whatever the case, I believe the professor has misread key points of our series.

"We did not say, for instance, that we concluded that exactly 100 killings had occurred in the last 50 years. We said, to the contrary, that 'the database does not include every attack of this type over the last 50 years.'

"We did not base our conclusion that rampage killings have increased on the database of 100 killers. Our story said: '...the incidence of these rampage killings appears to have increased, according to a separate computer analysis by the *Times* of nearly 25 years of homicide data from the Federal Bureau of Investigation.' Early on, we decided that no one could judge the prevalence of rampage killings from a search of newspaper clippings, as Professor Lott has done. It is remarkable how many of them are not covered, and how many small-town papers are not contained in databases.

"Finally, we leave the debate over gun control to Professor Lott, who feels passionately about it, and others, including the *Times*'s editorial page. We drew no conclusion 'that the nation needs tighter gun control laws,' and, as professional journalists, we don't see such assertions as part of our role."

28. Fox Butterfield, "Hole in Gun Control Law Lets Mentally Ill Through," *New York Times*, 11 April 2000, A1.

29. This is from a discussion that I had with Fox Butterfield at a symposium on gun control sponsored by the University of Arizona Law School on Friday, 26 January 2001.

30. The second letter that I sent was kept to around 120 words, so length could not have been an issue. The first was around 150 words.

31. Fox Butterfield, "National Briefing Washington: Link Between Gun Use And Limits," New York Times, 30 August 2001, A14; Fox Butterfield, "U.S. Crime Figures Were Stable in '00 After 8-Year Drop," New York Times, 31 May 2001, A1; Fox Butterfield, "The Woman Who Changed the Illegal-Gun Landscape," New York Times, 23 December 2000, A12; Fox Butterfield, "2 Economists Give Far Higher Cost of Gun Violence," New York Times, 15 September 2000, A24; Fox Butterfield, "Guns: The Law As Selling Tool," New York Times, 13 August 2000, Section 4, 4; Fox Butterfield, "Questions on Brady Law," New York Times, 6 August 2000, Section 4, 2; Fox Butterfield, "Study Disputes Success of the Brady Law," New York Times, 2 August 2000, A12; Ford Fessenden, "They Threaten, Seethe and Unhinge, Then Kill in Quantity," New York Times, 9 April 2000, Section 1, 1; Fox Butterfield, "Massachusetts to Enforce Strict Gun Safety Laws," New York Times, 3 April 2000, A12; Fox Butterfield, "Firearms Agency Intensifies Scrutiny of Suspect Dealers," New York Times, 4 February 2000, A12; Eric Nagourney, "Mapping Out Gun Hazards for Children," New York Times, 26 February 2002, F7; Associated Press, "Multiple Slayings Now More Likely In School Violence," New York Times, 5 December 2001, A25; David Stout, "Man Charged In Killings Evaded Strict Gun Laws," New York Times, 28 December 2000, A20; Reuters, "FBI Lists Caution Signs For Violence In Classroom," New York Times, 7 September 2000, A20; New York Times, "Study Says Gun Traffickers Arm Criminals," New York Times, 25 June 2000, Section 1; 22.

32. The news reports provided equal coverage to the positions of activists, with Wayne LaPierre, executive director of the NRA; Bill Powers, the NRA's director of Public Affairs; and Robert Delfay, president of the National Shooting Sports Foundation being balanced off against Tom Diaz, Violence Policy Center; Douglas Weil, Handgun Control; and Scott Harshbarger, president of Common Cause.

    Despite the fact that half of the period covers the Clinton administration and half covers the Bush administration, all the federal government officials quoted with respect to these studies served during the Clinton administration. These officials were James Johnson, Stuart Eizenstat, and Lawrence Summers, who all served in the Treasury Department.

33. "Illegal gun arrests mirror rising city homicide rate," Associated Press State & Local Wire, 10 August 2001.

34. For example, Cook stated that "[i]f you introduce a gun into a violent encounter, it increases the chance that someone will die." Editorial, Cincinnati Enquirer, 23 January 1996, A8.

35. Dave Kopel, "$100 Billion Mistake," National Review Online, 25 August 2001.

36. *Florida Times-Union*, "Rapes, assaults rise as drop in U.S. crime rate levels off," 19 December 2000, A4.

37. I asked all the presenters at a National Academy of Sciences panel on 18 September 2002, entitled "Gun Violence and Kids," whether they agreed with the statement.

38. For James Alan Fox see "The Crime Debate," *Buffalo News*, 1 September 2000, 2C. For Garen Wintemute see David Olinger, "Massacre energizes gun debate but not lawmakers," *Denver Post*, 19 April 2000, A14. Daniel Webster is discussed at length in my previous book, *More Guns, Less Crime*. For Matthew Miller, see quotes like "The differences in violent death rates to children are large, and are closely tied to levels of gun ownership" (Alison Ashton, "Research Proves Mom Right About Veggies," Copley News Service, 4 March 2002).

39. Terry L. Anderson, Montana State University; Charles W. Baird, California State University, Hayward; Randy E. Barnett, Boston University; et al. (Letter signed by 290 academics), "Disarming good people," *Washington Times*, 16 June 1999, A17. The correct number of 294 was noted in John R. Lott, Jr., "More Gun Controls?: They Haven't Worked in the Past," *Wall Street Journal*, 17 June 1999, A26.

40. If the set of stories in this survey were expanded to gun issues more broadly and extended to cover a longer period of time, there are three times when I was interviewed for stories in the *New York Times* during 1999. Of course, increasing the number of articles covered would increase the number of academics on the other side by an even larger unknown amount. One story that I was interviewed for involved the suits against the gun makers (Barry Meier, "It just looks like a smoking gun," *New York Times*, 12 December 1999, Section 4, 6), the school shooting in Colorado (Barry Meier, "Terror in Littleton," *New York Times*, 26 April 1999, A17) and the other involved an initiative that was being voted on in Missouri (Dirk Johnson, "Divided Missouri to Vote on a Right-to-Carry Concealed Guns," *New York Times*, 2 April 1999, A16). None of the other signers of the open letter were interviewed on any issue involving guns during the last few years.

41. The national surveys studied here were:
Newsweek Poll conducted by Princeton Survey Research Associates, 21–22 April 1999
Newsweek Poll conducted by Princeton Survey Research Associates, 12–13 August 1999
Gallup/CNN/USA Today Poll, 13–16 January 2000
Fox News/Opinion Dynamics Poll, 22–23 March 2000
ABC News/*Washington Post* Poll, March 30-April 2, 2000
ICR/ABC/*Washington Post*, April 2000
Associated Press conducted by ICR, 14–18 April 2000
Pew/Princeton Survey Research, April 2000
ABC News, August 30–September 2, 1999
CBS News, 15 August 1999
Yankelovich Partners, April 1995

LA Times, Times Mirror Center, 16–21 March 1994

LA Times, Times Mirror Center, 2–5 December 1993

USA Today, 17–21 December 1993

PEW conducted by Princeton Survey Research Associates, 12–16 April 2000

PEW, March 1994

PEW, December 1993

The national surveys studied here were:

Field Poll, California, 16–22 August 1999

Buckeye State Poll, November 1999

University of South Alabama, May 2000

North Carolina Statewide Poll, May 1994

Tennessee Survey/UT Social Science Research Institute, March 1994

Georgia/Survey Research Center, Spring 1993

Virginia Department of Criminal Justice Service's Criminal Research Center, 1992

42. Amos Tversky and Daniel Kahneman, "The Framing of Decisions and the Rationality of Choice." *Science*, 1981, 453–58.

43. ABC News/*Washington Post* poll was conducted by telephone August 30–September 2, 1999, among a random national sample of 1,526 adults. The results have a three-point error margin. Fieldwork by TNS Intersearch of Horsham, Pa.

44. ABC News/*Washington Post* Poll, 4–6 September 2000. N=1,065 registered voters nationwide. MoE ± 3. Field work by TNS Intersearch. (http://www.pollingreport.com/prioriti.htm).

45. The other options given in these surveys regarding "handling crime," protecting Social Security, encouraging morals, patients' rights, protecting Medicare, and protecting the environment, are also interpreted the same way. No reasonable person supports more crime or wants to discourage morals. And anyone who thinks that environmentalists are "wacko" would be reluctant to answer "yes" when asked whether "protecting the environment" is important. When people hear that these questions generate greater percent of those polled answering "yes," the only reasonable interpretation is that there is greater support for that position.

46. Ibid.

47. Ronald Brownstein, "NRA, Unions Fight for Blue-Collar Voters," *Los Angeles Times*, 22 October 2000, A1.

48. John Mintz, "Politics: With a Poll-Tested Message, NRA Aims to Counter Labor Efforts in Midwest," *Washington Post*, 5 October 2000, A20.

49. Other surveys ask extremely similar questions. For example, the PEW Research Center asks: "Which do you think is more important...more strictly enforcing current gun laws and punishing people who break them or passing new laws to increase gun safety and further restrict the sale of guns?" [Princeton Survey Research Associates, Public Opinion Online (Roper Center at University of Connecticut), 19 April 2000.]

50. CBS News, Public Opinion Online (Roper Center at University of Connecticut), 16 August 1999.

51. Zobgy International, "Zogby's Real American Poll," Public Opinion Online (Roper Center at University of Connecticut), March 2000.

52. Of course, this bias shows up most directly when pollsters ask people whether they support more gun control. *Time* magazine and *CNN* wanted to know: "Do you favor or oppose stricter gun control laws?" (Yankelovich Partners, Inc., "*Time, CNN*, Yankelovich Partners," Public Opinion Online (Roper Center at University of Connecticut), January 2000.) ABC/*Washington Post* and the Associated Press inquire about virtually identical questions. There are slight variations on the allowed responses, but options are limited to either saying you "favor" or "oppose" stricter gun laws. These pollsters provide no alternative for those who seek to reduce the level of regulation. However, it should be mentioned that in this case a few surveys have inquired whether people would like a reduction in the level of regulation and some surveys have recorded quite high levels of support. For example, in June 1999, Lou Harris sought to find out how people would answer the question: "In general, would you say you favor stricter gun control, or less strict gun control?" Twenty-five percent of respondents claimed that they wanted less strict regulations (Louis Harris and Associates, " Harris Poll," Public Opinion Online (Roper Center at University of Connecticut), 23 June 1999. (The *Los Angeles Times* also conducted a similar survey that was released on 31 July 2000.)

53. Tom has also worked closely with the Joyce Foundation, which extensively funds gun control research, though I don't believe that their funding has caused Tom to alter his views on guns.

54. This is based upon a discussion that I had with Rendell in 1999. See John R. Lott, Jr., "On guns, Ed Rendell can't seem to shoot straight," *Philadelphia Daily News*, 6 June 2002 (http://www.philly.com/mld/ dailynews/news/opinion/3410712.htm).

55. An informal survey by reporters at the *Richmond Times-Dispatch* found that: "In almost every case, the legal use of the gun has left the user shaken and angry. Firing a gun at another person, even in self-defense, can be as traumatic as it is heroic. The shooters, almost always, were reluctant to shoot, and when they did, they were angry at being forced to do it. But they were all grateful they were able to defend themselves." Gordon Hickey and Michael Martz, "Bearing Arms: Defensive use of guns can prevent crime," *Richmond Times-Dispatch*, 5 May 2002. (http://timesdispatch.com/news/ MGB3CT49U0D.html).

56. Because of my work for the *Los Angeles Times* and the *New York Post* (which I discussed earlier in Chapter 1) where I examined defensive gun uses during two different weeks in 2001, I realize that these two sources are hardly exhaustive (KeepandBearArms.com and the NRA Armed Citizen archives account for about 60 percent of the stories that I was able to find and I did not do a complete search).

57. Including duplicate stories, 344 of the defensive gun users were identified as men and 64 as women. In five cases a victim was killed, and in 82 they were injured. The criminals were virtually always men: 419 men and 2 women.

Most stories entail criminals in their teens (70), twenties (128), and thirties (74). And again, twenty-seven cases involved multiple male attackers.

58. Conversation with Dale Lezon on 15 April 2002.

59. Any mentions of woundings or brandishing to scare off criminals would be published when those who weren't regular staff were running things on a weekend.

60. Daniel J. Wakin, "Robbery Is Thwarted," *New York Times*, 10 July 2001, B4. KeepandBearArms.com and the NRA Armed Citizen implied that the *Times* carried no stories about defensive gun use, but I was able to find one very brief story by searching through the newspaper myself.

61. These three stories were missed by KeepandBearArms.com and the NRA. They all involved the gasoline station robberies and were published on 30 August 2001, 12 December 2001, and 13 December 2001. The one story reported by these websites was from the *Washington Post* police blotters. It involved a woman protecting herself from a criminal trying to break into her home (20 March 2001). I did not include the police blotters in the news story coverage, but doing so for the *Washington Post* would create a total of three short stories that total together 267 words.

62. "Gunman Kills 2," *New York Times*, 15 April 2001, Section 1, 23, and Timothy Egan, "Santee is Latest Blow to Myth of Suburbia's Safer Schools," *New York Times*, A1.

63. To be included in the search, news stories had to discuss guns that were either fired or brandished to cause or prevent harm. To conduct these searches the following search terms were used: "New York Times Company" and "gun" or "firearm" and "Metropolitan Desk;" "New York Times Company" and "gun" or "firearm" and "National Desk;" "*Washington Post*" and "gun" and "crime" restricting the responses by month (to keep the responses under 1,000); and "*USA Today*" and "Gannett Company" and "gun" or "firearm."

64. Thomas Sowell seems to believe that there is a conscious effort to shape what crime news is covered by the media. For example, in the case of crime between races, he writes:

"For example, vicious crimes committed by white people against black people are big news because these stories fit the shibboleths which establish the moral identity of the journalists who tell these stories. Vicious crimes committed by blacks against whites are not big news because these stories undermine the shibboleths—or, as it is phrased, 'feed stereotypes.' Ditto with stories about the homeless, homosexuals and others favored by current shibboleths." (Thomas Sowell, "Political 'shibboleths' a dangerous breed," *Windsor Star*, 23 February 2002, A7.)

65. The *Post* also provides a blotter of local crimes in the District of Columbia and the neighboring counties in Virginia and Maryland. The biggest difficulty with these very short discussions is that frequently little effort is made to distinguish whether the shooting was defensive or was part of a crime. In these brief records, 87,547 words were devoted to crimes committed with guns. By comparison, only 267 words were devoted to these cases of defensive gun use.

These three defensive gun use examples involve cases on 20 March 2001;
6 July 2001; and 6 October 2001.

66. More precisely, 46 percent, or 23,165 words, of the gun crime stories were
national stories.

67. For the *Post*, over 10,000 words involved national news stories.

68. For example, *Newsweek* recently noted that "...it's the [*New York*] *Times* that
drives the nation's news agenda." Seth Mnookin, "The Changing 'Times,'"
Newsweek, 9 December 2002 (http://www.msnbc.com/news/
841753.asp?cp1=1).

69. When I expressed to Fessenden my concern that the real imbalance was the
lack of coverage that defensive gun uses received, he made a dismissive sound
and our conversation quickly ended.

70. Admittedly, however, pictures showing what would have happened to people
without a gun to defend themselves don't exist and these would be more comparable in newsworthiness to the pictures of harm.

71. Many other similar quotes can be provided.

"What does it say about the United States Congress and your colleagues that
you can't even pass childproof locks on guns?"

Charles Gibson talking to Representative Carolyn McCarthy (D–NY), *Good
Morning America*, 2 March 2000.

Charles Gibson [speaking to a child]: And what do you wish for?

Franklin Gillespie (ten years old): I wish for no violence, only peace. To tell
the president to tell the people to stop selling guns.

Good Morning America, 29 May 2001.

72. The search terms for the evening news segments were:

GUN AND (CBS NEWS AND CBS EVENING NEWS) AND DATE AFT 31
DECEMBER 2000 AND DATE BEF 1 JANUARY 2002

GUN AND (ABC NEWS AND World NEWS Tonight) AND DATE AFT 31
DECEMBER 2000 AND DATE BEF 1 JANUARY 2002

GUN AND (NBC NEWS TRANSCRIPTS AND NIGHTLY NEWS) AND
DATE AFT 31 DECEMBER 2000 AND BEF DATE 1 JANUARY 2002

73. The breakdown of the 190,089 total was as follows:

NBC *Today Show*: 24,637

CBS *Early Show*: 44,088

ABC *Good Morning America*: 76,843

NBC *Evening News*: 14,206

CBS *Evening News*: 16,869

ABC *World News Tonight*: 13,447

74. The mentions of this one case were reported on *Good Morning America*, 7
March 2001. Even in this one case, Diane Sawyer emphasized in her discussion with the off-duty officer: "I know you're a professional. You've been a
member of SWAT teams for seventeen years."

75. As was done for the newspaper reports, broadcast news stories were counted
involving either the actual or threatened use of guns to cause or prevent harm.
The stories were also limited to cases in the United States, and excluded

articles about guns on planes as none of the weapons appear to have been brought on board with the intent to commit harm. One difference from the newspaper stories is that discussions involving cases before the courts were counted here, though this primarily involved two cases: Nathaniel Brazill, the thirteen-year-old who shot his teacher, and Sean "Puffy" Combs for firing a handgun in New York City. Yet, even this misses many negative stories on guns ranging from "militias" to the trafficking of guns. The television stories tend to contain about half as many words as those run in newspapers.

Because of the war on terrorism, 2001 had relatively few stories on guns. Coverage of the war drowned out other news, and very few stories on gun crimes were covered after September 11. On ABC's *Good Morning America,* 95 percent of the words devoted to gun crimes were covered during the slightly more than eight months preceding the attack on the World Trade Center. For NBC's *Today Show* and CBS's *Early Show,* the percentages are also very high, with 91 and 98 percent respectively.

The search terms used for *Good Morning America* were: Gun and ABC News and Good Morning and date aft December 31, 2000 and bef January 1, 2002. The search terms used for the *Today Show* and the *NBC Evening News* were: gun and NBC news transcripts and show and today and date aft December 31, 2000 and bef January 1, 2002. The same was done for the evening news.

The search terms used for the CBS *Evening News* and *Early Show* were: CBS and Evening News and firearm or gun and date aft December 31, 2000 and bef January 1, 2002 and gun and CBS and Early Show and date aft December 31, 2000 and bef January 1, 2002.

76. One difference with the *Today Show* is that Katie Couric interviewed Charlton Heston about guns and even asked Tom Selleck for his views, though Selleck declined to get into a debate on guns.
77. While this discussion focuses on television programs in 2001, Katie Couric did give Rosie O'Donnell a relatively hard time in a segment on 1 June 2000. Among other issues, Couric asked Rosie about her bodyguards obtaining permits to obtain concealed handguns.
78. Bryant Gumbel, "Senator John McCain Talks about PSAs He Is Showing in Movie Theaters," *The Early Show,* CBS News Transcripts, 9 May 2001.
79. Katie Couric, "Rosie O'Donnell Talks about Her Broadway Show 'Seussical,' Her Magazine *Rosie,* and the Tom Selleck Issue," *Today Show,* NBC News Transcripts, 15 January 2001.
80. For at least a couple of examples see: "Study: Guns No Safer When Locked Up," *Special Report with Brit Hume,* Fox News Channel, 5 July 2002 and *Special Report with Brit Hume,* Fox News Network, 1 May 2001. There was also a segment during 2001 on the *Fox Report with Shepard Smith* that I was not able to locate the exact date for. The segment examined specific recent cases of defensive gun use.
81. Associated Press, "Boy, 4, Kills Playmate with Fake Gun," *Newsday* (New York, NY), 27 April 1998, A4.

82. Pamela Hill, "Man whose gun killed stepson, 4, gets 10 years; Dad, a felon, not supposed to own weapon," *Arkansas Democrat-Gazette*, 14 February 2000, B3. See also Pamela Hill, "Grieving family warns against guns," *Arkansas Democrat-Gazette*, 3 November 1999, B9.

83. Associated Press, "Girl who shot mother's abusive boyfriend won't be charged," *The Advocate* (New Orleans), 2 May 2001.

84. Headlines in major newspapers reassure readers that "Fatal air accidents reach lowest level since 1945" (Mark Odell, *Financial Times* (London), 7 January 2002, 10) and that "Airplane crashes tragic, but rare" (Barbara Karkabi, *Houston Chronicle*, 10 September 1998, 7).

85. The segment was also rebroadcast on ABC's *This Week*. Diane Sawyer, "Children and Guns," 30 May 1999.

86. Ibid.

CHAPTER 3: HOW THE GOVERNMENT WORKS AGAINST GUN OWNERSHIP

1. NCJ182993 BJS

2. NCJ180752 BJA

3. NCJ148201 BJS

4. NCJ155284 BJS

5. NCJ178994 OJJDP

6. See *More Guns, Less Crime*, 7–10.

7. Ibid.

8. Dave Kopel and Glenn Reynolds, "Political Science," *National Review Online*, 29 August 2001.

9. Richard Rosenfeld, "Impact of the Brady Act on Homicide and Suicide Rates," *Journal of the American Medical Association*, 6 December 2000, 2721.

10. Dave Kopel and Glenn Reynolds, ibid., 347. Levitt apparently tried to overcome this image by writing his first op-ed about a week before his name was publicly nominated for the panel. Given that panel members are supposed to not have strong views on the topic that they are studying, it was strange that Levitt would write his first op-ed piece at this time. The op-ed argued that swimming pools posed a greater risk to children than guns, but it is hard to understand why he would choose this very time to write his very first op-ed on this particular topic when this would normally be considered the least appropriate time to do so. When I raised concerns about Levitt's strong opposition to guns to John Pepper, who was serving as the staff director for the panel, Pepper pointed to the op-ed piece that Levitt had written as evidence that Levitt believed the same things that I believed on guns. Personally knowing Levitt, I know that was not true and one could point to several of Levitt's academic papers. But the op-ed served its purpose.

11. The paper was given at the Australian & New Zealand Society of Criminology, 16th Annual Conference in Brisbane, Australia on 2 October 2002.

12. Henry I. Miller, "The National Academy of Junk Science," *National Review Online*, 8 October 2002 (http://www.nationalreview.com/comment/comment-hmiller100802.asp).

13. Editorial, "Rethinking Ballistic Fingerprints," *New York Times*, 11 November 2002, A16.

14. Copies of the ads in order were obtained from Advertising Information Services, Inc.; http://www.unloadandlock.com/psapics.htm; and the last two from the Ad Council.

15. U.S. Consumer Product Safety Commission, *Consumer Product Safety Review*, Fall 2002 Vol. 7 no. 2.

16. Robert Goldrich, "Gratification," *Shoot* (BPI Communications, Inc.), 6 October 2000, 4.

17. http://www.mcgruff.org/guns.htm

18. During the 1990s the Centers for Disease Control never identified more than 265 handgun suicides for this age group in any given year, a rate of one every thirty-three hours. Obviously, many firearm suicides listed in the CDC data never identify the type of firearm actually used, but even assuming that handguns make up the same percentage of unidentified cases as they do for identified cases still implies an average of fewer than one handgun suicide a day during the 1990s.

19. http://www.mcgruff.org/guns.htm

20. http://www.unloadandlock.com/neigh.htm

21. http://www.unloadandlock.com/storage.htm

CHAPTER 4: THE SHIFTING DEBATE: TERRORISM, GUN CONTROL ABROAD, AND CHILDREN

1. http://michaelmoore.com/2001_0922.html

2. "Some in Congress Contemplate Moving Families," *Roll Call*, 27 September 2001, 1.

3. Steve Marantz, "State Lawmakers Look at Guns Under New Light," *Boston Herald*, 1 November 2001, 1.

4. The Capitol Police Board sets the regulations pursuant to 40 U.S.C. §193f. The current Capitol Police Board Regulations in effect since 1998 state that "nothing contained in them shall prohibit any Member of Congress from maintaining firearms within the confines of his or her offices or from any Member of Congress or any employee or agent of any Member of Congress from transporting within the Capitol grounds, firearms unloaded and securely wrapped."

5. Jim Baron, "Panel Targets Gun-Toting Lawmakers," *Pawtucket Times*, 11 January 2002.

6. John R. Lott, Jr., "Will Suing Gunmakers Endanger Lives?" *Chicago Tribune*, 17 November 1998, 19. There are some politicians who say that they are sensi-

tive to these contradictions in their stands. One such politician is California senator Dianne Feinstein who used to have a permit to carry a concealed handgun. She no longer retains the permit, and she has pointedly raised this issue during committee hearings in the Senate. Others still criticize Feinstein by saying that she only gave up her permit when she became mayor of San Francisco and was given a police bodyguard.

7. John R. Lott, Jr., "When It Comes to Firearms, Do As I Say, Not As I Do; Guns: Rosie O'Donnell, Who Opposes Handgun Permits for Others, Doesn't See Problem with Her Bodyguards Having Them," *Los Angeles Times*, 1 June 2000, 11.

8. http://www.vpc.org/studies/roofcont.htm.

9. The McCain-Lieberman-DeWine bill is S.890, while the Reed bill is S. 767.

10. Anti-terrorism Policy, U.S. Senate Judiciary Committee, 6 December 2001, FDCH Political Transcripts: Washington, D.C.

11. Some examples include Fox Butterfield, "Gun Foes Use Terror Issue in a Push for Stricter Laws," *New York Times*, 13 November 2001, B6; Editorial, "Gun Shows Give Terrorists Easy Access to Firearms," *USA Today*, 12 December 2001; Editorial, "Gun Shows and Terrorists," *Washington Post*, 16 December 2001, B6; and Eric Holder, "Keeping Guns Away From Terrorists," *Washington Post*, 25 October 2001, A31.

12. David Shepardson, "Arab Americans criticize use of FBI informants," *Detroit News*, 6 May 2001 (http://detnews.com/2001/wayne/0105/06/c03-220841.htm).

13. Editorial, "Gun Shows Give Terrorists Easy Access to Firearms," *USA Today*, 12 December 2001.

14. Ibid. and Fox Butterfield, "Gun Foes Use Terror Issue in a Push for Stricter Laws," *New York Times*, 13 November 2001, B6.

15. Editorial, "Gun Shows Give Terrorists."

16. Jeremy Schwartz, "Pakistani merchant enters a guilty plea," *Corpus Christi Caller-Times*, 30 October 2001 (www.caller.com/2001/october/30/today/localnew/16238.html) and Jeremy Schwartz, "Alice man pleads not guilty," *Corpus Christi Caller-Times*, 22 September 2001 (www.caller.com/2001/september/22/today/localnew/12261.html); and Vanessa Santo-Garza, "Safety steps taken in offices," *Corpus Christi Caller-Times*, 20 September 2001 (www.caller.com/2001/september/20/today/localnew/12068.html).

17. Bob Herbert, "More Guns for Everyone!" *New York Times*, 9 May 2002, A31.

18. http://www.millionmommarch.org/features/timeout/index.asp?record=11

19. Nicholas Kristof, "'Chicks' and others with Guns," *Chattanooga Times/Chattanooga Free Press*, 9 March 2002, B6.

20. An example of belittling gun buyers can be found in Dan K. Thomasson, "Lax U.S. Gun Control is a Benefit to Terrorists," *Detroit News*, 30 December 2001. For a typical example of the news articles linking increased gun sales to the risk of having a gun in the home see Lois Romano, "At Tulsa Gun Show, Searching for Safety; U.S. Sales on the Rise Since Sept. 11 Attacks," *Washington Post*, 22 October 2001, A3.

21. There are currently about 6.5 million people living in Israel. Of those, 81 percent are Jews and 63 percent are over twenty years of age (http://www.jafi.org.il/agenda/2001/english/wk3-1/14.asp and http://www.un.org/Depts/unsd/social/youth.htm). Arabs are restricted from obtaining concealed handgun permits. At the time of this writing Israel had 340,000 handgun permit holders, though they were planning on issuing 40,000 more permits ("Army Issuing 40,000 Handgun Permits," IsraelNN.com, 6 March 2002, http://www.israelnationalnews.com/news.php3?id=19628). Related information can be found at (http://www.jpost.com/Editions/2002/03/06/LatestNews/ LatestNews.44715.html), though this second story appears to include only a portion of all the permit holders.

22. Abraham Rabinovich, "Israel OKs 60,000 more gun permits in terror fight," *Washington Times*, 7 March 2002 (http://www.washingtontimes.com/world/20020307-8478768.htm). See also Etgar Lefkovits, "Gun Demand Up 75 percent," *Jerusalem Post*, 8 March 2002 (http://www.jpost.com/Editions/2002/03/07/News/News.44732.html).

23. Similar examples involving "dozens of incidents where the intervention of private gun owners prevented or mitigated terrorist attacks" are claimed to exist in Dan Williams's piece "Under the Gun," *Jerusalem Post*, 2 January 2001.

24. "Armed Israeli Civilian Stops Terrorist Attacker," Fox News Channel, 4 November 2001.

25. Amos Harel, "Israeli seriously hurt in W. Bank shooting attack," *Ha'aretz*, 25 December 2001.

26. Celean Jacobson, "Armed Worshippers to Guard Synagogues," Associated Press, 19 March 2002 (http://story.news.yahoo.com/news?tmpl=story&u=/ap/20020319/ap_on_re_mi_ea/israel_synagogue_security_5).

27. David G. Grant, "Gunman found dead after police standoff," *Detroit News*, 13 March 2001. http://www.detnews.com/2001/metro/0103/13/d10-198791.htm

28. The Zogby poll is discussed in a press release, "Bush Best Man For Crisis; Airline Anti-Terrorism Measures Rate Well With Americans; Second Amendment Freedoms Important," Associated Television News, Washington, D.C. (Internet Wire), 15 October 2001 (http://biz.yahoo.com/iw/011015/02033037_1.html).

29. The exact date is not publicly available.

30. William M. Landes, "An Economic Study of U.S. Airline Hijacking, 1961–1976," *Journal of Law and Economics* 21 (April 1978): 1–32.

31. "'Major Disaster' Averted: Shoe Bomb Suspect Had Explosive Material to Bring Down Plane," ABCnews.com, 24 December 2001. (http://abcnews.go.com/sections/us/DailyNews/airplane_explosives011224.html)

32. David Harrison, "Britain drops plan to use armed guards on aircraft," *Daily Telegraph* (London), 6 January 2002 and Terri Judd, "Campaign against terrorism: Journalists took knives on to plane as test of security," *Independent* (London), 7 January 2002, 9.

33. The unions include the Air Line Pilots Association, the Allied Pilots Association, the Southwest Pilots Association, and the union for cargo pilots.

34. Captain Jim Lortscher, a Shuttle America pilot expressed this sentiment: "I will flip the plane over, turn it upside down. You don't have to do it for long. You just roll over, and people will hit the ceiling, and they are injured. It is very effective." (Sally Jacobs, "New Flight Plan Airline Pilots have a Take-Charge Attitude about Defending Planes," *Boston Globe*, 10 October 2001, C1.)

35. Amotz Asa-El and Dan Baron, "Harsh words, big cash," *Jerusalem Post*, 12 October 2001, 3; and Claudia Cowen, "Against All Odds," Fox News Channel, 26 December 2001. The Airline Pilot's Security Association claims that they have been informed by a gun manufacturer that El Al arms its pilots. Locked doors are not Nirvana. They also create safety problems: sealed doors with the plane designs we use can create differential pressures between the cockpit and cabin and produce "explosive decompression." Locked doors can further make it difficult for pilots to help passengers after crashes and can eliminate the cockpit windows as an escape route for passengers.

36. Statement by Airline Pilots' Security Alliance vice president in meeting at the Office of Management and Budget on 26 March 2002. He also claimed that El Al still armed its pilots.

37. Sara Kehaulani Goo and Greg Schneider, "Fewer Marshals on Flights At National, Pilots Say," *Washington Post*, 5 March 2002, A1. The facts for this and the following paragraph are taken from this article in the *Washington Post*.

38. Ibid. At that time there were about 35,000 flights operating in the U.S. The article quoted pilots saying the true number is "quite a bit less than 100%" and falling.

39. Among those whom I have talked to are Al Aitken and Gary Boettcher of the Allied Pilots Association and Steve Luckey of the Air Line Pilots Association.

40. This is based upon comments made to me by Gary Boettcher and Al Aitken of the Allied Pilots Association, Tracy Price of the Airline Pilots' Security Alliance, and Steve Luckey of the Air Line Pilots Association.

41. Ibid. The pilots unions in the *Washington Post* article argued that it would "require a force the size of the U.S. Marine Corps," but they assumed that there would only be one marshal on each plane.

42. Ibid.

43. Tom Ramstack and Kristina Stefanova, "Not much turbulence in baggage screening," *Washington Times*, 19 January 2002, A1.

44. This is from repeated conversations that I have had with the Air Line Pilots Association, the Airline Pilots' Security Alliance, and the Allied Pilots Association.

45. Larry King, "The Rodney King/LAPD Trial," CNN, 25 March 1993 and Jon Dougherty, "'No substitute for firearms' on aircraft: Expert believes stun gun would not have prevented 9-11 hijackings," WorldNetDaily.com, 22 January 2002.

46. Ian Ith, "Taser fails to halt man with knife," *Seattle Times*, 28 November 2001, A1; and Michael Burge, "Transit district may arm guards," *San Diego Union-Tribune*, 5 December 2001, NC1.

47. Michael Cooper, "Grand Jury to Hear Case Of Brooklyn Man's Death," *New York Times*, 2 September 1999, B3. This experience should actually be given a great deal of weight because other police departments experience similar problems (Robin Topping, "Cops cleared in fatal shooting," New York *Newsday*, 9 October 1998, A29).

48. Discussion with Steve Tuttle, a founder of Taser International of Scottsdale, Ariz., as cited in the Allied Pilots Association's filing with the U.S. Department of Transportation on the rule governing whether pilots can carry guns.

49. Dave Kopel, "Arms in the Air," *National Review Online*, 26 September 2001.

50. Hearing of the Subcommittee on Aviation of the House Committee on Transportation and Infrastructure, chaired by Representative John L. Mica, 2 May 2002.

51. Hinderberger also notes that "Commercial airplanes can land safely after the loss, or blow out, of a passenger window. In the event a cabin window is blown out, the ensuing decompression could result in a passenger injury or fatality to a nonbelted passenger near the window. But there would be little hazard to the continued safe flight and landing. Aircraft are designed to survive and land after a rapid decompression resulting from the loss of a cargo door, and have done so." Ibid.

52. Two articles in just the *New York Times* are: Michael Janofsky, "Traces of Terror: Travel," 12 July 2002, A1, and Matthew L. Wald, "Traces of Terror: Air Security," 11 July 2002, A1.

53. http://www.fbi.gov/ucr/ucr.htm. During at least the five years from 1995 to 1999, the handgun rate never reaches 21 percent. In one year it comes close, but on average it is less than half the value claimed.

54. Ibid.

55. John Quinones, "Local Heroes," *Primetime Live*, ABC News, 8 March 2001.

56. Ted Dees, "'Hero' Off-Duty Officer Saves Lives at Santee School Shooting," Law Enforcement Alliance of America: Falls Church, Va., 7 March 2001.

57. Legislation has passed the House of Representatives to change this by a whopping 372 to 53 vote, but it has never made it through the Senate.

58. John Bresnahan, "Cunningham Pushes Discharge Petition for Gun Bill," *Roll Call*, 5 November 2001, and Will Shuck, "Bill would allow off-duty cops to be armed everywhere," Recordnet.com, 23 March 2002 (http://www.recordnet.com/daily/news/articles/3news032302.html). In Seattle, Washington "Several off-duty police officers and sheriff's deputies recently have been barred from Key Arena, Husky Stadium and the Stadium Exhibition Center—all public, big-event venues in Seattle…" Lewis Kamb, "Armed Police Being Barred from Games," *Seattle Post-Intelligencer*, 12 March 2002 (http://seattlepi.nwsource.com/local/61853_guns12.shtml).

59. Staff Reports, "Assembly Oks Off-Duty Guns," *Sacramento Bee*, 25 May 2002 (http://www.modbee.com/local/story/2884555p-3704293c.html).

60. Sebastian Rotella, "French Shooting Suspect Plunges to His Death," *Los Angeles Times*, 29 March 2002, A1.

61. Fiona Fleck, "Swiss Massacre Spurs Calls for Gun Law Reform," *Sunday Telegraph* (London), 30 September 2001, 29, and Xinhua General News Service, "Switzerland's Image Under Scrutiny," Xinhua General News Service, 26 November 2001.
62. The International Crime Victimization Survey provides detailed evidence on robbery, sexual assault, and assaults across twenty-three countries (http://www.unicri.it/icvs/statistics/index_stats.htm).
63. Edmund L. Andrews, "Germany's Columbine," *New York Times*, 28 April 2002, Section 4, 2; and Sebastian Rotella, "Ominous Cracks Seen in Gun Control Utopia," *Los Angeles Times*, 28 April 2002, A3.
64. Rotella, "Ominous Cracks Seen in Gun Control Utopia."
65. Ibid.
66. Robert Graham, "Memory of shootings haunt people of Nanterre," *Financial Times* (London), 22 April 2002, 2.
67. Jon Henley, "Eight die in French council massacre," *Guardian* (London), 28 March 2002, 20.
68. Jim Wurst, "U.S. Agenda Dominates U.N. Plan to Control Small Arms," Inter Press Service, 21 July 2000.
69. William Alex Pridemore, "Using Newly Available Homicide Data to Debunk Two Myths About Violence in an International Context," *Homicide Studies*, August 2001, 267.
70. Stephen Robinson, "Dunblane gun law has been failure, says marksman," *Daily Telegraph* (London, United Kingdom), 28 December 2001. (http://www.portal.telegraph.co.uk/news/main.jhtml?xml=/news/2001/12/28/ngun28.xml&sSheet=/news/2001/12/28/ixhome.html)
71. Ibid.
72. "London Gun Crime Up 90%," *Sky News*, 19 December 2001. http://www.sky.com/skynews/article/0,,30100-1038794,00.html.

    The British Broadcasting Corporation put the problem pretty succintly: "While Britain has some of the toughest firearms laws in the world, the recent spate of gun murders in London has highlighted a disturbing growth in armed crime." (BBC News, "A country in the crosshairs," 4 January 2002, http://news.bbc.co.uk/hi/english/uk/ newsid_1741000/1741336.stm).
73. Sophie Goodchild, "Britain is now the crime capital of the West," *Independent Digital* (UK), 14 July 2002 (http://news.independent.co.uk/uk/crime/story.jsp?story=314832). The article notes that "'contact crime,' defined as robbery, sexual assault and assault with force, was second highest in England and Wales: 3.6 per cent of those surveyed. This compares with 1.9 per cent in the US."

    Of twenty-three major countries studied by the International Crime Victimization Survey during 2000, England and Australia had the two highest victimization rates, with 54.5 and 54.3 offenses per 100 inhabitants. Robberies and sexual assaults were two to three times higher in both countries than they were in the United States. (http://www.unicri.it/icvs/statistics/index_ stats.htm)

74. Nicholas Rufford, "Official: more muggings in England than US," *Sunday Times* (London), 11 October 1998.

75. Ed Johnson, "Mobile Phone Shootings Shock Britain," Associated Press, 9 January 2002.

76. The Australia Bureau of Statistics can be found at: www.abs.gov.au.

77. Nathan Vass, "Handguns declared public enemy No. 1," *Sunday Telegraph* (Sydney, Australia), April 2002. (http://www.dailytelegraph.news.com.au/common/story_page/0,5936,4128008%255E701,00.html#)

78. Steve Miller, "Gun Rights Groups Rip UN Chief's 'Hypocrisy,'" *Washington Times*, 22 February 2002, A3.

79. Ibid.

80. Ibid.

81. Julie McCormack, "Black man uses gun to stop three-man assault," *The Sun* (Western Puget Sound, Washington), 1 February 2001.

82. Lawrence Southwick, Jr., "Self-Defense With Guns: The Consequences," *Managerial and Decision Economics* (forthcoming): Tables 5 and 6. See also Gary Kleck's *Point Blank*. While the estimates are quite statistically significant for defense for all groups, small samples make it difficult to distinquish the differences by gender. Still the point estimates indicate that women benefit more than men from having a gun to defend themselves.

83. Bill Tattersall, "Toy Gun Exchange Turnout Decreases," *Morning Call* (Allentown, Pa.), 20 October 2000, B8.

84. Jennifer Morrison, "COPS, Community Take Bang Out of Street Violence," *Toronto Sun*, 20 July 2001, 10.

85. Valerie Richardson, "Zero tolerance takes toll on pupils," *Washington Times*, 13 May 2002 (http://www.washtimes.com/national/20020513-9519286.htm). Editorial, "Overreacting to gun games," *Rocky Mountain News*, 15 May 2002 (http://www.rockymountainnews.com/drmn/opinion/article/0,1299, DRMN_38_1146964,00.html).

86. Joseph Pereira, "EToys site back online," *Chicago Sun-Times*, 13 December 2001, 52.

87. Jeff Collins, "Guns Colored for Safety," *Orange County Register*, 7 January 2001.

88. The Associated Press, "Kmart to stop pistol ammo sales," *Charleston Gazette*, 29 June 2001, 3C.

89. John R. Lott, Jr., "'The Patriot' is right," *New York Post*, 22 June 2000.

90. See http://www.askingsaveskids.com/ask.html.

91. ABC News, "Americans Arm Themselves: Gun Dealers Report Many Sales to First-Timers,"1 October 2001 (http://abcnews.go.com/sections/us/DailyNews/WTC_terrorismgunrun_011001.html).

92. http://www.projecthomesafe.org

93. David Bean, "3 Million Free Gun Locks to be Distributed by Project Home-Safe," National Shooting Sports Foundation, 9 September 2001 press release.

94. "Firearms accidents in the home can result from an unauthorized individual, often a child, finding a loaded and unsecured gun in the home. The risk of

firearms-related unintentional injuries or deaths can be reduced when firearms owners are aware of and fully understand their responsibility to handle firearms safely and store them in a secure manner." http://www.projecthome-safe.org

95. While the numbers that I provided on this occasion were from 1996, the numbers in the text are the most updated numbers through 1998.

96. Sarah A. Klein, "AMA Push will Target Gun Lobby," *Crain's Chicago Business*, 30 April 2001, 1.

97. "Handgun Injury," *Reason*, 1 June 2001, 18.

98. The data is obtained from the Centers for Disease Control (http://wonder.cdc.gov).

99. The number of gun owners was obtained by multiplying the Zogby poll numbers by the number of adults in America in 2000. Press Release, "Bush Best Man For Crisis; Airline Anti-Terrorism Measures Rate Well With Americans; Second Amendment Freedoms Important," Associated Television News, Washington, D.C. (Internet Wire), 15 October 2001 (http://biz.yahoo.com/iw/011015/02033037_1.html).

100. Estimate from the National Safety Council (www.nsc.org).

101. The data is obtained from the Centers for Disease Control (http://wonder.cdc.gov).

102. Ibid.

103. David Byrd, "Kids, Parents, and Guns," *National Journal*, 8 April 2000, 1136.

104. For example, he claimed "Every single day Congress waits, we lose 12 children... to gun violence. Congress should follow Maryland's lead [and adopt built-in gun locks]." Jim Abrams, "House Oks Bill Backing Gun Laws," Associated Press, 12 April 2000.

105. One article that does a nice job breaking down these numbers for those under 15 versus including 16- to 19-year-olds is by Iain Murray, "Secrets and Lies Questionable Stats Plague Gun Debate," *Denver Post*, 18 June 2000, G1. See also David Byrd, "Kids, Parents, and Guns," *National Journal*, 8 April 2000, 1136.

106. The quote is attributed to Capt. George F. Paruch of the Richmond Police Department in Texas. (Robert B. Henderson, "Fort Bend Law Enforcement Agencies Distribute Gun locks," *Houston Chronicle*, 26 July 2001, 2.)

107. President Clinton even made this point when he was arguing for closing the so-called gun show loophole. From News Service Reports, "Clinton Urges Congress to Follow Maryland's Lead," *The Record*, 12 April 2000, A9.

108. National School Safety Center report, "School Associated Violent Deaths," (Westlake Village, California: National School Safety Center), 16 May 2001.

109. Ibid.

110. Chris Moran, "Union insures its teachers for homicide; Families will get $150,000," *San Diego Union-Tribune*, 28 July 2001, A1.

111. Frederick O. Mueller and Jerry L. Diehl, "Annual Survey of Football Injury Research," National Center for Catastrophic Sport Injury Research, February 2001 (http://www.unc.edu/depts/nccsi/SurveyofFootballInjuries.htm).

112. Richard Roeper, "Can't dodge the question: Aren't we overreacting?" *Chicago Sun-Times*, 20 June 2001, 11; and David Bloom, "Debate on Issue that Dodge Ball Should be Banned in Schools," *NBC Saturday Today*, NBC News Transcripts, 26 May 2001.

113. For a collection of the stories in these two paragraphs as well as numerous other cases see: http://opinionjournal.com/extra/?id=95000486.

114. Ibid.

115. Liz Cobbs, "Boy, 8, faces charges for pointing toy gun," *Ann Arbor News*, 2 March 2002 (http://www.mlive.com/news/aanews/index.ssf?/xml/story.ssf/html_standard.xsl?/base/news/10150548022833710.xml).

116. Fox News, "7-Year-Old Florida Boy Charged With Felony for Pencil Stabbing," FoxNews.com, 2 May 2002 (http://www.foxnews.com/story/0,2933,51730,00.html). In this case, "A 7-year-old boy has been charged with aggravated battery, a felony, for allegedly stabbing four elementary school classmates with a pencil after he was asked to share his crayons."

CHAPTER 5: EVALUATING EVIDENCE ON GUNS: HOW AND HOW NOT TO DO IT

1. The opposite of endogenous is exogenous. An exogenous change in something means it was an independent change, not a response to something else. In reality, almost everything is to some extent related to something else, so the distinction between exogenous and endogenous is a matter of degree. Since models and statistical methods must put a limit on how much to include, there will always be variables that are treated as "exogenously given" rather than dependent on another variable. For social sciences, this is a constant headache. Virtually any study is open to the criticism: "But if variable X depends upon variable Y, your results are not necessarily valid." In general, larger studies, relying on more data have better chances of being able to incorporate more relationships. Part of the process of doing research is finding out what possible relationships raise important concerns for the readers and then attempting to test for those concerns.

2. Raymond Bonner and Ford Fessenden, "States With No Death Penalty Share Lower Homicide Rates," *New York Times*, 22 September 2000, A1.

3. Terry Carter, "The Man Who Would Undo Miranda," *ABA Journal*, March 2000, 44.

4. With purely cross-sectional data, if one recognizes that there may be differences in crime rates even after all the demographic and criminal punishment variables are accounted for, there are simply not enough observations to take into account these regional differences. One cannot control for more variables than one has observations to explain.

   The problem with time-series data is the same. Time-series studies typically assume that crime follows a particular type of time trend (for example, assuming that crime rises at a constant rate over time or more complicated growth rates involving squared or cubic relationships). Yet, almost any crime pattern over time is possible and, like cross-sectional data, unexplained differences over time will persist even after all the demographic and criminal punishment variables are accounted for. Ideally, one could allow each year to have a different effect, but again with time-series data we would find that we had more variables to explain changes than observations to explain.

5. The first paper to do this was one that I coauthored with David Mustard ("Do Concealed Handgun Laws Deter Crime," *Journal of Legal Studies*, January 1997). Since then a large number of new studies have been done. Many are discussed in my book, *More Guns, Less Crime,* and other newer papers are discussed in the next section as well as the rest of this book.

CHAPTER 6: ACTS OF TERROR WITH GUNS: MULTIPLE VICTIM SHOOTINGS

1. http://www.nypost.com/news/worldnews/11845.htm. A similar version of events can be found at: http://www.washingtonpost.com/wp-dyn/articles/ A38430-2002Mar4.html and at http://www.coxnews.com/newsservice/stories/2002/0411-MIDEAST-ISRAEL-COX.html.

2. http://www.israelnationalnews.com/news.php3?id=24440

3. Philip Cook quoted in editorial, *Cincinnati Enquirer*, 23 January 1996, A8. Others share this belief. "It's common sense," says Doug Weil, research director at the Center to Prevent Handgun Violence and Handgun Control, Inc. "The more guns people are carrying, the more likely it is that ordinary confrontations will escalate into violent confrontations" (William Tucker, "Maybe You Should Carry A Handgun," *Weekly Standard*, 16 December 1996, 30).

4. See P. J. Cook, "The Role of Firearms in Violent Crime," in M. E. Wolfgang and N. A. Werner, eds., *Criminal Violence*, (Newbury, N.J.: Sage Publishers, 1982), and Franklin Zimring, "The Medium Is the Message: Firearm Caliber as a Determinant of Death from Assault," *Journal of Legal Studies*, 1 (1972), for these arguments.

5. Gary Kleck and Marc Gertz, "Armed Resistance to Crime: The Prevalence and Nature of Self-Defense with a Gun," *Journal of Criminal Law and Criminology* 86 (Fall 1995). For an extensive survey on this literature see Kleck (1997, Chapter 5) and Cook and Ludwig (1996).

6. Gary Kleck and Don Kates (288–290) present the most recent data from the Department of Justice's National Crime Victimization Survey from 1992 to 1998 and also indicate that the risk of serious injury from a criminal attack is lowest when one resists a criminal confrontation with a gun. There are problems with the National Crime Victimization Survey both because it doesn't directly ask people whether they used a gun defensively and its failure to adjust for many people not admitting to a law enforcement agency that they used a gun, even defensively. Unfortunately, this survey provides the only

available evidence how the probability of significant injury varies with level
and type of resistance.

7. Lott (1998b) finds these effects, but see related discussions by Bartley et. al.,
1998; Black and Nagin, 1998; Bronars and Lott, 1998; Plassmann and Tideman,
1998; Lott and Mustard, 1997; and Lott, 1998a. Ayres and Levitt (1998) discuss
related empirical evidence of spillovers for the issue of Lojack automobile
alarms.

8. Unfortunately, no data are available on whether handguns lawfully bought by
permit holders are used in crimes by another party at a later date.

9. One article gave a very detailed discussion of what happened that day in Pearl,
Mississippi: "Student eyewitnesses and shooting victims of the Pearl High
School (Mississippi) rampage used phrases like 'unreal' and 'like a horror
movie' as they testified Wednesday about seeing Luke Woodham methodically
point his deer rifle at them and pull the trigger at least six times. . . . The day's
most vivid testimony came from a gutsy hero of the day. Assistant principal
Joel Myrick heard the initial shot and watched Woodham choosing his victims. When Woodham appeared headed for a science wing where early classes
were already under way, Myrick ran for his pickup and grabbed his .45-caliber
pistol. He rounded the school building in time to see Woodham leaving the
school and getting into his mother's white Chevy Corsica. He watched its
back tires smoke from Woodham's failure to remove the parking brake. Then
he ordered him to stop. 'I had my pistol's sights on him. I could see the whites
of his knuckles' on the steering wheel, Myrick said. He reached into the car
and opened the driver-side door, then ordered Woodham to lie on the ground. 'I
put my foot on his back area and pointed my pistol at him,' Myrick testified."
(Bartholomew Sullivan, 'Students Recall 'Unreal' Rampage,' *The Commercial
Appeal*, 11 June 1998, A1.) See also CNN, 2 October 1997.

10. Reuters Newswire, 26 April 1998.

11. *Baltimore Sun*, 26 October 1991. As referenced in an article by Don Kates and
Dan Polsby. "Of Genocide and Disarmament," *Journal of Criminal Law and
Criminology* 86 (Fall 1995): 252.

12. http://www.jpost.com/Editions/2002/02/22/News/News.43961.html. For
another report on this case see: Middle East Newsline, "Israeli shopper kills
suicide attacker after bomb fizzles," WorldTribune.com, 22 February 2002.
(http://www.worldtribune.com/worldtribune/breaking_8.html)

13. http://www.nypost.com/news/worldnews/43051.htm. See also
http://story.news.yahoo.com/news?tmpl=story&ncid=578&e=4&cid=578&u=/
nm/20020524/ts_nm/mideast_dc_2296.

14. Many national publications have called for these types of laws in the advent of
public shootings. For example, the *New York Times* advocated "background
checks, trigger locks and gun show sales" restrictions as well as more comprehensive background checks as solutions to these attacks (*New York Times* editorial,13 April 2000, A30).

15. Ibid.

16. To illustrate, let the probability (p) that a single individual carries a concealed handgun be .05. Assume further that there are 10 individuals in a public place. Then the probability that at least one of them is armed is about .40 (= 1 − (.95)10). Even if (p) is only .025, the probability that at least one of ten people will be armed is .22 (= 1 − (.975)10). This calculation assumes that the individual's probability of carrying a gun is independent of how many people there are in a public place. One might argue that this probability would be negatively related to the expected number of individuals because each individual expects (with a positive probability) that another law-abiding citizen carrying a gun will protect him. Still, the main argument would still hold provided "free riding" doesn't wipe out the incentive for any party to carry a gun.

17. George Stigler (1970)

18. While the recent rash of public school shootings during the 1997–99 school years largely took place after the period of our study, these incidents raise questions about the unintentional consequences of laws. All the public school shootings took place after a 1995 federal law banned guns (including permitted concealed handguns) within a thousand feet of a school. The possibility exists that attempts to outlaw guns from schools, no matter how well meaning, may have produced perverse effects. It is interesting to note that during the 1977 to 1995 period, fifteen shootings took place in schools in states without right-to-carry laws and only one took place in a state with this type of law. There were nineteen deaths and ninety-seven injuries in states without the law, while there was one death and two injuries in states with the law.

19. In a recent paper (see T. Petee, K. Padgett and T. York, "Debunking the Stereotype: An Examination of Mass Murder in Public Places," [*Homicide Studies* 317 (1997)], the authors find felony related mass murders account for 36 percent and gang motivated mass murder incidents for 5.8 percent over the 1965 to 1995 period. That study defines mass murders as the killing of three or more persons (so it has much fewer incidents than our sample).

20. One concern that cannot be ruled out is that local or national news coverage reported in the Lexis-Nexis database may miss some local public shootings involving two or victims. Yet, especially given the earlier discussions in Chapters 2 and 3 it seems highly doubtful that local news coverage will miss public non-gang shootings involving at least two or, say, four people killed. To see whether it makes any difference, these different measures of public shootings are also examined, and, as it turns out, the results are not very sensitive to these different definitions. The way multiple victim public shootings are defined—requiring two or more killings or injuries, rather than three or more or four or more and so on—is somewhat arbitrary, and examining these different combinations overcomes that concern also.

However, as a comparison, we did use the FBI's Supplemental Homicide Report (SHR) data. While the results consistently indicated that concealed handguns laws reduced the level and severity of attacks, the results were rarely statistically significant.

Using four or more murders is the most problematic in that the results are no longer statistically significant for injuries. If negative binomials are used (as will be discussed later), the results for two or more injuries or murders and three or more murders are still consistently significant. Limiting the estimates to four or more murders and using the negative binomial regressions eliminates the statistically significant results, though the coefficients imply that there are drops in the number of attacks and number of people harmed.

Since there are well documented problems with the SHR, other researchers have also used news reports to document multiple victim killings. (See for example, Petee et al., 1997 and for a more popular discussion of using news reports to identify attacks see Fessenden, 2000.) In the SHR, some events are double-counted and others are left out. The SHR does not provide information on where or how the attacks took place or during the commission of a robbery or other crime. It also doesn't accurately report whether the shootings occurred during a gang fight. Our study has little to say about why gang fights over things like drug turf will be changing over time. Even if these cases were identified by the SHR data (and they are not) simply including a dummy variable for shootings due to gang fights would not properly account for all the impact that these changes might have. Indeed one would probably have to interact the dummy variable with all the variables used in the regressions that will be reported and thus it would be essentially the same as running a separate regression on these cases. Another problem is that the shootings we want to study make up only a small fraction of the number contained in the SHR.

21. Alschuler (1997, 369) claims that concealed handguns should only deter crimes involving strangers. Our response is that concealed handguns can deter crimes involving acquaintances as well as strangers, though deterrence involving acquaintances might be more easily thought of as similar to open-carrying of guns. The big effect of concealed handguns is that they may allow people to be able to now defend themselves outside of their home or business. The passage of the concealed handgun laws may deter crimes against acquaintances simply to the extent to which it increases gun ownership.

22. Most states allow private businesses to decide whether permit holders are allowed to carry concealed handguns on their premises. State rules may also vary with regard to other places such as government buildings, churches, and bars.

23. The results are statistically significant at least at the 4 percent level.

24. The year 1996 has an unusually high number of murders, injuries, and attacks. Prior to the 128 people who were killed in 1996, the largest number of deaths had been 87 in 1993. Injuries and the number of attacks showed the biggest increases in 1996. Prior to the 291 injuries recorded in 1996, the highest number was 92 in 1982. The year 1997 was also unusually dangerous, and includes some of the public school shootings.

25. http://papers.ssrn.com/sol3/papers.cfm?abstract_id=161637

26. The twenty-three states that enacted "shall-issue" or "right-to-carry" laws in the 1977 to 1997 period (dates in parentheses) are as follows: Alaska (1994), Arizona (1994), Arkansas (1995), Florida (1987), Georgia (1989), Idaho (1990), Kentucky (1996), Louisiana (1996), Maine (1985), Mississippi (1990), Montana (1991), Nevada (1995), North Carolina (1995), Oklahoma (1995), Oregon (1990), Pennsylvania (1989), South Carolina (1996), Tennessee (1994), Texas (1995), Virginia (1988), Utah (1995), West Virginia (1989), and Wyoming (1994). Some states such as Texas passed the law in 1995, but they did not go into effect until January of 1996. The following eight states had "shall-issue" laws over the entire period: Alabama, Connecticut, Indiana, New Hampshire, North Dakota, South Dakota, Vermont and Washington. Data on states having laws prior to 1993 are from Clayton E. Cramer and David B. Kopel, "Shall-issue: The New Wave of Concealed Handgun Permit Laws," 62 *Tennessee Law Review*, 679 (1995). We used a Nexis search to determine the state and date for states passing laws between 1993 and 1995. These two sources were also used in Lott and Mustard (1997). Because of objections raised to the dates for "shall-issue" laws in Maine and Virginia (see the discussion in Lott and Mustard), the regression analysis presented in Part III examines the sensitivity of our findings to alternative dates for Maine and Virginia.

27. The reverse—a particularly large upward trend—occurred in states that did not change their law (see Table 13).

28. Of course, there were zero multiple victim public shootings in individual states in particular years before the passage of concealed handgun laws. Appendix 6.1 provides a breakdown for the states that did not adopt right-to-carry laws.

29. Bombing data are available in the Bureau of Alcohol, Tobacco and Firearms annual publication entitled "Arson and Explosives: Incidents Report."

30. See Tracy L. Snell, "Prisoners executed under civil authority in the United States, by year, region, and jurisdiction, 1977–1995," Bureau of Justice Statistics, 14 May 1997.

31. This refers to fixed year and state effects.

32. See Lott (2000) for a discussion of these variables. For the source of penalties imposed for when a gun is used in a commission of a crime see Thomas B. Marvell and Carl E. Moody, "The Impact of Enhanced Prison Terms for Felonies Committed with Guns," *Criminology* 33 (May 1995): 247, 258–61.

33. These types of variables are normally referred to as fixed year and state effects.

34. This approach may actually understate the impact of right-to-carry laws since the estimates may attribute some of the drop to these other control factors when the drop is actually due to the right-to-carry laws.

35. The variable takes the value of one if a state has a concealed handgun or "right-to-carry" law, but zero if it does not have such a law.

36. The states and years of the missing observations are as follows: Florida (1988); Illinois (1993-95); Iowa (1991); Kansas (1993-95); Kentucky (1988); Montana (1994-95); New Hampshire (1984 and 1995); Pennsylvania (1995) and Vermont

(1978-79). As a further check on our results, we reestimated the regressions in
Tables 6 and 7 deleting the arrest variable and adding the sixteen missing
observations. The coefficients and levels of significance on the right to carry
law dummy variable were virtually unchanged.

37. If the variance doesn't equal the mean, the appropriate test is to use a negative
binomial, which no longer requires this assumption. Redoing the results presented in this chapter with a negative binomial produces extremely similar
results to those that will be reported. For example, redoing the right-to-carry
estimates for Table 6.6 with a negative binomial produces:

   Estimate corresponding to regression 1: 71%, z= 2.496, significant at the 1.3
   percent level

   Estimate corresponding to regression 2: 83%, z= 3.414, significant at the 0.1
   percent level

   Estimate corresponding to regression 3: 81%, z=3.277 , significant at the 0.1
   percent level

   Estimate corresponding to regression 4: 67%, z= 3.821, significant at the 0.1
   percent level

38. Appendix 6.2 shows the incidence rate ratios and z-statistics for specification 3
and 4 in Table 6.5.

39. Fessenden, 9 April 2000, 28.

40. We note that the arrest rate variable understates the actual (or expected) arrest
rate of individuals who go on shooting sprees. More than 90 percent of these
offenders are either arrested or killed, which is slightly greater than the overall
arrest rate for murder. The 90 percent figure (which comes from a Nexis
search) represents perpetrators who were immediately captured or killed. We
do not know whether those who escaped were apprehended later.

41. The first trend that takes the value 0 in the year the law is passed (and 0 in all
years following passage), -1 in the year before passage, -2 in the second year
before passage and so forth. The second variable takes the value 0 in the year
the law is passed (and 0 in all years before passage), 1 in the first year after passage and so on.

42. We note three other points related to Table 6.6.

   (1) Eight states in our sample had shall-issue laws during the entire period.
   All eight passed their laws before 1960 and so should have reached their equi-
   librium level of permits before 1977 (the first year in our sample). The value
   assigned to two time trend variables for these states and states that never
   enacted laws is zero.

   (2) A second reason for the split time trend specification is that if (relative to
   other states) shootings in states that pass right to carry laws are rising before the
   law goes into effect and falling thereafter, a dummy law variable would underes-
   timate the law's impact (even though the regression contains year dummy variables). For example, imagine that the increase in shootings before the law is
   symmetrical with the decline after the law. A simple dummy variable for the
   presence or absence of the law could indicate that the law had no effect yet the
   law might well have caused a change in the trend from positive to negative.

(3) We also estimated regressions adding two time-squared variables for the law variables. Here we find the same pattern of declining murders and injuries after passage of the law with the decline flattening out by the sixth year after enactment of the law.

43. Lott, 1998b, 75.

44. The F-test for the differences in these time trends is always significant at least at the 0.002 percent level.

45. We also tried adding in a variable for the Brady Act, but it was essentially zero and had no effect on any of the other estimates.

46. Also note that the execution variable is probably only weakly related to the probability that a mass murderer will be executed, given the long delays before execution, its over-inclusiveness (i.e., the variable measures the execution rate for all murders not mass murders) and the fact that many of these offenders are killed during their attack. Because of this we also tried including a simple dummy variable for whether the death penalty was in effect. The coefficient on this variable was never statistically significant, and it did not alter any other results.

47. The results are statistically significant at better than 0.01 percent level. The county level estimates with the execution rate correspond to the estimates in Table 4.13 (Lott, 1998b), and the coefficient on the execution rate is -7.21, with a t-statistic of -3.218. The smaller 4 percent effect is associated with the state level data. For similarly deterrence effects from capital punishment see Isaac Ehrlich, "The Deterrent Effect of Capital Punishment: A Question of Life and Death," *American Economic Review* 65 (1975): 397–417; Isaac Ehrlich, "Capital Punishment and Deterrence: Some Further Thoughts and Additional Evidence." *Journal of Political Economy* 85 (August 1977): 741–88; and Isaac Ehrlich and Zhiqiang Liu, "Sensitivity Analyses of the Deterrence Hypothesis: Let's Keep the Econ in Econometrics," *Journal of Law and Economics* (forthcoming).

48. Even in the three cases where the coefficient is no longer statistically significant it is still negative. The three cases correspond to specifications 5, 6, and 8 in Table 6.7, where the f-statistics for the difference in trends are 2.61, 0.09 and 1.59 respectively. The other thirteen estimates are very similar to those already reported.

49. This involved sixty-four different regressions for each of the specifications reported in Table 6.6.

50. In Tables 6, 7 and 8, we assumed that the passage of a right-to-carry law was an exogenous event. Following Lott and Mustard (1997, 39–48), we now assume that the likelihood that a state will enact a law depends on several political influence variables. These variables include: the National Rifle Association membership (as a percentage of the population), the percentage of votes received by the Republican presidential candidate in the state, fixed regional effects, and lagged violent and property crime rates plus changes in those rates between the two most recent periods. (Since presidential elections occur every four years, we interacted the percentage voting Republican with

dummy variables for the years adjacent to the relevant elections. Thus, the percentage of the vote obtained in 1980 is multiplied by a year dummy for the years 1979–82, and so on, through the 1996 election.)

The first stage (see the bottom half of Appendix 6.3) implies that states adopting these laws tend to be Republican, with low but rising violent crime rates. Higher NRA membership rates increase the likelihood of a law being adopted, but it is only significant at the twenty percent level. The second stage regressions support our earlier results. Adopting a right-to-carry law is associated with a significant decline in the combined number of multiple killings and injuries (both absolutely and per 100,000 persons). In the separate murder and injury regressions, the coefficients are always negative and either significant or marginally significant (a t-statistic greater than 1.65).

As a test of whether the shall-issue laws were passed because of a shooting, we reestimated just first stage regression by itself after including the lagged murder or injury rate from the shootings to see if the law was adopted because of the shooting. While the coefficients on these lagged values were positive, neither variable was ever statistically significant.

51. There is a chance that the killer at the University of Arizona on 28 October 2002 had a permit to carry a concealed handgun (John M. Broder, "Arizona Gunman Chose Victims in Advance," *New York Times*, 30 October 2002, A1). The killer is said to have "bragged to fellow students last year that he had received a permit to carry a concealed weapon in Arizona." This is the one example of this that I know of.

52. Note that there are 234 observations in the deaths or injuries per shooting regressions although Table 1 indicates that there were 396 shootings in the sample period. The dependent variable in equations (1) – (3) in Table 10 equals the average number of deaths or injuries per shooting in a state in a year. Hence, if there were two or more multiple victim public shootings in a state in a year, this counted as one observation in the regression.

53. While individuals with permits produce a large social benefit, they risk being shot by the attacker. We have no instances where people with permits have indeed been shot, but this risk surely raises the prospects of whether citizens with permits should be compensated or at least not have to pay large fees for obtaining a permit.

54. Fessenden, 2000.

55. For a discussion of the *New York Times* series see John R. Lott, Jr., "Rampage killing facts and fantasies," *Washington Times*, 26 April 2000, A15.

56. The results are statistically significant at the 5 percent (or lower) level for a two-tailed z-test (except for the first specification where the significance level is at the 12 percent level).

57. The results are significance at around 20 percent. The simple means also showed that the states that adopted right-to-carry laws during the 1995 to 1999 period experienced similar reductions in rampage killings. The average number of murders and injuries per state fell from 3.17 to 1.36 and the average number of attacks per state fell from .42 to .20.

58. Because the Poisson regressions with state specific effects did not converge, we substituted in regional dummy variables. The second column also presents OLS estimates that include state fixed effects variables. Regional and state fixed effects may be important if the *New York Times* has a regional or state bias in its coverage of shooting events. Both set of estimates have problems. State fixed effects are more desirable than regional fixed effects but OLS estimates are significantly biased towards zero because of many observations with zero values. The results here are more mixed. The Poisson estimates show a significant decline in the number of time-reported multiple victim public shootings after states pass right-to-carry laws, but the OLS estimates show no change (the coefficient is quite small at .0089 with a t-statistic of only .045).

The Northeast includes Connecticut, Delaware, D.C., Maine, Maryland, Massachusetts, New Hampshire, New Jersey, New York, Pennsylvania, Rhode Island, and Vermont; the South includes Alabama, Arkansas, Florida, Georgia, Louisiana, Mississippi, Missouri, North Carolina, Oklahoma, South Carolina, Tennessee, Texas, and Virginia; the Midwest includes Illinois, Indiana, Iowa, Kansas, Kentucky, Michigan, Minnesota, Nebraska, North Dakota, Ohio, South Dakota, West Virginia, and Wisconsin; the Rocky Mountains include Arizona, Colorado, Idaho, Montana, Nevada, New Mexico, Utah, and Wyoming; and the Pacific states include Alaska, California, Hawaii, Oregon, Washington.

59. Petee et al., 1997.

60. Again, the Poisson estimates do not converge when state fixed effects are used for there is not enough variation in the data to distinguish the law's impact on these shootings with state fixed effects. Consequently, the state fixed effects are replaced with regional dummies [Northeast, Midwest, South, and West (the left-out region)].

61. Whether the results for four or more murders are statistically significant depends on the type of statistical test used. If Poisson regressions are used, the results are marginally significant for murders and the number of attacks but not for injuries. If negative binomial regressions are used, the results are not statistically significant.

62. In explaining the per capita number of people killed, the shall-issue concealed handgun dummy incidence rate ratio was .325 (z-statistic = 3.1) and the difference in the before-and-after trends equaled .18 (z-statistic = 4.55).

63. A Tobit regression explaining the percent of the adult population with permits as a result of the number of hours of training required, the real permit fee, the number of years that the right-to-carry law has been in effect and the number of years squared, as well as the murder rate yields the following relationship:

Percent of the adult population with permits	-0.00134
	(4.278)
Hours of Training	-0.0507
	(4.278)
Real Permit Fee	0.00313
	(11.417)

Number of Years	-0.000198
	(3.360)
Number of Years Squared	0.00095
	(1.546)
Murder Rate	0.0278
	(2.503)
Chi-Square	63.47
	(9.926)
Log Likelihood	-198.2
N=36	

64. Kim Murphy, "Utah Gun Packers Don't Leave Home Without It," *Los Angeles Times*, 10 February 2002, http://www.latimes.com/news/printedition/front/la-oly-021002guns.story?coll=la%2Dhome%2Dtodays%2Dtimes

65. Timothy Egan, "Utah Colleges Fight To Keep Weapons Out," *New York Times*, 25 January 2002, A12.

66. Dan Harrie, "U. Professor to Quit If Campus Has Guns," *Salt Lake Tribune*, 18 April 2000, B2.

67. Amy Joi Bryson, "No-guns Petition Revived," *Deseret News*, 23 April 2002 (http://deseretnews.com/dn/view/0,1249,380014580,00.html).

68. Aaron Sheinin, "Hodges to kill school guns bills: Governor says he'll veto any bill allowing concealed weapons on school grounds," *The State* (Columbia, South Carolina), 9 February 2002.

69. http://ap.tbo.com/ap/florida/MGADM19ULZC.html

70. Egan, ibid.

71. Ibid, Bryson, fn. 10.

72. Similar debates over "gun-free zones" regularly occur over terrorism. For example, during June 2002 many Brooklyn Jews were alarmed by a CBS *60 Minutes* report that the terrorists who targeted the World Trade Center in 1993 first planned to blow up Jewish neighborhoods in Brooklyn. The terrorists apparently switched to the Trade Center only because they believed most of its occupants were Jewish. A terrorist interviewed by CBS gave the impression that Brooklyn Jews were still a prime target.

Rabbi Yakove Lloyd, founder of the Jewish Defense Group, tried organizing armed patrols in some heavily Jewish areas of Brooklyn, saying they "will be a very effective deterrent against terrorism directed at American Jews and other targets" (Ted Shaffrey, "Jewish group to start armed patrols in parts of New York City, rabbi says," Associated Press, 10 June 2002). Lloyd and some local politicians asked police for more protection, but the police never publicly offered additional patrols. Other New York City Jews, concerned about people running around with guns, even off-duty police officers or those with permits, opposed the Brooklyn patrols (Neil Graves and Kirsten Danis, "Rabbi Defies City on Patrols," *New York Post*, 11 June 2002, 28). New York City Police Commissioner Ray Kelly said that "anyone attempting to patrol the streets armed with a weapon will be arrested" [Derek Rose and Owen Moritz, "Armed Citizen Patrols in B'klyn Opposed," *Daily News* (New York), 11 June 2002, 5]. Mayor Bloomberg declared, "We will not tolerate people going around with guns in this city, acting unto themselves" (ibid).

73. Greg Jeffrey, "Licensed to Carry: An Analysis of 30 State Concealed Firearm Laws," published by Missouri: Greg Jeffrey, 2000, 33–39.

74. Jeffrey's index actually ranges from 0 to 74, where 74 is the most restrictive. Purely to have our coefficients agree in sign with our other measures of concealed handgun laws, we reversed the order of the index so that higher scores now imply fewer restrictions, which changes the index so that it ranges from 1 to 75.

75. The results are statistically significant at least at the 1 percent level.

76. We also tried running a simple Poisson regression on only those states that had the right-to-carry law in effect in a particular year. The number of deaths, injuries, deaths and injuries, and attacks was regressed on either a dummy variable that equaled one for the states that had an index value above the median and zero otherwise or the index. In both cases, the states with fewer gun-free zones had fewer attacks and the differences were always significant at better than the 0.1 percent level. Using the simple dummy implied that the states with above the median level of freedom to carry concealed handguns had 58 percent fewer killings and injuries and 52 percent fewer attacks.

77. William M. Landes, "An Economic Study of U.S. Airline Hijacking, 1961–1976," *Journal of Law and Economics* 21 (April 1978): 1–32.

78. This was a simple dummy variable that equaled one if the law is in effect and zero otherwise.

79. Note that October appears to be the most dangerous month although the number of shootings in October is only significantly greater than the number in January, September and November. Note, however, that the monthly dummy variables are not jointly significant.

80. One reason we may not find significant evidence of faddish behavior is that lagged shootings and lagged stories on shootings in the *New York Times* are so highly correlated that it is impossible for the statistical analysis to separate out their different effects. To account for this strong relationship, the last two sets of estimates in Table 6.11 use either lagged shootings or lagged stories by themselves. However, the results remain unchanged: lagged values of shootings are positively related to monthly shootings, while lagged differences are negatively related to differences in monthly shootings. Again, the percent of the population covered by right-to-carry laws continues to have a statistically significant reduction on the number of monthly shootings.

81. Daniel Vasquez, "Judge expected to rule in bomb plot trial Friday," *San Jose Mercury News*, 25 April 2002, 1B; Rachel Morgan, "Pupil Involved in School Slaughter Plot is Charged," *Birmingham Post* (Alabama), 29 November 2001, 8; Alan Maimon, "Barren officials say they foiled student gun plot," *Courier-Journal* (Lexington, Kentucky), 20 December 2001, 1B; David Rogers,

"Dr. Elliot Aronson Discusses his New Book, 'Nobody Left to Hate,'" *The Early Show* (CBS), 3 September 2001; and Cindy Wong, "Anxiety about School Security Leads to the Questioning," *Sun-Sentinel* (Fort Lauderdale), 5 September 2001, 6.

CHAPTER 7: GUNS AT HOME: TO LOCK OR NOT TO LOCK

1. Morley Safer, "Is there a gun in the house?" *60 Minutes* (CBS), 12 May 2002.
2. David Ottway, "A Boon to Sales, or a Threat?" *Washington Post*, 20 May 1999, A1; "John McCain Profile," *National Journal*, 6 November 1999.
3. Mark Schauerte, "Gov. Ryan Signs Bill that Requires Firearm Owners to Store Guns," *St. Louis Post-Dispatch*, 8 June 1999, A1; Editorial, "Trigger Locks," *The Record* (Bergen County, N.J.), 14 October 1999, L10; and Rene Sanchez, "The Battle for California," *Washington Post*, 23 October 1999, A1.
4. There is an issue of whether deaths are properly classified as accidental, but the bias frequently appears to err on the side of classifying deaths as accidental.
5. The study argued that older children could frequently remove or disable mechanical locks with a screwdriver or smash them with a hammer. "Accidental shootings: many deaths and injuries caused by firearms could be prevented," United States General Accounting Office, March 1991.
6. Recent new legislation in California is sufficiently restrictive in terms of what locks qualify that it prevented guns from being sold after the beginning of 2002. See Jason Kandel, "Lack of Gun Locks Halts Local Sales of Weapons," *Daily News* (Los Angeles), 12 January 2002. http://www.dailynews.com/NEWS/articles/0102/12/NEW02.asp
7. Putting a lock on a loaded gun actually makes an accidental discharge possible (e.g., by dropping the gun) that wouldn't be possible if a loaded gun were not locked.
8. Gerald Mizejewski, "Glendening shows off trigger lock," *Washington Times*, 23 March 2000, C1.
9. Data that we have from the National Opinion Research Center's General Social Survey does indicate a drop in state gun ownership rates coinciding with the passage with safe storage laws.
10. For example, Kleck (1997) and Kopel (1992 and 1999) provide international evidence on hot burglary rates.
11. Wright and Rossi (151) interviewed felony prisoners in ten state correctional systems and found that 56 percent said that criminals would not attack a potential victim that was known to be armed. They also found evidence that criminals in those states with the highest levels of civilian gun ownership worried the most about armed victims.

   Examples of stories where people successfully defend themselves from burglaries with guns are quite common (see Lott, 1998 and Waters, 1998). For example, see "Burglar Puts 92-Year-Old in the Gun Closet and Is Shot," *New York Times*, 7 September 1995, A16. George F. Will, "Are We 'a Nation of

Cowards'?" *Newsweek*, 15 November 1993 discusses more generally the benefits produced from an armed citizenry.

12. While I know of no empirical evidence that has been provided to support this
claim, it has been an issue that has been raised in legislative debates over safe
storage laws. Legislative hearings on safe storage laws have raised this issue in
both Hawaii (15 February 2000) and Maryland (16 February 2000).

13. W. Kip Viscusi, "The Lulling Effect: The Impact of Child-Resistant Packaging
on Aspirin and Analgesic Ingestions," *American Economic Review* (May
1984).

14. This is part of a more general phenomenon. As Peltzman (1975) has pointed
out in the context of automobile safety regulations, increasing safety restrictions can result in drivers offsetting these gains by taking more risks in how
they drive. Indeed, recent studies indicate that drivers in cars equipped with
air bags drove more recklessly and got into accidents at such sufficiently
higher rates that it offset the life-saving effect of air bags for the driver and
actually increased the total risk of death posed to others (Peterson, Hoffer, and
Millner, 1995).

15. Peter Cummings, David C. Grossman, Frederick P. Rivara, Thomas D.
Koepsell, "State Gun Safe Storage Laws and Child Mortality Due to Firearms,"
Journal of the American Medical Association, 1 October 1997, 1084–1086.

16. David Klein, Maurice S. Reizen, George H. Van Amburg, and Scott A. Walker,
"Some Social Characteristics of Young Gunshot Fatalities," *Accident Analysis
and Prevention*, Vol. 9 (1977): 181.

17. David Klein, "Societal Influences on Childhood Accidents," *Accident Analysis and Prevention*, Vol. 12 (1980): 277.

18. There is a large literature on the ability of guns to deter criminals including:
Ayres and Donohue, 2000; Bartley and Cohen, 1998; Black and Nagin, 1998;
Bronars and Lott, 1998; Kleck, 1997; Lott, 1998; Lott and Mustard, 1997; Plass-
mann and Tideman, 1999; Southwick, 1997; and Wright and Rossi, 1986.

19. Gary Kleck, *Targeting Guns: Firearms and Their Control*, New York: Aldine
de Gruyter Publishers, 1997, 306–307.

20. Julian A. Waller and Elbert B. Whorton, "Unintentional Shootings, Highway
Crashes, and Acts of Violence," *Accident Analysis and Prevention*, Vol. 5
(1973): 351–356.

21. We did find one case from 1999 that is not included in the list because it was
not listed by the CDC as an accidental death case. The case in Baltimore was
mentioned in forty-three different news articles because it generated a lawsuit against Strum Ruger & Co. and the store where the gun was purchased.
The lawsuit claimed that the manfacturer was liable for the death because of
a failure to make the weapon child proof. Despite the plaintiffs viewing this
case as a strong one to bring before a court, there are significant reasons to
believe that it was not an accidental death. Supposedly the three-year-old
child found his father's semi-automatic gun under the mattress in his parents
bedroom, obtained the magazine from the shelf in the closet, loaded the clip
into the gun, pulled back the slide, and accidentally shot himself in the head.

It is questionable whether most children under ten, let alone a three-year-old, have the strength to pull back the slide on a semi-automatic pistol. (For information on this case see Stacey Winakur, no title, the *Daily Record* (Baltimore) 1 December 2001, 15A; and Laurie Willis, "Judge rejects gun suit," *Baltimore Sun*, 14 October 1999, B1.)

22. Kleck (1997, 287) summarizes his take on this research by claiming that, "On the whole, previous studies failed to make a solid case for the ability of gun controls to reduce the total suicide rate." Geisel et al (1969, 676) find evidence of a reduction in suicide with respect to an index that they create on gun control, but they could find no significant or even meaningful results when they used dummy variables for the different laws. Martin S. Geisel, Richard Roll, and R. Stanton Wettick, "The Effectiveness of State and Local Regulations of Handguns," *Duke University Law Journal*, Vol. 4 (1969): 647–676; Douglas R. Murray, "Handguns, Gun Control Laws, and Firearm Violence," *Social Problems*, Vol. 23 (1975): 81–92; Matthew R. DeZee, "Gun Control Legislation: Impact and Ideology," *Law and Policy Quarterly*, Vol. 5 (1983): 367–379; Myron Boor and Jeffrey H. Blair, "Suicide and Implications for Suicide Prevention," *Psychological Reports*, Vol. 66 (1990): 923–930.

23. There is a debate within criminology and the medical literature over whether the accessibility of guns leads to higher suicide rates, but this literature does not address the impact of safe storage laws, and the evidence is fairly primitive. For example, a recent medical journal study compared the rate of gun suicides during the first week after people buy a gun with the suicide rate during any given week for people who do not own guns. It concluded that the rate for people who just bought the gun was 57 times higher [Garen J. Wintemute, Carrie A. Parham, James Jay Beaumont, Mona Wright, "Mortality among Recent Purchasers of Handguns," *New England Journal of Medicine*, Vol. 341, No. 21 (November 18, 1999)]. The authors took this as strong evidence that suicides could be prevented if guns had not been purchased. However, the research in criminology is more mixed. (For an extensive survey, see Kleck, 1997, 265–288), it often has to rely on rather imprecise variables, such as the number of federally licensed firearms dealers in a county to proxy for gun ownership (Lin Huff-Corzine, Greg Weaver, and Jay Corzine, "Suicide and the Availability of Firearms Via the Retail Market: A National Analysis," University of Central Florida Working Paper, November 1999).

24. Kleck, 1997, 269–275.

25. The states in order of adoption are: Florida (10/1/89), Iowa (4/5/90), Connecticut (10/1/90), Nevada (10/1/91), California (1/1/92), New Jersey (1/17/92), Wisconsin (4/16/92), Hawaii (6/29/92), Virginia (7/1/92), Maryland (10/1/92), Minnesota (8/1/93), North Carolina (12/1/93), Delaware 10/1/94), Rhode Island (9/15/95), and Texas (1/1/96).

26. Peter Cummings, David C. Grossman, Frederick P. Rivara, Thomas D. Koepsell, "State Gun Safe Storage Laws and Child Mortality Due to Firearms," *Journal of the American Medical Association*, 1 October 1997, 1084–1086.

27. www.handguncontrol.org.

28. More precisely, the data excludes accidental gun deaths for children under age 1, though it is our understanding that the number of accidental gun deaths in that category are exceedingly rare relative to even the small number of accidental gun deaths in the 1- to 4-year-old range.

29. I also examined county level data from 1977 to 1994, but could not find a relationship between safe storage laws and total accidental gun deaths or suicides. Because of obvious objections to using these aggregate numbers, since only a small share of accidental deaths or suicides involve juveniles, we will focus on the state level data. The safe storage laws are also statewide laws, though county level data could be useful in differentiating the impact of these laws on different population groups.

30. Indeed, the first agreement that President Clinton made with gun makers to voluntarily include locks was made with respect to handguns. See also for example, Amanda Ripley, "Ready. Aim. Enter Your Pin." *New York Times Magazine*, 21 November 1999, 82–3, which discusses the need for handgun locks.

31. The average law went into effect in early July, so that the law was in effect, on average, for half a year during the year that it is adopted.

32. The Cummings et al. (1997) research provides evidence of a 23 percent drop in juvenile accidental gun deaths after the passage of safe storage laws. Juvenile accidental gun deaths did decline after the passage of the law, but what Cummings et al. miss is that these accidental deaths declined even faster in the states without these laws. While the Cummings et al. piece examined national data, they did not use fixed year effects which would have allowed them to test whether the safe storage states were experiencing a drop relative to the rest of the country. The simple dummy variable that they use is only picking up whether the average juvenile accidental death rate is lower after the passage of safe storage laws. One potential problem with this approach is that any secular decline in accidental gun deaths would produce a lower average rate after the law even if the rate of decline was not affected by the law. The smaller drop that they observe than we do for the states that pass the law is due to the shorter period of time that they examine. Finally, because they did not break down the results by type of gun or, as we shall do later, by a more detailed age breakdown, they never observed some of the anomolies that we will show for some categories of accidental gun deaths (e.g., for handguns) actually rising after the passage of safe storage laws.

    In a recent interview with *USA Today*, Cummings stated "that, unlike Lott, he didn't explore the possibility that gun-storage laws actually cause crime. 'I guess I wouldn't have, because it seems like a very implausible connection,' Cummings says. 'But I guess anything's conceivable.'" (Martin Kasindorf, "Study: Gun-lockup laws can be harmful," *USA Today*, 11 May 2000, 8A.)

33. If the base years had been made using Year -1 in Figure 1 (the last full year before the safe storage was enacted) and 1990 in Figure 2, the differences in accidental handgun deaths for those under age fifteen is truly dramatic. At the same time that accidental handgun deaths are exploding in safe storage states

(increasing four fold by Year 3 and still being 2.25 times higher in Year 4), the accidental handgun death rate is plummeting in states without the law (declining by 56 percent in 1994 and 81 percent in 1996).

34. United States General Accounting Office, "Accidental shootings: many deaths and injuries caused by firearms could be prevented," United States General Accounting Office, March 1991.

35. The general specification that we will use is:

Accidental Gun Death Rate$_{ijk}$ = β^1 Safe Storage Law Dummy$_{jk}$ + β^2 Accidental Non-gun Death Rate$_{ijk}$ + β^3 Accidental Gun Death Rate for Adults$_{jk}$ + β^4 Control Variables$_{jk}$ + β^5 State Fixed Effects + β^6 Year Fixed Effects + α + ϵ_{ijk} where the "Accidental Gun Death Rate" is that rate for age group i in state j and year k. Besides the law dummy, the accidental non-gun death rate for the same age group, and the accidental gun death rate for adults, we account for vectors of control variables and state and year fixed effects.

36. Recent editorials in medical journals have called for research on whether waiting periods impact suicides [M. L. Rosenberg, J. A. Mercy, and L. B. Potter, "Firearms and Suicide," *New England Journal of Medicine*, Vol. 341 (18 November 1999)].

37. http://www.detnews.com/2002/oakland/0201/28/b04-400957.htm.

38. These estimates use Poisson regressions because of the count nature of this data. Indeed Poisson estimates are used throughout when dealing with the issues of accidents or suicides. Using Tobit regressions with accident rates per person in an age category produce even less statistically significant results and imply even more strongly that the safe storage law has no effect on accidents or suicides.

39. Consistent with the raw data, rerunning the results for accidental handgun deaths implies that these deaths actually rose after the passage of the safe storage laws.

40. I also tried year fixed effects by region so as to pick up different year to year trends in accidental gun deaths for each region, but this tended to further reduce the statistical significance of the results. The regions were broken down as follows: The Northeast includes Connecticut, Delaware, D.C., Maine, Maryland, Massachusetts, New Hampshire, New Jersey, New York, Pennsylvania, Rhode Island, and Vermont; the South includes Alabama, Arkansas, Florida, Georgia, Louisiana, Mississippi, Missouri, North Carolina, Oklahoma, South Carolina, Tennessee, Texas, and Virginia; the Midwest includes Illinois, Indiana, Iowa, Kansas, Kentucky, Michigan, Minnesota, Nebraska, North Dakota, Ohio, South Dakota, West Virginia, and Wisconsin; the Rocky Mountains include Arizona, Colorado, Idaho, Montana, Nevada, New Mexico, Utah, and Wyoming; and the Pacific states include Alaska, California, Hawaii, Oregon, Washington.

41. For example, the estimates for accidental handgun deaths that correspond to those reported for specifications 3, 6, 9, and 12 in Table 3 were: -1.5e-6 (t-statistic = 0.646) for children under age five; 4.00e-7 (t-statistic = 0.239) for chil-

dren from five to nine; -1.33e-6 (t-statistic 1.358) for children from 10 to 14; and -1.12e-6 (t-statistic = 1.149) for people age fifteen to nineteen.

42. Because people might be the least likely to store their guns safely when they feel the most threatened and the survey data provided in Section V.D. confirms this, we also re-estimated the earlier regressions for accidental gun deaths and suicides by interacting the violent crime rate with the safe storage law dummy variable. If people are more likely to feel threatened in high crime rate areas, higher crime rates should be associated with smaller reductions in accidental gun deaths and suicides. The coefficients are slightly more negtiave than reported earlier, but the results are qualitatively unchanged. Our interpretation of these results is that accidental gun deaths and gun suicides are simply not a problem in the law-abiding households who are most likely to alter their behavior.

43. http://www.orlandosentinel.com/news/opinion/orl-edped211072102jul21.story?coll=orl%2Dopinion%2Dheadlines.

44. Including lagged values of the crime rates as an explanatory variable does not alter these findings. The coefficients for rape, robbery, and burglary still remain positive and statistically significant and the signs of the other coefficients remain unaltered. The results for the later regressions upon which the figures are based actually become more significant and the pernicious impact of the safe storage law more pronounced.

45. Poisson estimates were also employed for the murder and rape regressions and this actually implied an even stronger relationship between safe storage laws and crime rates. The incidence rate ratio estimates were: murder 1.0496 (z-statistic = 4.082) and rape 1.1048 (z-statistic = 18.213). The other crime variables could not be estimated using Poisson simply because so few observations had zero values.

46. Not including the other gun control variables for a set of regressions that correspond to those in Tables 3 and 6 produced a slightly different change in crimes: 3,819 more rapes, 21,000 more robberies, and 49,733 more burglaries.

47. Ted R. Miller, Mark A. Cohen, and Brian Wiersema, *Victim Costs and Consequences: A New Look*, National Institute of Justice, Washington, D.C. (February 1996).

48. The graphs use linear and squared trends. Using individual year dummies also produces a breakpoint at year zero. While none of the predicted violent crime values prior to year zero exceeds 645 violent crimes per 100,000 people, the values for four of the next five years are above that and eventually rise above 700 for years eight and nine.

49. The graphs also make it clear why rape and robbery rates were the only violent crime categories using the simple dummy variable to show a statistically significant increase in crime after the passage of safe storage laws. While all the violent crime categories increase when safe storage laws go into effect, rape and robbery were the only categories whcre the crime rates rose above the previous before law averages.

50. "A regiment of (anti-gun) women," *The Economist*, 13 May 2000.

51. Simple regressions running the percentage of these crimes committed in resi-
    dences on time trends for the years and including fixed state and year effects
    provides some additional support. An F-test for the difference in before-and-
    after trends equals 1.72 for homicide and 1.47 for robberies.

52. "13-year-old foils robbery with shotgun," *Daily News* (Bogalusa, Louisiana), 26
    January 2001. (http://www.dnewsnet.com)

53. Jeff Piselli, "Girl shoots mother's assailant, police say," (Mississippi) *Clarks-
    dale Press Register*, 30 April 2001. (http://www.zwire.com/site/
    news.cfm?newsid=1747736&BRD=2038&PAG=461&dept_id=230617&rfi=6)

54. "Alleged intruder shot, in critical condition," *Gainesville Sun*, 11 March 2001.

55. The omitted characteristics picked up in the intercept are for an employed,
    married, veteran, Protestant, weekly church attending, white male with no
    education living in the open country who feels very safe at home and makes
    less than $15,000 per year.

56. The endogenous variable for whether a gun is stored unlocked and loaded
    equals one when this is true and zero otherwise. Because these regressions use
    a variable that takes only these two values, we will estimate logit regressions.

57. The result is now: -0.0995 (t-statistic = 1.995).

58. Because the General Social Survey reports national weights, the state level
    percentages were reweighted to reflect the composition of people in that state
    using the thirty-six demographic groupings that we have used in the earlier
    regressions.

59. The result was significant at the 17 percent level for a two-tailed test.

60. Criminologists questioned using gun magazine sales as an accurate representa-
    tion of the stock of gun ownership (Lester 1989 and Kleck 1997).

61. Another recent study in the *Journal of Trauma* examined accidental gun
    deaths, gun suicides, and gun homicides for 5- to 14-year-olds over the period
    from 1988 to 1997. The biggest problem is how the study measures what gun
    ownership rates are. The first two measures used were: 1) the adult firearm
    homicide and firearm suicide rates and 2) the adult firearm suicide rate, under
    the assumption that those rates are higher where guns are more common.
    Unfortunately, juvenile firearm homicides or suicides could be related to those
    measures for reasons unrelated to gun ownership. Assume two areas have the
    same gun ownership rates, if one had more adult firearm homicides, is it really
    surprising that it would also have more juvenile firearm homicides? When
    they used survey data it is either for a "nonrandom" set of states or aggregat-
    ing survey data from the General Social Survey to the region leave even
    though that data is available at the state level. Instead the survey data used in
    this book is for all states available from the General Social Survey. (Mathew
    Miller, Deborah Azrael, and David Hemenway, "Firearm Availability and
    Unintentional Firearm Deaths, Suicides, and Homicide Among 5–14 Year
    Olds," *Journal of Trauma*, Vol. 52, No. 2, 2002: 267–275.)

62. The estimates using either the accidental gun death or gun suicide rates were
    substantially smaller and less significant when we used weighted-least squares

than when we used Poisson estimates so we report the Poisson estimates here. (The coefficients are reported as incident rate ratios.)

63. However, one economics study claims that the sales of the fourth largest gun magazine, *Guns & Ammo*, is a good proxy for gun ownership rates by criminals. Why only this one magazine is used is not adequately explained. Duggan claims that it is for two reasons: 1) that *Guns & Ammo* is more heavily oriented towards handguns than other magazines and 2) that it is the only magazine for which county level data is available. While 50 percent of *Guns & Ammo*'s reviews are of handguns, 43 percent of the *American Rifleman*'s reviews are of handguns and 100 percent of the reviews in *Handguns Magazine* and *American Handgunner* are of handguns. Other magazines also provide county level data. For example, *Handguns Magazine* provides both county level sales data as well as a complete emphasis on handguns.

CHAPTER 8: DO GUN SHOWS AND ASSAULT WEAPONS INCREASE CRIME?

1. Jim Kessler, *No Questions Asked: Background Checks, Gun Shows and Crime*, Americans for Gun Safety Foundation, Washington, D.C., 2001.
2. "Wayne LaPierre, NRA, and Dennis Henigan, Brady Campaign, Discuss Senator McCain and the Issue of Gun Control," *Hardball*, CNBC, 19 June 2001.
3. The quote is from Mary Lee Blek, the Million Mom March President, during a debate that I had with her at McKendree College in southern Illinois on 28 November 2001.
4. Lois Hess, "Bush Undermining Gun Control Laws," *Baltimore Sun*, 31 July 2001, A11.
5. "Sen. Smith Chides Gingrich For Voting To Repeal Assault Weapons," *New York Beacon*, 8 May 1996, 13; and "Church Body Joins in Opposition To Weapons Ban Repeal," *Washington Informer*, 27 December 1995, 26.
6. For a very useful reference see David B. Kopel, "Should Gun Shows Be Outlawed?: McCain Bill Does Much More than Impose Background Checks," Issue Paper no. 1–2002 (Golden, Colo.: Independence Institute, 23 January 2002), http://www.davekopel.com/2A/IP/gunshows2.htm.
7. Caroline Wolf Harlow, "Firearm Use by Offenders," Bureau of Justice Statistics, U.S. Department of Justice, November 2001. An earlier study using the same survey data found slightly higher rates of criminal guns acquired from gun shows (1.7 percent) or flea markets (1.7 percent), but a discussion with Ms. Harlow indicated that their later study had used a "cleaned up" version of the survey data. Apparently there had been several coding and other errors in the original version of the data. The earlier study was by John Scalia, "Federal Firearm Offenders, 1992–98," Bureau of Justice Statistics, U.S. Department of Justice, June 2000.
8. Wright and Rossi, 1986.
9. "Gun Shows: Brady Checks and Crime Gun Traces," Bureau of Alcohol, Tobacco, and Firearms, January 1999.

10. Keith Bea, "Assault Weapons: Military-Style Semiautomatic Firearms: Facts and Issues," Cong. Research Serv., Rep. No. 92–434, 65 (1992).
11. David Kopel, "Gun Games," *National Review Online*, 21 May 2002 (http://www.nationalreview.com/kopel/kopel052102.asp).
12. James Bovard, "Gun control decoys on the firing range," *Washington Times*, 2 July 1998, A17.
13. *More Guns, Less Crime* (199–201); Jens Ludwig and Philip Cook, "Homicide and Suicide Rates Associated with Implementation of the Brady Handgun Violence Prevention Act," *Journal of the American Medical Association*, 2 August 2000, 585–591; Letters to the Editor, "Impact of the Brady Act on Homicide and Suicide Rates," *Journal of the American Medical Association*, 6 December 2000, 2718–2721.
14. One issue that has come up is over the length of time that background check records are kept. The Government Accounting Office released a report in July 2002 stating that record-keeping may have affected the sales of seven guns nationally from July 2001 to January 2002. For those seven guns problems were noticed after more than one day. (Jesse J. Holland, " GAO says keeping gun records for only a day may put guns in the hands of the wrong people," Associated Press, 24 July 2002, http://www.sfgate.com/cgi-bin/article.cgi?f=/news/archive/2002/07/24/national0443EDT0494.DTL.)
15. Roth and Koper tried accounting for state juvenile gun possession bans and "murder trends, demographic and economic changes, the Federal juvenile handgun possession ban, or California and New York initiatives."
16. Timothy J. Burger, "Gun Control Advocate May Have Violated Gun Laws," *New York Daily News*, 21 March 2002 (http://www.miami.com/mld/miami/news/politics/2909641.htm).
17. Jim Kessler, Research Director of the Americans for Gun Safety Foundation, in E-mail dated 8 January 2002.
18. Americans for Gun Safety lists sixteen states as having closed the gun show loophole in 1999 (plus two additional states, Colorado and Oregon, in 2000), but the difference is due in part to Tennessee eliminating its background check for private sales in November 1998. The other differences are Iowa, which according to E-mail correspodence with Jim Kessler, Americans for Gun Safety, accidentally lists as "open" and South Dakota which it accidentally lists as "closed." Other differences involve Minnesota which Americans for Gun Safety classifies as "closed" and Indiana which they classify as "open." As to Minnesota, 624.7132 provides an exception for those who are not licensed dealers. Section 609.66 Subd. F says that "A person, other than a federally licensed firearms dealer, who transfers a pistol or semiautomatic military-style assault weapon to another without complying with the transfer requirements of section 624.7132, is guilty of a gross misdemeanor if the transferee possesses or uses the weapon within one year after the transfer in furtherance of a felony crime of violence, and if: (1) the transferee was prohibited from possessing the weapon under section 624.713 at the time of the transfer; or (2) it was reasonably foreseeable at the time of the transfer that the transferee was likely to use

or possess the weapon in furtherance of a felony crime of violence" (added in 94). The key here seems to be "reasonably foreseeable." As long as one has no reason to believe that the person to whom they are transfering the gun has criminal intent, it would appear that the transferer is protected.

While Americans for Gun Safety has not spent a lot of time trying to determine the exact dates of passage (indeed this information is not usually necessary for their tasks), we did ask Kessler for any information that he had on dates. In two cases, Massachusetts and New Jersey, we had dates that were different than what Kessler told us. Kessler said that New Jersey closed its loophole in 1978, but the requirement for handguns dates back to 1927 and for long guns to 1968. The date for Massachusetts also preceeds the 1977 period for our study.

19. Surprisingly, the Bureau of Alcohol, Tobacco, and Firearms used the same source when examining 1998 and claimed that there were 4,442 such shows, when the total given to me by Bruce Wolberg, advertising manager for the Gun Show Calendar, was 2,630. The differences across some states was substantial and affected the rankings. For example, Texas is 213 instead of the BATF's 472. Pennsylvania is now 138 instead of 250, Florida 178 instead of 224, and Illinois 103 instead of 203.

After repeated attempts, my research assistant James Knowles finally got John D'Angelo at the BATF to answer questions about these discrepancies. According to Knowles, D'Angelo stated that "it would be better to use our own numbers than the numbers from the report, unless I hear otherwise from him. He asks what we expect from him in response to our question. He explained that he could not find the exact documentation for the manual counts and said that he will look into it a little further but that he is not optimistic that he will find it. He said that he would "call back," but he never did.

20. The exact regression was the weighted least squares of ln(Per Capita Gun Show rate) on ln(General Social Survey's Gun Ownership rate weighted by state information on race, age, and sex). The coefficient was 0.58 and the t-statistic was 7.916.

21. See the website for Americans for Gun Safety: http://ww2.americansforgunsafety.com/myths.html.

22. Even the claim that these three states rank in the top five on the basis of the total number of gun shows has problems. It is based upon the claim in the January 1999 Bureau of Alcohol, Tobacco, and Firearms study that also used the Gun Show Calendar, but, as already noted, their numbers were not the same as those provided by the Gun Show Calendar people themselves.

23. Americans for Gun Safety, "No Questions Asked: Background Checks, Gun Shows, and Crime," Americans for Gun Safety Foundation: Washington, D.C., April 2001.

24. The legal history of the law is somewhat complicated. From the Act's effective date it contained a provision allowing the California Attorney General to sue to add additional guns to the Act. The first time that the state attorney general attempted to do this, Don Kates brought a suit which was deferred in a

compromise by which any action under that particular provision was enjoined for the pendency of his suit. In 1998 the intermediate appellate court not only upheld Kate's original suit, but declared the rest of the Act invalid as well. However, an injunction prevented this appellate decision from going into effect. Still the court's decision appears to have prevented enforcement of the parts of the Act that had been in effect until 1998.

25. Operations Report, National Instant Criminal Background Check System, U.S. Department of Justice, Criminal Justice Information Services Division, April 2001, 6.

26. For example, the longest single down time lasted over sixty hours during 11–14, 17, and 22 May 2000; Ibid., 6.

27. Operations Report, National Instant Criminal Background Check System, U.S. Department of Justice, Criminal Justice Information Services Division, March 2000, 9.

28. Operations Report, 2001, Ibid, 27. The report does note that "During calendar year 2000, approximately 22 percent of appeals (2,013) were overturned by the NICS appeal team," but the percent of appeals that were awarded based on cases in 2000 is not mentioned.

29. Elaine S. Povich, "Revised Bill Targets Gun Shows," Newsday, 16 May 2001, A6.

30. Gun Show Loophole Closing and Gun Law Enforcement Act of 2001, s.890, 15 May 2001, sponsored by McCain, Lieberman, Schumer, DeWine, and Carper.

31. Daniel Weintraub, "Sniper case has Lockyer in political cross hairs," 27 October 2002, E1; and Paul M. Rodriguez, "Terror's Blueprint," Insight, 12 November 2002, 18.

32. Dave Kopel and Paul H. Blackman, "Not So Fast," National Review Online, 23 October 2002.

33. Caroline Wolf Harlow, "Firearm Use of Offenders," Bureau of Justice Statistics, revised 31 December 2001.

34. Dave Kopel and Paul H. Blackman, ibid., 23 October 2002.

35. Based on a conversation with Sgt. D'Allaird of the N.Y. state police.

36. Based on a conversation between James Knowles and Sgt. D'Allaird of the N.Y. state police and the Maryland State Attorney General's office.

37. Robert M. Thompson, Jerry Miller, Martin G. Ols, and Jennifer C. Budden, "Ballistic Imaging and Comparison of Crime Gun Evidence by the Bureau of Alcohol, Tobacco and Firearms," National Integrated Ballistic Information Network (NIBIN) Program, BATF, U.S. Department of the Treasury, 13 May 2002.

38. Jeff Johnson, "Police Challenge Gun Control Advocates on Ballistic Imaging," CNSNews.com, 29 October 2002 (http://www.cnsnews.com/ViewNation.asp?Page=\Nation\archive\200210\NAT20021029a.html).

39. Frederic A. Tulleners, "Technical Evaluation: Feasibility of a Ballistics Imaging Database for all New Handgun Sales," Bureau of Forensic Services, California Department of Justice, 5 October 2001.

40. http://ww2.americansforgunsafety.com/who_is_ags.html
41. There are practical problems with the proposal. For example, gun shows would worry that once the regulations were successfully enacted, any payment would soon be eliminated.

CHAPTER 9: CONCLUSION

1. Some academics believe that the arguments are a façade for less noble reasons. For example, John Donohue, at the Stanford Law School, writes that "National Rifle Association's preference is to maximize the number of guns (after all, that is in the best interest of gun manufacturers)." John J. Donohue, "Tough Target," *American Prospect*, 16 December 2002, 35.
2. Ted Shaffrey, "Jewish group to start armed patrols in parts of New York City, rabbi says," Associated Press, 10 June 2002.
3. Neil Graves and Kirsten Danis, "Rabbi Defies City on Patrols," *New York Post*, 11 June 2002, 28.
4. Derek Rose and Owen Moritz, "Armed Citizen Patrols in B'klyn Opposed," *Daily News* (New York), 11 June 2002, 5.
5. Ibid.
6. Don Thompson, "Handgun Purchases Down in California," *Modesto Bee*, 19 March 2002 (http://www.modbee.com/local/story/1892991p-1999989c.html); Brian MacQuarrie, "Firearms interest soars in Bay State," *Boston Globe*, 24 November 2001; and Eric Bailey, "State Handgun Sales Head for a Record Low," *Los Angeles Times*, 12 November 2001, 6, Part 2.
7. The quote is from Luis Tolley of the Brady Campaign. James P. Sweeney, "California handgun sales pushing record low," Copley News Service, 6 November 2001.
8. Glocks were the one type of gun specifically exempted from the requirements because they are popular among police and it was known before hand that the sixty-foot drop would severely damage the gun. Susan McRoberts, "New Laws Slow Sales of Guns," *Whittier Daily News*, 19 November 2001, A1. (http://www.whittierdailynews.com/default.asp?puid=1599&spuid=1599&indx=1212354&article=on).
9. Brian MacQuarrie, "Firearms interest soars in Bay State," *Boston Globe*, 24 November 2001, A1.
10. Actual personal contact with gun opponents has convinced me the most that gun control advocates want the total elimination of private gun ownership. For example, in 1999, I was on a panel debate about cities suing gun makers with Ed Rendell (he was the mayor of Philadelphia at the time, and was elected governor of Pennsylvania in 2002). During the presentations, Rendell said that he didn't want to take guns away from hunters or law-abiding citizens and that he just wanted to use the suits to make gun-makers responsible for the costs that guns impose on cities. Yet, after the debate I saw Rendell put his arm

around an activist who wants to ban handguns and heard him say, "I just can't say publicly what we want to do, we have to take these things slowly." I was standing right behind Rendell when he said it.

When Rendell saw me, he angrily turned toward me, asking what I wanted. I said that I had hoped we could talk more about the issues raised by the panel. I said that I understood the costs to cities of the bad things that happen with guns, but I wanted to know why he didn't consider the benefits of defensive gun use and of victims defending themselves. Still quite angry, Rendell said that, as a city prosecutor, he had never seen a defensive gun use, and that as far as he was concerned, he had never heard of a defensive gun use. He said that he didn't believe they occurred.

I started to offer to provide him examples, but he said that he didn't need any evidence and walked away.

Rendell's actions have already had a big impact on gun ownership. He was the first mayor to foresee how simultaneously filing suits by dozens of cities against gun companies could impose a massive cost of legal defense and bring the industry to its knees. By making it financially impossible for many companies to defend themselves, even lawsuits that have consistently been thrown out by judges across the country have driven many gun-makers into bankruptcy. (I have written about this experience previously in the *Philadelphia Daily News*, 6 June 2002, http://www.philly.com/mld/dailynews/news/opinion/3410712.htm.)

11. Richard Harris, "A Reporter at Large: Handguns," *New Yorker*, 26 July 1976, 58.

12. Jill Barton, "Student Who Shot Teacher a Reluctant Witness in Gun Trial," Associated Press, 31 October 2002.

Appendix 1: Some Recent Evidence on Guns and Crime

1. Ian Ayres and John Donohue, "Nondiscretionary Concealed Weapons Laws: A Case Study of Statistics, Standards of Proof, and Public Policy," *Am. Law & Econ. Rev.* 436 (2000); William Bartley and Mark Cohen, "The Effect of Concealed Weapons Laws: An Extreme Bound Analysis," *Econ. Inquiry* 259 (1998); Daniel Black and Daniel Nagin, "Do Right-to-Carry Laws Deter Violent Crime," 27 *J. Legal Stud.* 209 (1998); Stephen Bronars and John R. Lott, "Criminal Deterrence, Geographic Spillovers, and Right-to-Carry Laws," 88 *Am. Econ. Rev.* 475 (1998).

2. Mark Duggan, "More Guns, More Crime," *Journal of Political Economy*, October 2001: 1086–1114.

3. In fact, there is frequently much more variation in crime rates or other individual characteristics across counties within a state than there are across states. For example, 80 percent of the counties in the U.S. have zero murders in any given year and even the highest murder rate states contain many counties without any murders.

4. Michael Maltz and Joseph Targonski, "A Note on the Use of County-Level UCR Data," University of Illinois at Chicago working paper, 2001.

5. See Jens Ludwig and Philip Cook, "Homicide and Suicide Rates Associated with Implementation of the Brady Handgun Violence Prevention Act," *Journal of the American Medical Association,* 2 August 2000, 585–591 as well as my own work in the two editions of my book.

6. For survey information on this see: John R. Lott, Jr., *More Guns, Less Crime* (Chicago: University of Chicago Press, 2000); Edward L. Glaeser and S. Glendon, "Who Owns Guns?: Criminals, Victims, and the Culture of Violence, *American Economic Review* papers and procedings, May 1998: 458–462; and Philip Cook and Jens Ludwig, *National Study of Private Ownership of Firearms in the United States,* 1994: Washington, D.C: Police Foundations, 1997.

7. John R. Lott, Jr., "Impact of the Brady Act on Homicide and Suicide Rates," *Journal of the American Medical Association,* 6 December 2000, 2718.

8. Duggan also claims that he focused on *Guns & Ammo* because it was the only guns magazine to provide county level data on magazine sales, yet that is clearly not true.

9. See Appendix 2.

10. This is based on a conversation with Skip Johnson, who is a vice president with Primedia which owns *Guns & Ammo* magazine.

11. See Appendix 2.

12. Of the two significant positive coefficients, one by Black and Nagin includes separate nonlinear time trends for each state (see 209–210 from *More Guns, Less Crime* for a discussion of this). The one significant result from Duggan uses differences even though he doesn't do any tests for whether this is the appropriate specification. [In fact, Moody (805) tests for unit roots and finds that county crime rates are stationary.]

   There is one paper by Dezhbakhsh and Rubin that is critical of my work, but I have not included it in Appendix Table 1.1 because they do not investigate the differences in crime rates before and after right-to-carry laws are adopted (Hashem Dezhbakhsh and Paul H. Rubin, "Lives Saved or Lives Lost?: The Effects of Concealed-Handgun Laws on Crime," *American Economic Review Papers and Proceedings,* May 1998, 468–474). What they do is run a regression over only those observations where the right-to-carry law is in effect, they then take this regression and plug in those observations during 1992 for which the right-to-carry laws are not in effect. This last step generates what they claim are predicted values for what the crime rates would be in those counties without the laws if they had the law. They then compare what the actual crime rates were in the counties without the laws with their predicted crime rates and take the difference. If the actual crime rate is greater than the pre-dicted, they claim that this shows that the law would have lowered the crime rate. If the actual crime rate is less than the predicted value, they claim that this shows the law would have raised the crime rate.

   This approach makes no sense to me. It throws out all the information on the before-and-after change in crime rates that occurs when states change their laws. The method also eliminates the role of fixed effects. All the predicted crime rates in the counties without right-to-carry laws in 1992 are assumed to have the same intercept value from the regression since there is no county dummy to use in making the predicted value. If the omitted county that is represented by the intercept happens to have a low crime rate, it will make the right-to-carry laws look good. If the reverse is true, the right-to-carry laws will look as if the law is increasing the crime rate. On average randomly picking one will produce no systematic effect and the predicted values will lie on both sides of the actual crime rates.

13. Black and Nagin mark only the levels of statistical significance at the 5 percent level. There are a number of negative coefficients whose levels of statistical significance lie between the 5 and 10 percent level.

14. For example, Ayes and Donohue write (22) that: "Note that for a number of the violent crime categories, very large negative estimated coefficients are found on some of the dummies for more than six years after passage. As noted, only a small portion of the entire array of shall-issue states contribute to these estimates, thereby allowing a substantial drop in crime in an early passing state (whether caused by the shall-issue law or not) to have a disproportionate effect in estimating a post-passage dummy or linear trend."

15. http://www.apbnews.com/cjsystem/1999/09/24/shoottrans0924_01.html

16. Another example involved Mary Lee Blek of the Million Mom March during a debate at McKendree College on 28 November 2001. Ms. Blek also accused me of doing my work because of funding that I obtained from the gun industry.

17. As of this writing, the Violence Policy Center still has a section of its website entitled: "Funder of the Lott CCW Study Has Links to the Gun Industry" at http://www.vpc.org/fact_sht/lottlink.htm.

18. Stephen Chapman, "A Gun Study and A Conspiracy Theory," *Chicago Tribune*, 15 August 1996, 31.

19. John R. Lott, Jr., "Does A Helping Hand Put Others at Risk?: Affirmative Action, Police Departments, and Crime," *Economic Inquiry*, April 2000: 239. The conclusion also noted: "it would be a serious mistake not to realize that this simple relationship is masking that the new rules reduce the quality of new hires from other groups."

20. Ibid.

APPENDIX 2: OTHER MEASURES OF GUN OWNERSHIP

1. Marnie Ko, "Law-abiding Criminals," *Alberta Report*, 30 July 2001, 24; and Bill Kaufmann, "Critic Says War on Gun Law Still Has Ammo," *Calgary Sun*, 20 March 2001, 10. Responses by the Canadian government to these concerns can be found at: David Austin, "Still Time," *National Post*, 17 February 2001, A19; and David Austin, "Number of Tardy Gunowners Exaggerated," *StarPhoenix*, 16 February 2001, A15.

2. Mark Duggan, "More Guns, More Crime," *Journal of Political Economy*, October 2000, 1089.

3. The data for the *American Rifleman* were collected by examining individual issues of magazine. The data for *Guns & Ammo* was obtained directly from Skip Johnson, the vice president and executive director at the magazine.

4. Not all the gun magazine sales are available for all years. I obtained *Guns & Ammo* sales data from 1977 to 1998 (in contrast, Duggan uses the data from 1980 to 1998); *American Handgunner*, 1978 to 1998; *American Hunter*, 1981 to 1998; *American Rifleman*, 1981 to 1998; *North American Hunter*, 1985 to 1998; and *Handgun*, 1990 to 1998.

5. This data is available from the Audit Bureau of Circulation.

6. Florenz Plassmann and John R. Lott, Jr., "More Readers of Gun Magazines, but Not More Crime," State University of New York working paper, January 2002.

7. Globe Research Corp., "*Guns & Ammo* Magazine Subscriber Survey Results for 1994," emap-USA: New York, N.Y., 1995.

8. The data is available from the Audit Bureau of Circulation.

9. This is based on a conversation with Skip Johnson, who is a vice president with Primedia which owns *Guns & Ammo* magazine.

10. This is derived from running the natural log of per captia magazine sales for either of these three magazines on the natural log of the per capita sales of the five largest non-gun magazines and the natural log of the per capita sales of *Guns & Ammo*.

11. The regression is: natural log of gun ownership given by General Social Survey on the natural log of per capita magazine sales and state and year fixed effects.

12. The survey was not conducted every year. Initial years where the gun questions were not asked are 1972, 1975, 1978, 1983, and 1986. Beginning in 1988, the gun questions were asked every year but to only two-thirds of the total survey sample. There was no funding for surveys in 1979 and 1981 and beginning in 1994 the survey was switched to biennial (even years). The survey data is also weighted by the demographics in each individual state. Over the entire period, "own gun" was "refuse to answer" for 156 out of the total 24,855 observations with a response to that variable.

13. See *More Guns, Less Crime*, Chapter 3.

14. Compared to other surveys such as the CBS General Election Exit Poll with over 36,000 observations in 1988 and the Voter News Service Poll with over 3,400 people surveyed in 1996, the General Social Survey only surveys 899 to 1973 in any given year. While the General Social Survey will not provide a very accurate picture of gun ownership in any given state in a year, the much larger number years over which the survey is provided allows us to investigate trends.

15. The household rate was calculated by assuming that married women owned guns at the same rate as married men of the same race and age grouping.

16. Using weighted least squares where the weight was the state population, I estimated:

ln(murder rate) = a0 + b1 ln(magazine sales for the preceding year) + b2 ln(magazine sales two years previously) + b3 arrest rate for murder + b4 death penalty execution rate + b5 state population + b6 state population squared + b7 unemployment rate + b8 poverty rate + b9 real per capita income + b10 real per capita unemployment insurance payments + b11 real per capita welfare payments + b12 real per capita retirement payments + b13 36 different demographic variables that measure the percent of the state population in different age, sex, and race divisions + state fixed effects + year fixed effects

To deal with the endogeniety issues involved in using the arrest rate for murder in explaining the murder rate, I also tried using the arrest rate for violent crime and the results were virtually identical. Removing the arrest rate entirely also produced similar results.

17. Duggan, "More Guns, More Crime," *Journal of Political Economy*, October 2001, 1100.
18. When one looks at the violent crime, rape, robbery, and aggravated assault categories for the five other gun magazines there are a total of forty lagged sales coefficients. Of these forty, four are significantly positive and significant and three are significantly negative.
19. Mathew Miller, Deborah Azrel, and David Hemenway, "Firearm Availability and Unintentional Firearm Deaths, Suicide, and Homicide among 5–14 Year Olds," 52 *Journal of Trauma*, February 2002, 267–274.
20. "Bang, bang, you're dead," *The Economist*, 2 March 2002.

BIBLIOGRAPHY

Alschuler, Albert W. "Two Guns, Four Guns, Six Guns, More Guns: Does Arming the Public Reduce Crime?" *Valparaiso Law Review* 31 (Spring 1997): 365–373.

Ayres, Ian, and John J. Donohue. "Nondiscretionary Concealed Weapons Laws: A Case Study of Statistics, Standards of Proof, and Public Policy," *American Law and Economics Review*, Vol. 1 (Fall 2000).

———. "Shooting Down the More Guns, Less Crime Hypothesis," working paper (2002).

Bartley, William Alan. "Will Rationing Guns Reduce Crime?" *Economics Letters*, Vol. 62 (1999): 241–243.

Bartley, William Alan, and Mark Cohen. "The Effect of Concealed Weapons Laws: An Extreme Bound Analysis," *Economic Inquiry* (April 1998): 259.

Bartley, William Alan, Mark A. Cohen, and Luke Frobe. "The Effect of Concealed Weapon Laws: Estimating Model Uncertainty." *Economic Inquiry* 36 (April 1998): 258–265.

Black, Dan A., and Daniel S. Nagin. "Do 'Right-to-Carry' Laws Deter Violent Crime?" *Journal of Legal Studies* 27 (January 1998): 209–219.

Boor, Myron, and Jeffrey H. Blair. "Suicide and Implications for Suicide Prevention," *Psychological Reports*, Vol. 66 (1990): 923–930.

Bronars, Stephen G., and John R. Lott, Jr. "Criminal Deterrence, Geographic Spillovers, and the Right to Carry Concealed Handguns," *American Economic Review*, 82 (May 1998): 475–478.

Cook, P. J., and Jens Ludwig. "You Got Me: How Many Defensive Gun Uses Per Year?" Paper presented at the annual meeting of the Homicide Research Group, Santa Monica, California (17 May 17 1996).

Cook, P. J. "The Role of Firearms in Violent Crime," in M. E. Wolfgang and N. A. Werner, eds., *Criminal Violence*. Newbury, N. J.: Sage Publishers, 1982.

Cramer, Clayton E., and David B. Kopel. "'Shall Issue': The New Wave of Concealed Handgun Permit Laws," *Tennessee Law Review* 62 (Spring 1995).

Cummings, Peter, David C. Grossman, Frederick P. Rivara, and Thomas D. Koepsell. "State Gun Safe Storage Laws and Child Mortality Due to Firearms," *Journal of the American Medical Association*, 1 October 1997, 1084–1086.

DeZee, Matthew R. "Gun Control Legislation: Impact and Ideology," *Law and Policy Quarterly*, Vol. 5 (1983): 367–379.

Donohue, John J. "The Impact of State Laws Permitting Citizens to Carry Concealed Handguns," presented at Brookings Institution conference, December 2001.

Duggan, Mark. "More Guns, More Crime," *Journal of Political Economy*, Vol. 109 (2001): 1086–1114.

Ehrlich, Isaac, and Zhiqiang Liu. "Sensitivity Analyses of the Deterrence Hypothesis: Let's Keep the Econ in Econometrics," *Journal of Law and Economics*, Vol. 42 (April 1999) 455–487.

Ehrlich, Isaac. "Capital Punishment and Deterrence: Some Further Thoughts and Additional Evidence." *Journal of Political Economy* 85 (August 1977): 741–88.

———. "The Deterrent Effect of Capital Punishment: A Question of Life and Death," *American Economic Review* 65 (1975): 397–417.

Geisel, Martin S., Richard Roll, and R. Stanton Wettick. "The Effectiveness of State and Local Regulations of Handguns," *Duke University Law Journal*, Vol. 4 (1969): 647–676.

Goodstein, Laurie, and William Glaberson. "The Well-Marked Roads to Homicidal Rage," *New York Times*, 10 April 2000, A1.

Harlow, Caroline Wolf. "Firearm Use of Offenders," Bureau of Justice Statistics, revised 31 December 2001.

Huff-Corzine, Lin, Greg Weaver, and Jay Corzine. "Suicide and the Availability of Firearms Via the Retail Market: A National Analysis," University of Central Florida working paper, November 1999.

Kates, Don, and Dan Polsby. "Of Genocide and Disarmament," *Journal of Criminal Law and Criminology* 86 (Fall 1995): 247–256.

Kleck, Gary, and E. Britt Patterson. "The Impact of Gun Control and Gun Ownership Levels on Violence Rates," *Journal of Quantitative Criminology*, Vol. 9 (1993), 249–288.

Kleck, Gary, and Marc Gertz. "Armed Resistance to Crime: The Prevalence and Nature of Self-Defense with a Gun," *Journal of Criminal Law and Criminology* 86 (Fall 1995): 150–187.

Kleck, Gary. *Targeting Guns: Firearms and Their Control.* New York: Aldine de Gruyter, 1997.

Kleck, Gary, and Don B. Kates. *Armed: New Perspectives on Gun Control,* New York: Promethus Books, 2001.

Klein, David, Maurice S. Reizen, George H. Van Amburg, and Scott A. Walker. "Some Social Characteristics of Young Gunshot Fatalities," *Accident Analysis and Prevention,* Vol. 9 (1977): 177–82.

Kopel, David B. "Lawyers, Guns, and Burglars: Lawsuits Against Gun Companies and the Problem of Positive Externalities." Paper presented at the American Criminology Meetings (1999).

Kopel, David B. *The Samurai, the Mountie, and the Cowboy.* New York: Prometheus Books, 1992.

Kopel, David, and Paul H. Blackman. "Not So Fast," *National Review Online,* 23 October 2002.

Landes, William M. "An Economic Study of U.S. Airline Hijacking, 1961–1976," *Journal of Law and Economics* 21 (April 1978): 1–32.

Lester, David. "Gun Ownership and Suicide in the United States," *Psychological Medicine* (1989): 519–521.

Lott, John R., Jr. and David Mustard. "Crime, Deterrence, and Right-to-Carry Concealed Handguns," *Journal of Legal Studies* 26 (January 1997): 1–68.

Lott, John R., Jr., "The Concealed Handgun Debate," *Journal of Legal Studies* 27 (January 1998a): 221–243.

———. *More Guns, Less Crime: Understanding Crime and Gun Control Laws.* Chicago, University of Chicago Press, 2000.

———. "Guns, Crime, and Safety: Introduction," *Journal of Law and Economics,* Vol. 44 (October 2001): 605–614.

Lott, John R., Jr., and John E. Whitley. "Safe Storage Gun Laws: Accidental Deaths, Suicides, and Crime," *Journal of Law and Economics,* Vol. 44 (October 2001): 659–690.

Marvell, Thomas B., and Carl E. Moody. "The Impact of Enhanced Prison Terms for Felonies Committed with Guns," *Criminology* 33 (May 1995).

Miller, Mathew, Deborah Azrael, and David Hemenway. "Firearm Availability and Unintentional Firearm Deaths, Suicides, and Homicide Among 5–14 Year Olds," *Journal of Trauma*, Vol. 52, no. 2, 2002: 267–275.

Miron, Jeffrey A. "Violence, Guns, and Drugs: A Cross-Country Analysis," *Journal of Law and Economics*, Vol. 44 (October 2001): 615–634.

Moody, Carlisle E. "Testing for the Effects of Concealed Weapons Laws: Specification Errors and Robustness," *Journal of Law and Economics*, Vol. 44 (October 2001): 799–813.

Murray, Douglas R. "Handguns, Gun Control Laws, and Firearm Violence," *Social Problems*, Vol. 23 (1975): 81–92.

Mustard, David B. "The Impact of Gun Laws on Police Deaths," *Journal of Law and Economics*, Vol. 44 (October 2001): 635–658.

Olson, David E., and Michael D. Maltz. "Right-to-Carry Concealed Weapons Laws and Homicide in Large U.S. Countries: The Effect on Weapon Types, Victim Characteristics, and Victim-Offender Relationships," *Journal of Law and Economics*, Vol. 44 (October 2001): 747–770.

Parker, Jeffrey A. "Guns, Crime, and Academics: Some Reflections on the Gun Control Debate," *Journal of Law and Economics*, Vol. 44 (October 2001): 715–724.

Peltzman, Sam. "The Effects of Automobile Safety Regulation," *Journal of Political Economy* (August 1975): 677–725.

Petee, Thomas A., Kathy G. Padgett, and Thomas York. "Debunking the Stereotype: An Examination of Mass Murder in Public Places," *Homicide Studies* 1 (November 1997): 317–337.

Peterson, Steven, George Hoffer, and Edward Millner. "Are Drivers of Air-Bag-Equipped Cars More Aggressive?: A Test of the Offsetting Behavior Hypothesis," *Journal of Law and Economics* 38 (October 1995): 251–264.

Plassmann, Florenz and T. Nicolaus Tideman. "Does the Right to Carry Concealed Handguns Deter Countable Crimes?: Only a Count Analysis Can Say," *Journal of Law and Economics*, Vol. 44 (October 2001): 771–798.

———. "Geographical and Temporal Variations in the Effects of Right-to-Carry Laws on Crime," Virginia Polytechnic Institute and State University working paper (1999).

Police Foundation. "National Study of Private Ownership of Firearms in the United States, 1994," National Institute of Justice (1997).

Rosenberg M. L., J. A. Mercy, and L. B. Potter. "Firearms and Suicide," *New England Journal of Medicine*, Vol. 341 (18 November 1999).

Southwick, Lawrence, Jr. "Self-Defense with Guns: The Consequences," State University of New York at Buffalo working paper, 1997.

Stigler, George J. "The Optimum Enforcement of Laws," *Journal of Political Economy* 78 (May/June 1970): 526–536.

Tulleners, Frederic A. "Technical Evaluation: Feasibility of a Ballistics Imaging Database for all New Handgun Sales," Bureau of Forensic Services, California Department of Justice, 5 October 2001.

Viscusi, W. Kip. "The Lulling Effect: The Impact of Child-Resistant Packaging on Aspirin and Analgesic Ingestions," *American Economic Review* (May 1984).

Waller, Julian A., and Elbert B. Whorton. "Unintentional Shootings, Highway Crashes, and Acts of Violence," *Accident Analysis and Prevention*, Vol. 5 (1973): 351–356.

Waters, Robert A. *The Best Defense: True Stories of Intended Victims Who Defended Themselves With a Firearm*. New York: Cumberland House Publisher, 1998.

Wintemute, Garen J., Carrie A. Parham, James Jay Beaumont, and Mona Wright. "Mortality Among Recent Purchasers of Handguns," *The New England Journal of Medicine*, Vol. 341, No. 21 (18 November 1999).

Wright, James D. and Peter H. Rossi. *Armed and Considered Dangerous: A Survey of Felons and Their Firearms*. New York: Aldine de Gruyter, 1986.

Zimring, Franklin, and Gordon Hawkins. "Concealed-Handgun Permits: The Case of the Counterfeit Deterrent," *The Responsive Community*, Spring 1997.

Zimring, Franklin. "The Medium is the Message: Firearm Caliber as a Determinant of Death from Assault," *Journal Legal Studies* 1 (1972): 97–123.

ACKNOWLEDGMENTS

I must particularly thank Chris DeMuth and David Gerson at the American Enterprise Institute who provided me with the opportunity to write this book. Valuable comments have been provided by Gertrud Fremling, Bill Landes, Dana Leavitt, Bruce Nichols, Mitch Polinsky, John Whitley, and Don Kates. Extremely helpful research assistance was provided by Jill Mitchell, James Knowles, Maxim Lott, Lydia Regopoulos, and Grant Rabenn. I have also received valuable help in putting together some of this data by David Mustard and John Whitley.

Two chapters in this book draw heavily on my research with other academics. In particular, William Landes, a professor at the University of Chicago Law School, coauthored Chapter 6 on multiple victim public shootings. Chapter 7 updates and expands research that I did with John Whitley, an assistant professor at the University of Adelaide in Australia, who coauthored previous research with me on safe-storage gun laws ("Safe-Storage Gun Laws: Accidental Deaths, Suicides, and Crime," *Journal of Law and Economics*, October 2001). Work on those two chapters began while I was at the University of Chicago and continued while I was at Yale University.

I have also had the opportunity to present parts of this research at a variety of academic forums, and I appreciate the useful comments I received. A partial list of these places includes: American Enterprise Institute, Arizona State University, Auburn University, University of Chicago, Claremont Graduate School, George Mason University Law School, Hoover Institution, University of Houston, University of

Illinois, University of Kansas, University of Miami, New York University, University of Oklahoma, University of Southern California, Rice University, University of Texas at Austin, University of Texas at Dallas, the College of William and Mary, Yale University (Business and Law Schools), and Yeshiva University School of Law.

I also wish to thank participants at the Economics of Law Enforcement Conference at Harvard Law School, Association of American Law Schools Meetings, American Economic Association Meetings, American Society of Criminology Meetings, Midwestern Economic Association Meetings, Southern Economic Association Meetings, and Western Economic Association Meetings.

INDEX

Page numbers in **bold italics** refer to citations in tables and figures.